Women, 

This book is a pathway, a journey of discovery. It takes you through the looking glass into a world of deep erotic desires, awakening the dormant energies of your own unspoken sexual needs. It will enable you to both respect and trust your sexual instincts, and share moments of intimacy more honestly with others.

Women, Sex and Astrology

SARAH BARTLETT

BLACK
lace

This Black Lace book contains sexual fantasies.
In real life, make sure you practise safe sex.

First published in 1998 by
Black Lace
332 Ladbroke Grove
London W10 5AH

Typeset by SetSystems Ltd, Saffron Walden, Essex
Printed and bound by Mackays of Chatham PLC

ISBN 0 352 33262 X

CONTENTS

INTRODUCTION

'Also she loves the howling of wolves
And the growling of bright-eyed lions . . .'
Homeric hymn to the mother of the gods

*T*his book is a unique and richly evocative guide to understanding the mysteries and wisdom of female sexuality. By drawing on myth, astrology and psychology you can begin to discover the secrets of your desire, and reconnect to your hidden sexual energies. This book explicitly discloses how to honour your own erotic needs. It guides you deep into the darker realms of your sexuality and shows how these wild, instinctive urges can be channelled into the light.

This book is a pathway, a journey of discovery. It takes you through the looking glass into a world of deep erotic desires, awakening the dormant energies of your own unspoken sexual needs. It will enable you to both respect and trust your sexual instincts, and share moments of intimacy more honestly with others.

Women, Sex and Astrology looks also at how male partners may express their sexual needs and responses, and how their erotic desire is triggered, often very differently from your own.

Female Sexuality

For thousands of years, female sexuality has been distorted, misunderstood or repressed by cultural and religious expectations. Sexuality has come to be regarded as profane rather than sacred. In the ancient past, gods and goddesses gave us purpose, direction and a means to channel and project our sexual energies. Here in the West we may no longer worship Aphrodite, nor follow the ecstatic cults of Dionysus to channel our ancient

1

wildness, but we still have instinctive urges, sexual needs, and a mission to discover who we are.

Honouring the ancient gods and goddesses is a means of honouring your sexuality: by discovering the secrets of these gods and goddesses, you can discover the true nature of your sexual desire and purpose. The mythic archetypes (the gods and goddesses) throughout this book are the essence of an understanding of female desire. They are at the core of your sun sign, and Venus and Eros placements in your birth chart.

Your sexuality is just one expression of who you truly are. By embracing it you may begin to discover your real values, and who, why and how you desire.

So What is an Archetype?

Throughout this book there are references to archetypes. An archetype is an original model, or pattern: a fundamental image which we all unconsciously carry from ancient time. It is buried deep within our unconscious due to thousands of years of selective mental processing. These archetypes are represented by the gods and the goddesses included in this book. Understanding them will help you understand your sexual identity.

Mythic Astrology

The position of the heavenly bodies in the sky at the moment of your birth defines that moment and sows the seed of who you are. Knowing the position of the planets that are associated with sexuality, eroticism and intimacy can guide you to a deeper awareness of your individual style and needs, as well as how to harmonise and blend these energies with those of your partner. These planets are personified by the gods and goddesses after whom they were named.

The Erotic-profile Chart

In your erotic-profile chart based on your date of birth, two major heavenly bodies, the sun and Venus, along with the tiny but highly potent asteroid Eros, reflect your sexual, intimate and erotic nature. Understanding these heavenly bodies will enable you to discover the mysteries of your own individual sexuality, as well as how to integrate your erotic needs with your partner's. By using astrology and the mythic archetypes associated with each sun sign, and the power of Venus and Eros, you can also access the darker areas of your sexual inhibitions or needs. You can begin to reconnect to the power of your ancient feminine passion, and start to enjoy the freedom of sensual pleasuring and mutual stimulation.

Astrology has always been a powerful journey of self-awareness. By creating your own astro-erotic-profile chart as you work through this book, you can begin to build up a distinct and unique sexual portrait.

The chart is divided into two sections: a zodiac-style wheel for filling in the planets and a separate section beneath to fill in personal phrases/key words found at the end of your relevant chapters.

This is a book of practical self-analysis and discovery of others. Interaction with yourself means you can begin to get in touch with your real erotic needs and sexual preferences, and begin to share these honestly with your partner.

How to Fill in the Chart

Fill in the chart found at the end of this introductory chapter as you follow your journey. First read your relevant sun-sign chapter and use the interactive sections to form a framework for your own self-awareness. Next, use the appropriate key words and phrases to begin filling in your profile. Also copy the symbol for the sun into the relevant portion of the zodiac. Then look up the Venus and Eros placements in your birth chart from the tables at the end of the relevant sections.

How to Find Your Venus and Eros Signs

Venus and Eros also move through the signs like the sun. Under the year of your birth in the appropriate tables, find your birth date. For example, you may have been born on 5 September 1960. If you look through the Venus tables, you will find your date and see that Venus was in the sign of Libra from 3 September to 26 September.

When looking up your Venus and Eros placements, you may find that you were born on the day that one of them has just moved into a sign, or a day when the planet moves out of a sign, just like some people are born 'on the cusp' when the sun was moving into another sign.

It is possible, due to time variations throughout the world, that Eros and/or Venus may be positioned in either the preceding or following sign. For example, say you were born on 3 September 1960. If you look in the table for Venus placements, you will see that on that day Venus moved into Libra. However, it is possible that your Venus placement might be in the preceding sign of Virgo. Also, if you were born at the end of the given period, for example, on 26 September 1960, Venus was at the end of Libra, and it may be that Venus is in the following sign of Scorpio. The same goes for Eros positions.

If this is the case, the simplest solution is to read the adjacent sign as well as the given one. You should be able to determine which you feel is most like you.

Remember: this is important only if you were born on a 'cusp' day (i.e. a day when a planet or asteroid has just moved into a sign, or the last day a planet is in a sign before it moves into the following sign). For all other dates, the planets will be in the right signs wherever you were born in the world and at whatever time.

The only way to ensure you know the exact position of every planet in your birth chart is to consult a professional astrologer, but that is not necessary in order to use this book.

Next, read the sections for Venus and Eros relevant to you and work through the interactive sections. Again, use the appropriate key words or phrases to fill in the rest of your chart, and again copy the symbols for Venus and Eros into the right segments of the wheel. If you have Eros in Taurus, for example, copy the glyph for Eros into that section.

As you gradually build up your own erotic profile you may begin to discover the secrets of your pleasure principle, your sexual style, needs and erotic triggers. You can also make an erotic profile for your partner in order to compare and communicate.

Use the questions in the interactive sections at the end of specific chapters to build up a profile of your sexual character. In this way you can increase your own self-awareness. You may wish to keep a personal notebook of thoughts and ideas as you work through this book.

Interactive Section

- Do you feel in tune with your sexual needs and desires? If so, can you connect to the ancient mysteries of female sexuality, to a time when the ecstatic cults and rituals were a safe channel for our instinctive needs?
- If not, have you ever considered how feminine instinct and sexual power have been distorted or sullied over the past thousands of years?
- What do you feel your sexuality is all about? Is it to enjoy pleasure, or do you feel there are deeper issues at stake?
- Does the idea of archetypes, of the fundamental images we all carry from an ancient time, seem disturbing?
- Does the idea of gods and goddesses personifying our desires, feelings and sexual nature align with your cultural and family heritage, or does this produce an uneasy reaction?

THE EROTIC-PROFILE CHART

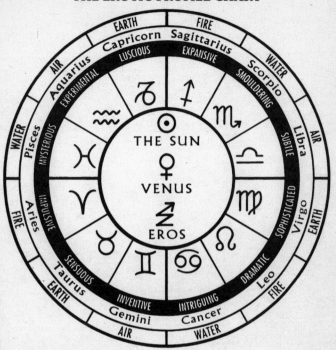

| MY SEXUAL IDENTITY IS |
| MY SEXUAL PURPOSE IS |
| I DESIRE WITH |
| I FIND PLEASURE IN |
| I AM SEXUALLY NURTURED BY |
| MY SEXUAL RESPONSES ARE |
| I HUNT MY PLEASURE |
| I AM TURNED ON BY |
| MY FANTASIES INCLUDE |
| MY EROTIC TRIGGERS INCLUDE |

PART ONE
SUN SIGNS

CHAPTER ONE:

WORKING WITH YOUR SUN SIGN

Your sun sign in astrology is the zodiac sign through which the sun was travelling on the day of your birth. Your sun sign reveals your purpose in life and the way you express your basic life energy. It is from this central point, the core of your personality, that your sexuality radiates. This sexual energy shines out from each of us in different ways, to attract or to exclude. A beacon of erotic connection for some, a warning light of potentially conflicting sexual energy to others. It gives many clues as to the kind of sexual partners and sexual experiences with which you can harmonise. The following twelve sun-sign chapters include the following:

1. How you express your sexuality, your sexual purpose and how you shine.

2. Your serpent power – how you desire.

The word 'desire' is rooted in the Latin *de sidera*, which literally means 'absence of stars'. Thousands of years ago, people used the stars to guide them on their travels. With no stars to guide us, we become lost. We seem to be compelled by something unknown, lost in the dark, looking for a star to guide us forward, or home. Following our desires is to navigate with no stars, no map, no logical system. We feel we are out of control and blind desire takes hold of us. It overwhelms us as if coming from nowhere, compelling us towards another person. This feeling from the inner place where there are no stars is triggered by another with whom we resonate. By acknowledging our sexual desires we are drawn into the unknown territory of our deeper selves. Through examining your sexual desire, you can become more aware of who and what you are.

The serpent woman of desire lies coiled and sleeping within each of us. She awakens to the call of Eros. Like Psyche, our serpent woman may lie in a dreamless sleep, unconscious, unaware of Eros's presence. When Psyche was rescued from eternal sleep by Eros, she awoke to the powerful desire for him. This is the moment when our serpent woman awakens: it is the moment when we are filled with sexual desire and longing.

It is the placement of Eros in your chart which represents what or who it is that awakens the serpent woman. See the Eros chapter to find out your own erotic triggers and fantasies.

Our serpent woman also operates differently from sun sign to sun sign, depending on the position of the sun in your chart. Knowing this enables us to clarify how we fashion our desire and follow it through. It is each sun sign's serpent woman who fashions desire into sexual reality for those of that sun sign.

Our serpent power is usually denied access to our day-to-day living, to the world of business meetings, social small talk and family crises. But our serpent woman is waiting. When the moment is right, she will respond to certain stimuli from Eros; she will unfurl her coils from the very centre of our being, inviting our sex to respond.

3. Beauty and beast within.

Sometimes we are seized by sudden passion, by erotic longing and erotic daring. This is when we are taken over by the invisible 'serpent woman' inside us who has been triggered by Eros.

Both her light and her darkness are hidden from us in our day-to-day lives. The light side of our serpent woman is our beauty, and the dark side our beast. If we acknowledge the complexities of our serpent woman, we can begin to enjoy the innate sexual needs that we may have not yet brought into the light of our consciousness. We may also begin to understand how, if we do not acknowledge the dark side of our serpent woman, she may manifest herself in our sexual expression through power trips, impotence, pain and guilt. Our beauty may be acceptable, but our beast is often something we would prefer to ignore.

4. Male sexuality.

Our partners, lovers and friends also have their own unique way of expressing themselves and responding sexually. We can become more aware of our own needs only if we can accept and integrate those of our partner. This section looks at male sexuality by sun sign.

5. Compatibility.

Obviously this is a general overview, for every birth chart includes more detail than can be noted in this book. Treat this section as a basic guide to those who may resonate more easily with your sexual preferences, rather than as an opt-out clause for those who may not.

This section can give you some clues as to those whose sexual chemistry may be in tune with your own. Remember: there are many other factors to be taken into consideration when considering the compatibility of two people. This is only a guide. Don't forget that, although you may seem to blend and harmonise your sexual expression with another sun sign, it may be that your Venus or Eros placements are not in such harmony. Alternatively, you may have very different sun-sign sexual expressions and seem on the surface incompatible, but if your Venuses are in harmony there will be much sexual and romantic pleasure between you.

Look at all the options. Work with yourself first, creating your erotic profile to discover the richness of your sexuality, then create your partner's or friends' profiles, too.

6. Interactive section.

This is where you start making the chart. There is a series of questions for you to work with your own awareness and self-discovery. Also key words and phrases for you to contemplate, reflect upon, and then start filling into your erotic-profile chart.

CHAPTER TWO:
ARIES

22 MARCH–20 APRIL

'The goddess with the gleaming eyes . . .'
Homeric hymn to Athena

Aries Woman – Purpose and Sexuality

Aries woman is acutely aware of her vulnerability, and her sexual purpose is to discover how she can welcome both intimacy and trust into her sexual lifestyle. Her nature is passionately bound up in her need to dominate, and this can often result in fiery relationships born out of frenzied physical desire. For the Aries woman, love and sex are usually separated, for her drive to find total pleasure can often distance her from her true needs. She thrives on the impulsive encounter, the spontaneous exchange of glances, the sensation of the moment. Hers is not a sexuality of commitment, for she wants to enjoy the challenge of the hunt, not the repetitiveness of long-haul relationships. However, for all her apparent independence, she is desperately searching for a partner who can provide her with honest stimulation, and the chance to involve herself totally.

The Aries woman rarely expects her male lover to play the dominant role in sexual encounter, and would prefer being the huntress, to seduce and capture. Her frantic pace and her passion for bodily contact are two ways she avoids the truth about her sensitive feelings. She needs sexual freedom, but she also needs someone who can give her the passion, the ecstasy and the confirmation of her own unique self.

Aries women are often drawn to anonymous sexual encounters, just to indulge their passion for stimulation and arousal. Yet she may find her greatest challenge, and she needs sexual challenge, is found in giving herself openly on a more intimate basis. The Aries woman needs to learn to let go sexually, to find herself through giving and receiving, rather than merely to dominate.

Key Word: Flow

For the Aries woman, the flow of pleasuring needs to fluctuate. Sometimes she would prefer someone who can move slowly at first, arousing her with gentle touching, with spoken fantasy, or by tonguing. Sometimes she would prefer wild abandon, fast and hard stimulation, to really feel she is being moved forcefully towards a climax rather than merely enjoying the anticipation of it. She would benefit from changing rhythms, from a partner who can both push her into fierce responses and quick orgasm if necessary, and allow her to enjoy a languid climax, where she can float with the feelings of her body rather than be overwhelmed by them.

The Aries woman is hungry for dangerous pleasure. Her inner sexual needs demand fantasy become reality. She has images in her mind of being aroused in public, or beneath the table of a candlelit dinner, or of exotic locations filled with hunters and huntresses. She needs a man who can share her fantasies, offer her new ones, and experience them with her. Hers is a world filled with visions of being driven to orgasm as her partner enters her with the full impact of his hardness. She is fire, and she must be lit from within.

How Aries Shines

The Aries woman enjoys making the initial seduction. She needs to take the initiative, to lure or hunt. Her games must be brief and highly suggestive. She will insist on no compromise: for the Aries woman a sexual experience is either all or nothing. But, because she must shine so brightly, monogamy is difficult. Aries women have childlike hearts and desires, and want everything now.

She may project a need to be dominated or lain on an altar of sexual initiation, but in reality it is she who will do the dominating. To really shine she needs to take on a role that lies within her dreams: a deep fantasy world where to be the goddess at the altar, naked and softly caressed by her priestess, is an enticement far greater than to be tied down and feasted upon by the lips of a vampire. To pursue and to lure, to provoke and then to turn and tame, is her game. She has a strong erotic magnetism, one that is a balance of male and female energy. Her power lies in her ability to take on the role of maleness, to impose her will over any adversary. She may fight with nails and teeth, punishing her partner with a torn back. This wild side of the Aries woman must shine: she needs a partner who can accept her forceful Yang, or masculine, nature. Her sexual purpose is not to receive but to give, and in doing so she may come closer to acknowledging the fragility that is truly her woman soul.

Serpent Woman Power

This is the way of the Aries woman's serpent of desire:

The serpent wakes at dawn. This is the time when she wants her sex to be warmed, fired into ecstasy. If there is no one who can share this moment then she will wait, impatient, hungry, watching for the time to strike. This serpent will strike fast and urgently for she wants it all, and she wants it now. She will look eagerly and hopefully for strength in a man's eyes, and the signs that he is willing to dedicate himself to her sexual needs. If she sees strength in her lover, she will move straight in, her passion and her arousal growing fast, too fast sometimes.

This serpent needs a lover who can accept her demand to be centre of attention. A lover who can assert his need for pleasure, yet give her endlessly of himself. Her serpent awakens quickly to the right contact. There is no prevarication. The moment must be spontaneous, and sexual stimulation must begin with the fantasy. She may carry her lover's image in her mind all day until she can no longer stand the overwhelming power of her serpent, tempting her to touch herself. She will want to release the image of his face and body, for she will not let it possess her. As she moves her fingers down to her silky mound she may imagine his willing submission. She would rather her fantasies were in full view of the world, for she avoids too much intimacy. This is her way.

Aries Woman – Her Beauty and Her Beast

Traditionally, Aries is ruled and guided by the planet Mars, the Roman god of both war and vegetation. His counterpart in Greek mythology was Ares. Ares was not so highly honoured nor revered as the Roman Mars. Ares was a personification of his mother's rage: he was born when his mother, Hera, became jealous of her husband, Zeus, giving birth to Athene from his head. Athene embodies foresight and wisdom. She was both a warrior goddess and one who protected those worthy of her attention.

The Aries woman's sexual beauty can be heard through the voice of Athene's honourable power. Her sexual beauty is acceptance of her feminine nature.

Her beast is aligned with Ares, an archetype of domination and sexual control, and like Ares at times aligns solely with passion and frenzy to cloak feeling.

Her Beauty

Athene was a warrior-protector and had the power of wisdom and foresight before entering into battle. This quality of the Aries woman's sexual beauty comes alive when she draws on her insight into the consequences of her seduction. If the Aries woman is in touch with her beauty, with Athene's strength to acknowledge the deeper vulnerability of humanity, she may forge her passion with conviction.

In her teens the Aries beauty may shine out through her sexual courage as she veers more towards male company than female. Later on she may experiment with her impulsive need for sexual release, taking on the toughest and most dynamic of partners to prove her worth and meet her need for sexual danger.

Her responses are quicker than most, attuned to fierce passion, enlivened by the flicking of a tongue or darting fingers across her velvet bud. She needs to act dangerously. She will provoke and tease, torment her partner into the highest and finest moment of abandon, until he must take hold of her sex and take vengeance on her. She will have the power, enclosing him in her hot embrace, her rhythm hard, her cries like the warrior returned. Her beauty is her fantasy world, for through it she lives passionately and fearlessly. She may enjoy the dominatrix role, or pressing on her lover's penis as she sits astride him yet holds herself back. Her beauty is that she can give all and take all, but only with whom she chooses. Then she will honour and protect that special moment of embrace.

Her Beast

The archetype of Ares lurks within the Aries woman, ready to strike with ruthless vanity, to sexually dominate and control. Ares symbolises rage and uncontrollable desire at its most rampant and compulsive. When the Aries woman aligns solely with Ares, she is controlled by the male, Yang, principle which is so alive within her passionate make-up. Her beast arises as a need to tear down the spirituality of her sex. She fears the unknown territory of her labia, of her arousal and her climax that can be so much more ecstatic than her partner's. By identifying with Ares, she can cloak herself in aggressive sex. She may enjoy sadistic pleasure, taking delight in her partner's pain as she mounts him again and again. He will take on the submissive role, bound to the iron bedstead or bent backward across a low velvet-cushioned stool. When the Aries woman is identifying with the Ares archetype, clitoral stimulation may be too close to the deep awareness of her femininity, and thus she may favour excessive penetration alone to fuel her power trip.

When she orgasms through power alone, she is lost, drawn down to her bestial nature. She may not respond easily to caresses, languid sensuality and the unfolding of her own moist bud. She may deny herself serenity in favour of potency. For it is the fear of her own femaleness that causes her beast to invade.

Her dark side is that she wants to be free from feeling, free from the burden of sexual responsibility and her womanness. If she blocks the true emotional vulnerability of her orgasm, she can become jealous and possessive, demanding her partners give all of themselves, and at the same time seeking out others to satisfy her hunger.

The Aries Male

The Aries male wants excitement. His is not an easy sexuality to bear, for he wants quick responses and he wants them now. For him the fantasy, the image, and the anticipation are what counts. The sexual build-up is the turn-on. The release and the moment of pleasure are short-lived and often an anti-climax. Many Aries males admit to having problems with orgasm.

At first he will be seduced too quickly by his own desire. He needs to satisfy his hot hardness first, and his partner second. His need for self-gratification is powerful. He may prefer hard penetrative sex because it can give him the sense of masculine potency that is his sexual purpose. Yet, when he sinks deeply into his partner's sex, the warm flesh clamping his penis and forcing him to push faster, his own moment of orgasm will be lonely. He keeps his pleasure for himself, and for himself alone.

His lover must be spontaneous enough to respond to his pace, his rhythms, his pulsating lingam. He seems the most primitive of all the sun signs, and his sexual purpose is to satisfy his primal needs. Yet he is the adventurer, the first to suggest public sex, the first to take a risk and play with danger. He is most likely to enjoy his orgasm when in a dangerous situation, about to be interrupted by an intruder, so others will see him displaying his superbly erect member, powerful and aching for release.

But he fears the exposure of his feelings, never allowing his partner access to his imagined world. He will always be driven to engage in his pleasure with furious passion, for in this way none can get close to his vulnerability. He ignites passion in others and is a superbly assertive lover, but he never stops to indulge in tenderness. Lacking the sensuality of some signs means that he adores the roughness and heat of the moment. This is his fire.

He is on a mission, a quest to satisfy his masculine pride. Such power, such mastery of penetration, is his that he may forget who it is who moans beneath him. Lost in a world of images, he would rather fantasise about whose labia he kneads with his rough hands, or whose erect nipples he covers with his lips. He would rather fantasise than know the woman he pleasures. For him, to be so intimate, so absorbed, so engulfed by the dark warmth of her sex is to be no longer alive. It is surrender. The Aries male does not willingly surrender to the abyss of sexual union.

Compatibility

The Aries woman often rushes too quickly into a sexual relationship. She is so intent on her passionate head-strong demands that she may not care who it is she has seduced with her fiery and provocative fantasy. She needs to find a lover who can stimulate her imagination, enjoy her erotic role-playing and her delight in vibrators, candles and fire. She needs a lover who can change from dynamic to passive, who can teach her to flow to varying rhythms and to give of herself both sensually and with feeling.

Aries Woman with the Fire signs (Sagittarius, Leo and Aries)

She may find the most imaginative foreplay and exotic locations with fire signs, for they share her impulse for fast arousal. Here is a mutual desire for self-gratification but an acceptance of the other's need to be first.

With Sagittarius she will be inspired by his need for danger. At worst, they will have too many moments of pure impulse, too many moments of needing complete freedom from the other. At best, she will take pleasure in ravishing him in the open air. She will force herself against him, take hold of his erect cock and press it slowly into her softness, the night air cold against their backs but the heat between them building to the cry of her climax.

With Leo she can enjoy the pleasure of a dramatic experience. He will kiss her nipples to hard aching points, savagely stirring her labia with his hands. She may respond eagerly, seeking his hardness against her belly. He may overwhelm her, but may also demand too much in return. She may become impatient with his need to be stroked, to make her carefully take her time and lick him all over when she would rather they were soaked with sweat and burning with the need for release.

With Aries she may enjoy mutual masturbation, fingers locked round his hard, aching penis as he fires her clitoris with firm strokes. He may use objects, candles, fruit, belts or dildos, to bring her quickly to a climax. They may prefer to arouse one another through penetration, both taking the dominant role when it suits them.

Aries Woman with the Air signs (Gemini, Libra and Aquarius)

The Aries woman will respond well to the intellectual eroticism of the air signs.

When Gemini phones her, begins to play with words as he feels his own maleness harden beneath his hand, he may suggest she reaches down to her warm sex. To feel beneath her silken panties for the mound of soft hair and twirl her fingers there. His voice will seduce her: his ability to communicate sexual arousal is awesome. He will be the master of erotic conversation, but he may not enjoy for long her need to dominate him.

With Libra she may entangle herself in his sophisticated games. At first, she will be drawn by the way he seems so passive, so waiting to be dominated. Yet she may discover, when they merge together, his need for refinement, that he is ethereal rather than carnal. She will enjoy his gently provocative caress, the way he can lick her all over, delighting in every orifice as if it were a feast. She may find this man most challenging of all, for they are opposite in their whole sexual expression. She must be willing to accept that, for him, her body is beautiful, a work of art to be gazed upon. He will spend hours watching her masturbate, but he may not allow her to spoil his ideals of aesthetic sexuality. She will become impatient without physical release and need the hard passion of deeper thrusting.

With Aquarius she may need to understand that his pleasure comes not so much from sensual stimulation and participation as from being a spectator. He may involve her in unusual group sex, or prefer a threesome where he can observe her passion as detached from himself. However, this is opposite to the Aries woman's need for intense passion on a one-to-one basis. She may fantasise about threesomes but is less likely than any other sign to actually involve herself in them in reality. The Aquarius male may offer her a new perspective on sexual dominance. His very detachment from the act allows him to observe and analyse what is occurring. He may take a long time to reach an orgasm, simply because he chooses to test himself out. She may become uneasy about his uninvolved and experimental approach to sexual encounters.

Aries Woman with the Earth signs (Taurus, Virgo and Capricorn)

If the Aries woman is in touch with her Athene archetype, she may discover a valuable sensual dynamic with the earth signs. Although not motivated by the same underlying sense of purpose, the earth signs have the power of sensuality and are a safe container in which the Aries woman can re-evaluate her connection to her body.

With Taurus she may find him as primal and as lustful as herself. Yet he will take his time to arouse her, pleasuring her with touch, sight and the delights of oral stimulation. She needs to make time for him to touch her not only with his fingers but with the delicate brush of his lips across her nipples, the featherlight glide of his hair across her tight bud as he moistens her inner thighs with his mouth. He will oil her toes, kiss his way to her throat until she will finally feel the power of his penis push hard against her heated clitoris. Like her, he has a desire for hard penetration, yet he can lengthen the ecstasy with his control within her secret place. His ability to seek pleasure rather than mere excitement will inspire her to an appreciation of the delicacies she often denies herself.

With Virgo, she must quickly discover the art of enslavement, for this man could prove too pure, too in need of accuracy and perfectly timed orgasm, for her passionate impulses. Virgo men aspire to be craftsmen, refining and polishing their sexual performance. A performance is what it becomes. He will move in time with her rhythms, undress her with his eyes and be quite frank about his intentions and his method of reaching ecstasy. This may be unerring, for the Aries woman loves the danger of the unknown, the risk of finding a male with a cock to match her hunger for deep penetration. If she opens up her fantasy world to him, suggests he be her slave as she commands him to rub his lingam between her breasts, to offer up his body to her every command, then perhaps they can share such pleasure. The Virgo male is all technique: his performance is superb, but he may hold back from true erotic intimacy.

When an Aries woman identifies with her Ares archetype, she may fiercely challenge the Capricorn man. Together they could have lengthy aggressive foreplay. The Capricorn male likes to control both his instinct and his orgasm at all costs. He is the most conventional of all the signs, fearful of the unusual but drawn to passionate women. The Aries woman may find he offers sexual strength and a skilled hand that guides her own to his always hard manhood. Her imagination knows no bounds, but he prefers preconceived techniques, automatic and repetitive stimulation. He may be fascinated by the loss of control her domination forces on him: he fears but secretly desires it. The Aries woman is probably the only sun sign to make him moan aloud as she sits astride him, her hair thrashing across his chest as she takes hold of his manhood, then kneads him, touching the tip against her sex, forcing him to surrender to her.

Aries Woman and the Water signs (Cancer, Scorpio and Pisces)

The water signs are probably the least able to resist the sexual magnetism of the Aries woman, and yet are the most likely to be the ones she misunderstands. These signs are opposite to the Aries woman: the Aries woman wanting total physical pleasure, the water signs seeking emotional ecstasy.

It is perhaps only fair to the Aries woman to remember she can easily seduce the Cancer male. She finds it simple to engage herself in a passionate encounter with this man and remain emotionally uninvolved. He, on the other hand, will find it virtually impossible to bond with her without involving his feelings. He is the connoisseur of oral sex. He seeks both to nourish his partner and to be nurtured through mutual oral stimulation. He would prefer her to take all of him in her mouth, for her to kneel before him, clasping his buttocks with her hands and her tongue slowly curling around his tortured penis. Yet she may not have time to indulge in his gradual unfurling and would prefer to burn inside with his deep thrusting.

If the Aries woman can acknowledge the vulnerability within her, she may find the Scorpio male a potent and satisfying partner. Their inner purposes are very different, but their strong sexual instincts may merge with erotic intensity. Both like to dominate, but he will do so using his darkly skilful mind. The Scorpio male shudders with an almost demonic frenzy when filled with raw sexual desire. She may find him alarmingly intense as his throbbing penis enters her like a black spear. But she may be able to combine her extraordinary fantasy world with his serious and powerful sexuality. He is hard to satisfy, but her pleasure will be his, and her reward will be a newfound connection to her deepest female self.

With the complex and sensual Pisces male the Aries woman may at first find a strange and compelling need to act out the role of aggressor. His sensitivity and elusive rhythms will stimulate her. She may enjoy his submissive ambivalence one day, then the next day his lush and extremely sensual demands. His is a sexual world of extraordinary dimensions. He may take her to the heights of abandon and to the torment of obsession, particularly if she has Venus in Pisces, or he has Venus in Aries.

Interactive Section
Aries Woman

The sun represents my sexual purpose.

My sexual purpose is to welcome closer sexual intimacy and trust my woman soul.

I need to learn to let go sexually, to give and to receive.

I sexually shine by taking the initiative and enjoying the pursuit.

My serpent power strikes fast when it is fired into ecstasy.

My beauty is heard through the voice of Athene and comes through honouring my own feminine sexual power.

My beast is heard through the voice of Ares when I avoid feeling and emotions, detaching myself from my sexual womanness.

27

Aries – sun-sign key words for your erotic chart

Fill in the blank spaces at the bottom of this page and the same area on your erotic-profile chart beneath the zodiac wheel. You can choose which words or phrase you most identify with, so that you begin to work with the images and meanings behind your sun sign.

The sun-sign section indicates your sexual identity, purpose and desire:

My sexual identity is _____

Choose from: spontaneous, impulsive, passionate, potent, demanding, fiery, assertive, impatient, provocative.

My sexual purpose is _____

Choose from: to develop self-awareness, to get in touch with my woman soul, to welcome emotional intimacy and trust, to learn to flow to the rhythms of my partner.

I desire with _____

Choose from: intention, impulse, purpose, dynamism, urgency.

Questions

- To what extent can you connect to your truly female side?
- Do you find it threatening or obliging? Warming or too fragile?
- Do you spend more time in male company or with female friends?
- Do you prefer to instigate sexual stimulation or have you rejected your spontaneity for fear of being too demanding?
- Does desire seem to take hold of you without giving you time to consider the outcome?
- Are you usually the first to be aroused?
- Do you get impatient with your partner if they can't keep to your pace?

CHAPTER THREE:
TAURUS

21 APRIL–21 MAY

*'I have decked my bed with coverings of tapestry, with
carved works, with fine linen of Egypt. I have perfumed
my bed with myrrh, aloes and cinnamon.'*
Proverbs 7:16–18

Taurus Woman – Purpose and Sexuality

When Taurus woman walks through a room she fills men's eyes with an image that stirs their unconscious longing for the archetypal Aphrodite. The image she projects, often unconsciously, is enough to make men want to kiss her face all over, to merge with the intense femaleness that arises from the ancient darkness of the earth.

To the Taurus woman, her body is a temple of beauty. For her, sexual experience is about self-pleasure and sensual awareness. Her sexual purpose is to uncover her true values, to find what it is that gives meaning to her, and to connect to her powerful sensuality. Sexual experience for the Taurus woman is deeply connected to her feelings. She may at first appear coy, unwilling to participate. But, when she finds a partner with whom she can both sexually and emotionally unite, she will genuinely offer herself.

At every twitch of her luscious mouth, at every glance of her knowing eye, she can seduce with the art of an instinctive huntress. She is a truly physically and sensual being, but she needs to open herself to the truth that sex and love are not always synonymous. The Taurus woman needs to learn to communicate her sexual preferences and to discover that her bodily responses are deeply connected to her emotions.

Key Word: Sensuality

The art of touch is the art of pure arousal to the Taurus woman. She thrives on the nurturing caresses that her hands and tongue can give to her partner. Fast, penetrative sex is not necessary for the Taurus woman. She uses all her senses to invoke climax for her and her partner. She will focus solely on her partner, sometimes obsessed with the need to control him with her mouth, her lips and her tongue, but always ready to give her sweetness to him. Wild abandon can be hers, but only after long and careful foreplay. She prefers a man who can take his time, not force her into penetration too soon. Her sexual desire is aroused only by beauty: delightful words, the richly evocative environment of velvets, silks, satins and lace.

She has much unbridled passion to express but finds it difficult unless her partner can understand her shyness. Masturbation is an option she'll choose in favour of involvement in a brief or one-night sexual encounter, for she fears the exposure of her emotions too soon. Yet she adores the beauty of a man's climax, of his lustful, animal quality which brings her closer to the fecundity of the earth. For she is of earth, this woman, and her nature is one that demands total exclusivity, so that her partner can truly plough her waiting furrow.

How Taurus Shines

She takes her time. She does not take the initiative easily, but she may seduce with her beautiful voice, her sensual touch and her need to offer pleasure. Her sexuality is deeply connected to nourishment, for she is the giver of life. She shines when she can offer herself as a sexual feast, so that many may come to her table and share in her exotic fruits, her honey, the sweetness of her moist sex, the warmth of her wine. She is the feasting table for her partner, but once he comes to eat with her he may find her own appetite insatiable. She hungers for sensual stimulation, and prefers simple pleasures to excitement or danger.

Her wildness lies in the deep fathoms of her nature, where she is willing to go to any lengths to please her partner. Anal or sadomasochistic sex is against her inner needs, but she will perform and indulge in any unusual play if it stimulates her partner and ensures he becomes hers. To truly shine she must be fondled slowly, her breasts teased, tenderly bitten, and the nipples aroused to euphoric hardness. She will enjoy playing a submissive role, especially one involving oral sex: having her

31

throat kissed, her labia tongued, or indulging her own need to lick and surround her partner's penis with her honey lips. She prefers her partner to orgasm first, for then she can feel most secure, when he is truly possessed by her sensual art.

Serpent Woman Power

This is the way of the Taurus woman's serpent of desire:

This serpent must attract. She must not pursue. She waits, coiled in her secret place, knowing that those who seek out beauty will come to her. This serpent may sleep for many days, pleasuring herself, for she is beautiful enough alone. When a man first walks into her landscape she will show no desire. She will play a deadly game, one where he must tread close enough to her serpent's nest before she can strike. Her strike is disguised by her soft voice and touch. He may be the first to put his hand upon her arm or kiss her cheek. Such hints for this serpent woman reveal intentions that cannot be forgotten. She will attach herself to any man who can offer her ecstasy, and any man whom she can ultimately possess.

Her serpent will rise slowly, in time with the motion of the earth. She may plan the first encounter, cover her body with perfumes, oils, massaged into her skin as she lies alone in the bath. Here she will watch the foamy water swirl across her pubic hair, where the serpents are waiting to be stirred. As the water caresses her sex she may find she cannot resist touching her erect bud, wet, oiled, ready for pleasure. She will feel the desire growing inside her, as her sex aches in anticipation of their meeting. She will plot every move of the seduction, even their final journey, as she rouges her nipples. Her serpent can only become powerful if she feels comfortable, warm, perhaps in her own bed and her own territory. Too many risks and her serpent returns to sleep alone. For this woman does not wish to dominate, but needs to feel unrestricted, to release her emotions through orgasm. Wherever the earth gives her a sense of grounding and centredness, there she will be ready to unleash her serpent. This is her way.

Taurus Woman – Her Beauty and Her Beast

Taurus has always been connected to, and symbolically ruled by, the planet Venus. The archetype of the planet Venus is multifaceted, as you will discover in the Venus section devoted to her. Venus energises and expresses herself through all of us. However, for the sun in Taurus, the Roman goddess Venus personifies grace, beauty and sensual love. Before her associations with the Greek Aphrodite, she was the simple guardian of flora and fauna. It is this gentle, serene and harmonious goddess who embodies the Taurus beauty. When the Taurus woman is in touch with this archetype, she will be intuitive and her emotions will flow. She will find the inner serenity of sexually enjoying the here and now.

Her beast is aligned to the dark side of the goddess Pasiphaë. Pasiphaë was cursed by the sea god Poseidon with an obsessive desire to be ravaged by the beautiful sacrificial white bull that her husband Minos refused to give up. Her obsession grew so strong that a trusted friend agreed to help her satisfy her lust. Her desire for copulation with an animal was such that her reputation for sexual bestiality was unrivalled by any other god. The product of this bizarre union between Pasiphaë and the white bull was the Minotaur, half-man half-bull. Pasiphaë eventually arranged her own revenge on Minos, ensuring that whenever he had sexual intercourse he ejaculated poisonous insects, snakes and scorpions, thus destroying his lovers in the process.

When the Taurus woman's beast is activated, she may too become obsessed with the object of her desire and, in her need to possess, she may in the end destroy her own true sensuality and deep affection, offering only greedy and manipulative sexual interaction. Her partner may literally reward her with poisoned sexual activity, contaminated not by snakes but by the Taurus woman's own possessiveness and jealousy.

Her Beauty

For the Taurus woman, her sexual questing may have begun as innocently as the Roman Venus, the spirit of the gardens. In her youth the Taurus woman finds great delight in the senses, what she sees before her, and what she feels and touches. This means she may develop sensual-sexual urges earlier than many, for her body is her shrine. Finding a self-image is important for the Taurus woman, and if she resonates to the inner rhythms of her body as it asks for sexual experience she may become quickly aware of what she has to offer, and what others may find compelling.

The Taurus beauty honours her sensuality by keeping in time with the ebb and flow of her body's responses. Like Venus in the garden tending her plants, she must craft her lovemaking and nurture her sexual finesse. If her garden of passion is well cared for then the feast will be the most exquisite. If the Taurean woman can access the secret of her garden of earthly delights, she will be the mistress of the erotic arts.

She will offer the gift of slow build-up, of courting her partner's phallus into sheer euphoria before he has even touched her. She will gently caress with the fingers of a genie who can rub magical fire into the darkest corners of his skin. She is the connoisseur of the senses. She may insist on visual stimulus: that he must watch her undress slowly, or be a voyeur as she takes a bath. She may suggest her partner shares this bath, sinks slowly into the musky oils, and face to face they sip champagne. Her beauty is that she gives time to indulge in all the senses. Her pleasuring has a rhythm all of its own and, if it is to be shared, her lover must be ready to repeat this sensual unfolding time and time again.

Her Beast

When the beast of the Taurus woman rises, the dark side of Pasiphaë can bring jealous imaginings and an obsessive need for sexual control. She has a deep-seated fear of rejection which can undermine her sexual responses. She may go to extremes, wanting only to control others and manipulate sexual experiences that have no emotional content. She may find herself choosing partners or lovers who retaliate with poisonous words.

When aligned only to Pasiphaë, she may rigidly resist her partner's needs and deny any communication about her own. She may become fixated on controlling her partner into orgasm, so that he becomes totally dependent upon her. She may withhold her own orgasm, refusing to be stimulated or aroused. If she has lured and attracted a partner who does not maintain the arousal she wordlessly demands, then like Pasiphaë she may seek revenge. She may choose to masturbate before him, knowing that he will be held under her power, unable to share in her climax. When her beast is active she cannot value herself. She may be hungry for constant stimulation, denying that she has become addicted to sex that is purely physical.

The Taurus Male

Hedonism and the delights of the senses drive the passion of the Taurus male. When he is drawn into a sexual encounter he will want to be certain of his enjoyment, as much as of his partner's. Each thrust of his phallus will be measured; each fingering of his lover's clitoris will be remembered. He will absorb himself in the highly tactile world from which he draws so much pleasure. The Taurus male wants to ravish first, then possess later. He may take his time to attune himself to his partner's needs, but once he has learnt about her sensual appetite he will spoon her with sexual delicacies.

This man feasts on close contact and heavy foreplay. He may be unabashed about his erection, and feels natural naked. The desire for earthy, instinctive sex makes him, at times, temperamental if he can't get enough stimulation.

The natural world is a source of infinite arousal, from the touch of a feather down his spine to his own nerve endings stirred by being massaged or by the water while bathing. He may prefer lying on his belly on the floor while his partner sits astride his buttocks. She may rub oils into his skin, push her fingers down the cleft to finger his penis from behind. This may be a most exquisite sensation for him, as she holds him tightly, not allowing him to turn over, not allowing him control. The Taurus male will enjoy sexual pleasure most when he is least in control.

He may not seek excitement, nor adventurous unusual sexual environments, but he will play slowly with his partner's nakedness. He will caress with true tenderness. His lips will travel every inch of her body before he gives more of himself. He is the serene sensualist who insists on using all five senses. With his ears he will be aroused by the sounds of their bodies, the slapping, gliding sounds as he rubs his penis between her breasts. The sight of her vulva, wide, inviting, enticing him in. The smell of her sex, arousing him to delicious frustration. His utter sensuality is his gift, yet he may withhold much of his deeper giving if his own pleasure is denied.

Compatibility

The Taurus woman moves slowly, takes her time to make certain she is giving herself to the partner who can reward her with self-worth. More than any other sign she fears failure in her sexual relationships. She needs to find a lover who will take pleasure with her, enjoy the sensual experiences for which she yearns, and has the patience and dedication to encourage her to experiment with her own sensual fantasies.

Taurus Woman with the Fire signs (Aries, Leo and Sagittarius)

If the Taurus woman is in touch with her Venus archetype she may well discover a potent and enriching sexual dynamic with these very different types.

If her Venus placement is in Aries then her encounter with the strident and potent Aries male could turn into a melange of languorous delicacies and powerful excitement. Any Taurus woman will be plunged into pleasure by the Aries male's potent arousal. Theirs is a passion built on her sensuality and his uncontrollable abandon. She may jerk her hips forward waiting for his strong hands to grasp her pubic mound. He will lead; she will follow. She may resist when he begins to finger the tight curve of her buttock down to her anus. She may prefer his penis to stay closer to her inner chalice, to rub against her swollen sex and tempt and tease. They may take turns to dominate, but essentially the Taurus woman will always be in control. If she becomes too possessive he may turn away from her as quickly as he arrived in her bed.

With Leo she may enjoy his need for constant attention. The Leo male is notorious for wanting to be sexually served. He will expect high standards and demand lengthy foreplay, filled with dramatic highs and lows. Sexual intimacy for the Leo male is like a theatrical production. There must be music, lights, scenery and performance. His pleasure is mostly for himself, but he will insist that he is the only male who can satisfy her desire. She may treasure his attention and adore caressing and massaging him for hours but, if her own needs are denied, their intimacy could be forced into chaotic outbursts and emotional scenes.

The Sagittarius male has a high sex drive. However fiery his outlook on life, his sexual expression may find easy sport in the arms of a Taurus woman, for a while at least. He is an adventurer and would rather enjoy intimacy in outdoor places: the wild mountainside or the park bench at dawn. The Taurus woman can release honey for his sweet tooth, and the Sagittarius male can release the joy of nature's bestial wildness for her. The Taurus woman may be driven by his passion and his love of oral stimulation, but she may become jealous of his need for freedom. She may tire of his need for dangerous locations and the brashness of his penetration. She may prefer the slow and the tried.

Taurus Woman with the Air signs (Gemini, Libra and Aquarius)

The Taurus woman may find the abstract ideals of the air signs out of tune with her own more animal and simple approach to sexuality. Although highly attracted by their free, detached and intellectual qualities, she may become too possessive and too demanding for their need for space, especially if she is aligning mostly to her Pasiphaë archetype.

With Gemini, unless she has Venus in Gemini (see Venus section) or he has Venus in Taurus, the attraction of this master of foreplay will perhaps prove a deadly obsession. She will enjoy his ability to play any role she desires. He could take her into romantic escapades, or introduce her to his fascination for watching two women pleasuring each other. She will shiver with desire because the Gemini male knows how to keep her secret jewel awakened, urging her to the brink of total pleasure as he astounds her with his nimble fingers. However, she may lead herself astray with this man, for she is always tempted to demand more, to possess him. This may not sit well with his need for freedom.

With Libra she may share all the pleasures of beauty. Yet the Libran male is more seduced by aesthetic beauty than the earthy reality of the body. He will enjoy his surroundings: the boudoir, rich colours, vibrant blues, and the sheen of black satin pillows. He will linger longer than any other man across the restaurant table, his eyes darting suggestions, his words enticing and ripe with meaning. He is the artisan of romance. The earthy sensuality of the Taurus woman may charm him into her lavish bed. The wine, the hazy smoke, the golden hue of her sex will inspire him. But when the reality of her body reminds him that he is only human, he may suffer from his fear of being sexually engulfed. This man is an idealist, and this woman stays close to nature: she does not need ideology. Yet she will please him longer than many.

The Aquarian male may love to watch her undress. To remove her tissue-thin chemise, her skin glowing in the light of a log fire. They will share black olives, mussels, food that caresses her tongue and throat and amuses his passion for the unusual. He may at first steer down her own pathway, lured by her very difference. He will enjoy her self-pleasuring, find great stimulus when she fingers her sex before him. She will feel safe with this man's rigidity but find fault with his cool detachment when he is testing out his own self-control. She may enjoy licking champagne from his belly button and the crevices between his thighs, tonguing the end of his penis. She will give him most pleasure with oral sex, but the way he achieves orgasm is in the power of his mind, rather than in the touching of his body. He may find her insatiable appetite for fellatio becomes routine and too demanding.

Taurus Woman with the Earth signs (Taurus, Virgo and Capricorn)

With her own sign, Taurus, she may discover untouched and secret areas of her body when she shares her sexual expression with him. Here is a mutual need for plenty of good hard sex, and the ability to understand each other's richly sensual needs. Together they can indulge in mutual masturbation, a favourite Taurean pleasure. They may prefer to enjoy bathing together, both able to massage and control the other until they climax together. Her sex will glisten with the swirls of the water and he will delight in his aching penis at the sight of her earthy beauty.

With Virgo she may enjoy his meticulous desire to service her with every pleasure imaginable. He will offer her the art of sexual perfection in his performance and in his impeccable grace. His is not passion and frenzy: there is no hard animal lust; there is only a desire to find order in his own instincts. He feels he must tame the animal side of his passion to align with method and discrimination. She may find this slightly disturbing at times, for Taurus needs natural rhythms rather than enforced timing and ritualistic orgasm.

With Capricorn she may find the pulsating quality of his desire overwhelming. She will be the chalice and he the blade, his body undulating to her own rhythms. Darkness is their ally for both fear the delicious ache they will experience the first time they discover the other. She may find she becomes more relaxed in his presence, that her nakedness glows and her desire enraptures her. She will feel as if his body is drawing her own from the ground. The magic of his power will arouse her sex until she is lost in the heavy delight of his thrusting raw passion.

Taurus Woman with the Water signs (Cancer, Scorpio and Pisces)

The water signs may stimulate a powerful erotic response from the Taurus woman, enriching her earthy sexuality with emotional intensity.

With Cancer she may find his ambivalence initially disturbing and yet awkwardly exciting. She may find herself drawn away from her serene sensuality by the gentle seduction of this secretive man. Both require tenderness and sensual arousal to evolve; both need time and patience to allow their pleasure to be shared and inhibitions relinquished. They have much to offer each other: she may show him the joys of tactility, oral sex and mutual masturbation; he may teach her to be submissive and receptive, and show her how safe she can feel in the arbour of his complete emotional passivity. His fantasy world will intrigue her and his exploration of her body will take a lifetime, but she has the patience and the desire for such languid pleasure.

Scorpio is her natural opposite in the zodiac. Like other polarities, this can be a highly erotic and transformative sexual relationship. The Scorpio male is the supreme master of seduction. The Taurus woman is the total sensualist, delighting in sexual pleasure that takes her to the depths of pure surrender. Both will ravish and possess the other, he drawn to her earthy demands, she to his extremes of passion and his love of oral stimulation. Together they will turn each sexual encounter into more than just physical pleasure. Both need to learn to respect the other's demanding sexual hunger.

With Pisces she may feel safe in the flowing caresses of this man's lingering touch. He may be aroused by her seductive and highly sensual aura. She may need to take the sexual initiative to ensure her arousal is maintained and that he can find pleasure in the submissive role he often prefers. She will enjoy dominating him and together they will find much joy in his desire for total surrender. She may well prove an enduring and deeply sensitive partner, able to intuitively respond to his changing sexual patterns and elusive desires.

Interactive Section
Taurus Woman

The sun represents my sexual purpose.
My sexual purpose is to discover the value and meaning of my sensual nature.
I need to learn to communicate my sexual preferences and to remember that love and sex are not always synonymous.
I sexually shine by adorning my lover with earthly beauty.

My serpent power rises rhythmically, paced to the flow of other.

My beauty is heard through the voice of Venus when I connect to the inner serenity of my ancient sensuality.

My beast is heard through the voice of Pasiphaë when I become possessive, jealous and obsessed, thus destroying true intimacy.

Taurus – sun-sign key words for your erotic chart

Fill in the blank spaces at the bottom of this page and the same area on your erotic-profile chart beneath the zodiac wheel. You can choose which words or phrases you most identify with, and so begin to work with the images and meaning behind your sun sign.

The sun-sign section indicates your sexual expression, purpose and desire.

My sexual expression is _____

Choose from: sensuous, indulgent, lush, seductive, emotional, ardent, possessive, romantic, affectionate.

My sexual purpose is _____

Choose from: to discover the value and meaning of relationship through my sensual nature, to acknowledge the depth of my emotions, to learn that sexual love does not mean possession, to begin to place trust in different patterns of sexual behaviour.

I desire with _____

Choose from: subtle artistry, secret passion, method and purpose, determination, gut instinct.

Questions

- What relationship do you have with your body? Is it a pleasurable one or do you fear the underlying power of your femininity?
- Once you have committed yourself to a sexual relationship, do you find you prefer sexual conventions to experimentation?
- Does a sexual relationship always have to be a loving one? If not, do you feel rejected if love is not all-inclusive?
- Have you ever denied your feelings are involved in a

sensual relationship, only to find you become possessive and jealous?

- How easy is it for you to flow with your partner's
  moods, rhythms and desires?
- If the object of your desire does not take the initiative,
  are you hurt or do you reject them before they have
  time to respond, for fear of your own vulnerability?
- Do you enjoy asserting your own sexual needs during
  arousal, or are you concerned only with pleasuring
  your partner?

CHAPTER FOUR:
GEMINI

22 MAY–22 JUNE

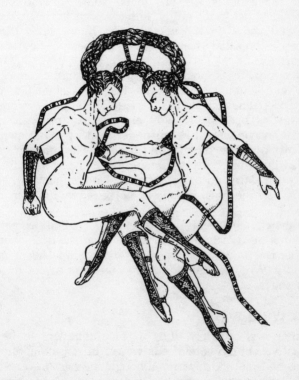

*'Sexual thoughts are like wild swallows that fly into her
mind to create fantasy, then leave with the speed of light
when the pleasure is over.'*
Anon

Gemini Woman – Purpose and Sexuality

The essential purpose of the Gemini woman is to find her elusive 'twin'. For a Gemini woman there often seems to be a gap, as if someone is permanently missing in her life, even though she may have a partner or be involved in a deeply sexual relationship. She is essentially lonely. She mirrors herself in those around her, until she believes she has found someone who can respond to her inner needs. In her search for her twin, she may move from lover to lover, in the hope that someone can satisfy her restless and sometimes neurotic sex drive.

Her sexuality is more about intellectual erotic connection than simple physical contact. If she cannot find a truly telepathic contact, the merging of souls and minds as well as bodies, her light and breezy approach to sexual encounter will be misunderstood by many men, and her inner needs torn and bruised. She often gives too easily of her body, assuming this is the key to love. She often dares not place emotional investment in her sexual relationships, for she is too sensitive, too fearful of pain.

Although she thinks she does, the Gemini woman does not need to find a soul mate. What she does need to discover is who she is and to truly know her own identity. Who Gemini is is more important to her than why she is.

Key Word: Variety

Gemini needs variety. It is a spicy stimulant in her sexual vocabulary. She needs variety of sensation, anything unusual and bizarre, although she may in reality find experimental or group sex distasteful. The Gemini woman is not overtly promiscuous but, if variety is lacking in one sexual relationship, she may well try as many partners or lovers as she can in her endless search for satisfaction, and her twin self.

She has a more intellectual approach to sexual encounters than any other sun sign. Her inner sexual needs demand that she 'think' about sex, and she will often enjoy her own fantasies more than the actual performance. This is why sexual communication must be verbally stimulating for her. She can become quickly bored with physical contact which does not involve mental excitement.

The Gemini woman may need to learn that her mind is the primary erogenous zone for her own pleasuring. Being turned on by a voice, by talking, by sharing fantasies, is more likely to heighten her sexual desire than silent sex. The phone was probably invented for the Gemini woman, and erotic phone conversations are an essential accessory for her sexual richness.

How Gemini Shines

The Gemini woman must shine. She must radiate her grace and her beauty and be the centre of lavish attention. Yet the Gemini woman often moves into a sexual relationship too quickly. If she is physically attracted to someone, and they are intellectually her equal, she will quickly signal her intentions. Giving all of herself in one swoop of desire can often engulf her intended lover and she needs to learn to slow down her emotional involvement. Because her emotional expectations of each sexual experience are high, she finds it difficult to separate love from sex.

She projects excitement and demands excitement in return. In some ways it is the type of encounter, or the involvement of the mind in her sexual experiences, that is her ultimate trigger for orgasm. In her dreams, in her fantasies, she may find it is often the thought of another woman which mysteriously brings her to climax. Bisexuality fascinates, entices and excites her mind. She may imagine herself as possessor of both a velvet yoni and a shaft of thrusting rigidity. To welcome both male and female to her erotic world is to her neither wicked nor unusual.

But, whatever the preference of her sexual fantasies, she will always chase after that elusive lost twin. Through her sexual encounters she may discover herself, but only if she can find a partner who can guide her to focus inwardly. Her purpose is to truly know who she is, and her sexuality can provide the answer.

Serpent Woman Power

This is the way of the Gemini woman's serpent of desire:

The serpent wakes quickly from her slumber, eyes searching, scanning the plane, the train, the bar, searching out the beauty she seeks. She may see a face across a room, hear a voice on the telephone, or touch the beautiful hand of a waiter (hands convey deeply erotic messages to Gemini). She feels the urgency of passion and attraction quicker than any other sun sign. She will be on the lookout for instant sexual experience. As an opportunist, the moment must be taken, the pleasuring taken where she can find it. She wants to taste the newness and originality of a variety of encounters, whether with many lovers or with her current partner. Arousing herself is often preferable, however, to waiting for a lover who cannot respond at her speed. Masturbation plays a large part in her sexual repertoire, both mutual and alone.

She seduces easily, preferring to tease, torment, and challenge. Her serpent power rises enflamed with mind-blowing expectations. She will keep her serpent nourished with fantasy, fiercely impassioned with the thoughts of her own verbal and oral talents, for she is the virtuoso of foreplay. Verbal and oral sex are inextricably linked for the Gemini woman. Her serpent demands communication, sexual words, erotic gestures, moving to engage in fellatio, to express herself with her tongue, for this is her most exquisite language. It is said that Cleopatra was a Gemini woman. She apparently enjoyed fellatio with thousands of men, once pleasuring several hundred men at one single feast. This is her way.

Gemini Woman – Her Beauty and Her Beast

In traditional astrology, the sign of Gemini is ruled, guided and nourished by the planet Mercury. The planet was named after the Roman messenger god, his Greek counterpart being Hermes. The son of Hermes and Aphrodite was Hermaphroditus. When Hermaphroditus was desired by the beautiful water nymph Salmacis, she bathed with him in the river, merging with him both sexually and physically for ever. Hermaphroditus was from then on both male and female. The Gemini woman is like this child: a harmonious blend of male and female qualities, and child of Aphrodite and Hermes.

The Gemini woman's sexual beauty is studded with Hermes' talent: like the messenger god, her purpose is sexual mastery and knowledge. The Gemini woman's sexual beast is aligned with Aphrodite: like Aphrodite her sexual purpose can be for self-pleasure and capricious seduction.

Her Beauty

Hermes is able to travel wherever he chooses. His journey is exciting, inspiring: he can play with mortals, deceive the gods and love recklessly. The Gemini woman's sexual beauty is expressed, like this archetype, through her mercurial mind, her seductive arts, her charm, her guile, her testing of the lover of her choice, the versatility of her sexual arousal, both given and taken. Like Hermes she may take risks and cross boundaries that few others would choose to. Sexually, she will be aware of herself at a young age, enjoying masturbation and discovering the joy of her own intimacy. She is a free spirit, searching for one who can live up to her ideals and perhaps mirror her true identity.

Her responses are attuned to the rhythms of thunder and lightning: sometimes she will strike fast, enjoying pure explosive penetration; yet at other times she will lead herself deeper into her mind, further away from the intensity of her lover's thrusts, until she cries for release.

She idealises every partner because, for her, love and sex are synonymous, locked together, interwoven between the jewel of her sex and the fantasies in which she lives. Her beauty is her ability to arouse every man, for she can be every woman. She is a trickster, playing the part of whoever she wants to be. Fantasy is her lover, and sexual stimulation the means to discovering who she really is. She finds the erotic in all thoughts; she finds the erotic in all images.

Her Beast

It may seem bizarre to associate the Gemini woman's beast, the dark side of her sexual purpose, with the goddess of desire. However, Aphrodite herself had a dark side. She was eternally self-pleasuring, eternally persuasive and eternally held up a mirror to remind herself she was the most beautiful and seductive of women. Aphrodite was intent only on her own sexual satisfaction.

She wore a girdle of desire which would arouse any man who had the privilege to see it. The Gemini woman carries her own girdle of desire. Her awakening to this incredible power plunges her often into promiscuity: she can learn to seduce and trap too soon, be too ready to give herself to another, too impatient to test her intuition.

Aphrodite needs to control, to be in power, and desperately hates to be controlled. Gemini's dark side is that at times she will please herself first and her lover second. Her cruel streak can manifest itself in teasing, controlling, coaxing, playing the dominant but never the dominated. Yet she fears sexual rejection so much that, if a man does not respond to her persuasion, she may feel betrayed, lost and alone. The Gemini beast arises because of her vulnerability, her low self-esteem, and her lack of compassion.

Although she plays the role of controller, she often finds it difficult to verbalise what she truly wants from her lover. Her expectations can be too high and she often assumes that her lover can read her mind. This can lead to unsatisfactory pleasure, fake orgasms and pretence, leaving her both physically frustrated and restless to explore an alternative means to fulfilment.

The Gemini Male

This is a childlike man who is innocently amused by his own sexual expression and needs. He is like a will-o'-the-wisp, ready to come and go as he pleases and ready to indulge or to abandon a sexual encounter on impulse. His spontaneity rivals that of the Aries male, but he needs excessive mental stimulation and communication. His is not a sexuality of sensual adventure. It is more a curiosity to see how stimulated or turned on he can be by words, gestures, ideas and thoughts. The actual bodily contact comes later. He does not want passion as such: he merely searches for some lost vision, some ideal twin who constantly eludes him. His sexual purpose is to discover who he is, and he may be promiscuous in his search for someone to mirror himself. He will masturbate regularly from an early age, aware of the need to pleasure himself with fantasy and erotic images.

He will be fascinated by a face, a gentleness, a seductive gesture. He will follow instinctively, knowing that the anticipation is more valuable than the encounter. A new lover may relieve his boredom and restless energy, but she will also seep into his mind so that he has sleepless nights and mood swings and he feels the need to take her one step further along the path. He will surprise her, take her when she least expects him to, perhaps while travelling in the car or the back of a taxi. He has the dangerous ability to be anyone, to take on roles and play out any sexual perversion if asked. His disconnection from his body makes it hard for him to be fully sensually aligned to his partner, unless he has Venus in Taurus.

Penetrative sex can be a big issue for the Gemini male. His mastery of oral stimulation and seduction are unprecedented, but he may find difficulty in lengthy thrusting to please his partner. To him, this becomes boring, for his mind is not engaged in the dynamics of repetitive sex. Orgasmic release makes him feel vulnerable. He will be most likely to enjoy climaxing in his partner's mouth or across her body. He will touch his partner's labia with the lightest of touches. Hovering like a bird of paradise, his tongue will alight for a second, sending ripples of pleasure across her pubis. Ask the Gemini man for sexual stimulation and he can give it all, as long as he is rewarded with variety and conversation. Try to possess or engulf him and he will put on his mercurial wings and fly by morning.

Compatibility

The Gemini woman believes she will arouse many men. But are there many men who can arouse her? She is often indiscriminate in her choice. The object of her desire may quickly lock into her passionate streak of lightning desire, his hardness only a barometer to boost her self-esteem. She may forget to think about who this man really is and whether he is worthy of her. She needs to find a lover who can help her focus inward, and be intellectually aligned to her sexual needs.

Gemini Woman with the Fire signs (Aries, Leo and Sagittarius)

When the Gemini woman is in touch with her Hermes archetype she will experience fluidity and ease of communication in encounters with the fire signs.

With the Aries male she can respond fast to his potency. He will inspire her with his passionate vision of sexual fulfilment, his chariot of fire driving wildly into her sex. Penetrative sex can be boring for the Gemini woman, but this man's brand of fire may scorch her mind and perhaps offer a challenging way to express her excessive energy. But both can become impatient with the other's hunger for very different feasts: hers is for outrageous mental sexual contact, and his for pure animal lust and pleasure.

With Leo she may be enflamed, but he may demand too much from her. Both need to plunge into the limelight of the other's desire, and thus their initial sexual liaison will be fraught with dangerous meetings and dramatic scenarios. But the Leo man has little time for the unusual: he is more inclined to use tried and tested methods of climax. The Gemini woman needs the freedom to explore the outer limits of sexual freedom. Her curiosity is insatiable. Theirs may be a short-lived but highly passionate merging of two attention-seekers.

A Sagittarius male can take her to those outer limits she so yearns for. These two are natural opposites in the zodiac, which makes for highly erotic sexual relationships, a blending and indulging of their differences. With a Sagittarius male she may discover a new release through oral ecstasy and wild abandon. The Gemini woman will stir extraordinary images in his imagination, but may also keep her true feelings deeply hidden. She can play the vamp, the barmaid, the dominatrix, the slave, the pimp, the bisexual, any role he chooses. Together, theirs is a pleasure of intense spontaneity. Both enjoy sexual adventure while travelling, and may hook into each other so powerfully that their net may be filled with tantalising expectations and unpredictable extremes of passion.

Gemini Woman with the Air signs (Gemini, Libra and Aquarius)

With the other air signs, the Gemini woman will feel comfortable and able to express her childlike and spontaneous need for communication. These may not be sexual relationships of deep, intense passion, but she can align herself with the intellectual energy she so desperately needs in order to enjoy her sex.

With a Gemini male she may believe she has found her twin soul. They will be breathless together, both intuitively understanding how the other is stimulated by erotic conversation and the surges of the mind. Another Gemini may be the closest to her ideal, but could at times be too absorbed in his own quest for self. They may enjoy erotic phone conversations. He will be at work, the office staff out to lunch, as he gazes down at his hardening penis beneath his trousers. He will utter words that touch her clitoris like his lips would do. A smile will cross her own mouth as she hears his enticing voice. She will press her sex hard against the wall as they lock in mutual verbal and sexual arousal.

Libra may hold the key to her beautiful fantasies and thoughts. With him there is silken conversation. A closed circuit of minds and hands. He will be enthralled by her mind, excited by her as an ideal lover. She will seduce him with her skilled hands and her artful tongue. She may find him easily aroused and closely aligned to her intellectual sexuality. The Libran male is the most likely to seek refinement. He will want to measure and balance their lovemaking. He will be fascinated by her bisexual inclinations. He may suggest she bring a friend so he can indulge his pleasure of being a voyeur. If she is uncomfortable in the reality of this, she may simply talk to him, tell him how it would be if she were with this female lover of his fantasy. This will provoke them both into a surge of mutual masturbation which both will be unable to control.

The Aquarius male may offer her a grander picture, a clarification of who she is in the universe. He may want to watch her as she closes her eyes, and he will begin to touch her nipples, circling them until they harden into red buds. Their bodies will glide in fusion, but their minds may be far apart: hers refining and questioning; his waiting for answers. Yet together they may sexually unite in a perfect solution. The Aquarian male's ambiguous words will arouse her beyond all expectation. For hers is a thirst for a climax of the mind and the pulsating release of her clitoris as she feels it rise between her unfolding lips to his kiss.

Gemini Woman with the Earth signs (Taurus, Virgo and Capricorn)

Although the Gemini woman is alert to change, to variety and difference, she may become restless with and disorientated by the sexual machinations of the earth signs.

With Taurus, unless she has her Venus placement in Taurus, the Gemini woman may fear the earthy sensuality and the silent seduction of this man. He has slow hands, intensely flickering fingers, caresses that demand all the time in the world. She may feel abducted, ravished, out of control. Not an easy energy for her to enjoy. Taurus prefers long periods of steady, deep penetration; she may not. He will be skilled at the art of bringing her to a climax with his fingers and tongue, but she may begin to grow restless with his need for repetition and slow, cautious paces.

Virgo seeks perfection rather than a frenzy of passion. She may prefer wild spontaneity to metronome love. She needs a place where there are no clocks ticking to remind him when to stop, no bathing away of the sweet fragrances of her passion when their intimacy is over. They may respond to each other intellectually but both are deeply committed to their own needs.

Capricorn may assume sexual control of her. Although he may infuse her with erotic connections when they meet, it may be difficult for her to establish her own needs in his scheduled world. For the Capricorn male there is a time and place for sex. He is not spontaneous unless there is a safe container for his vulnerability. He likes to see; not to speak. She would rather play with his penis for hours, biting and nibbling him into tormented longing, than endure his obsession with the length of his performance. With this Capricorn man, she may align with Aphrodite. At first she will impulsively seduce him but, when she begins to realise he seeks control, she will turn on him. There will be stormy encounters with this man. Maturity versus innocence. She plays the child and he will treat her like one. Bondage and anal sex are strong contenders for the Capricorn male's arousal with this woman, but she may remain unmoved and unwilling to share her self, resorting to fake orgasms and lies.

Gemini Woman with the Water signs (Cancer, Scorpio and Pisces)

Here their sexual energies are uncontrolled, a mingling of restless air and chaotic water. Yet somehow the powerful emotional intensity of these signs often allows the Gemini woman to reach into the deeper pockets of her own sexual needs.

With Cancer she may feel captivated and cherished. Her little-girl-lost appearance will appeal to his highly sensitive nature. He will offer her slow and skilful arousal, a nourishment of body and mind, while she may lead him into explosive passion that he may not ever have tasted. The emotional content of her sexual relationships often eludes the Gemini woman, but this man can show her how to integrate her deepest emotional needs with her sexuality. A powerful combination, but only if she is mature enough to accept his excessive attachment to her, and he can allow her the freedom to come and go as she pleases.

The Scorpio male has a powerful magnetic effect on the Gemini woman. She may at first find her feelings disturbed by the dark smouldering depths of this man. She is so light, so willing to enjoy conversation and short bursts of pleasure in spontaneous celebration, while he takes his time to indulge all his senses, demanding power and control over every move and every response. She may either allow herself to be possessed by this man or she will totally reject his overpowering and sometimes sadistic sexuality. She may be fascinated by his intense sexuality, but she will always fear his power.

The Pisces man can give and enjoy pleasure with the changeable and restless sexuality of the Gemini woman. Pisces will flow with her needs and may indulge in all her fantasies. Like Gemini, he would rather escape the earthly reality of human passion through dreams, illusions and pretence. He will bring her much pleasure, for he is the connoisseur of oral sex, finding deep arousal in licking her. He will explore every inch of her mind and her body, for he is ultimately sensual and yet able to talk through the night if she so desires.

Interactive Section
Gemini Woman
The sun represents my sexual purpose.

My sexual purpose is to discover who I truly am through my relationships.

I need to learn not to become emotionally involved in every sexual encounter.

I sexually shine by being the centre of lavish attention.

My serpent power is impatient and aroused quickly by any sexual opportunity.

My beauty is heard through the voice of Hermes when I honour my sexual mastery and my ability to arouse my partner.

My beast is heard through the voice of Aphrodite when I seduce without considering the consequences and deny my true emotional needs.

Gemini – sun-sign key words for your erotic chart
Fill in the blank spaces at the bottom of this page and the same area on your erotic-profile chart beneath the zodiac wheel. Choose which words or phrases you most identify with, and so begin to work with the images and meaning behind your sun sign.

The sun-sign section indicates your sexual identity, purpose and desire.

My sexual identity is _____
Choose from: inventive, versatile, adaptable, idealistic, erotic, exciting, multifaceted, entertaining, opportunist.
My sexual purpose is _____
Choose from: to discover my true identity in order to find wholeness, to get in touch with my true emotional needs, to welcome sexual intimacy as only one expression of self.
I desire with _____
Choose from: spontaneity, impulse, haste, intellectual pleasure, cunning, curiosity.

Questions

- To what extent do you feel you are on a quest to find your elusive 'twin'?
- Do you feel there is someone or something missing in your life, even when you are involved in a sexual relationship?
- Do you prefer male friends to female? If so, do you feel uncomfortable with women unless you are fantasising about bisexual experiences?
- Do you prefer to be in control of seduction and the initial romance?
- Do you put off physical sexual pleasure in favour of mental stimulation or masturbation?
- Do you leap into sexual encounters without considering the consequences? If so, are you usually disillusioned or hurt because your expectations are too high?
- Do you deny your emotional needs when embarking on a sexual encounter? Do you escape from sexual relationships that seem too intense and physically dependent?

CHAPTER FIVE:

CANCER

23 JUNE–23 JULY

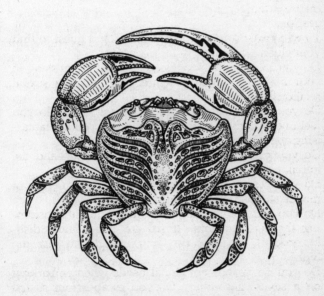

'She waited for his touch as if he were a marauder who
had come in, infinitely unknown and desirable to her.'
DH Lawrence, *The Rainbow*

Cancer Woman – Purpose and Sexuality

The Cancer woman projects an aura of total feminine mystique. There is something about her which is deeply bound to the ancient pre-patriarchal civilisations, as if the early goddess cults still live within her psyche. The Cancer woman's sexual purpose is to reconnect to the ebb and flow of her body, the natural rhythms of her femaleness, and learn to allow her feelings to flow with them, too.

Her nature is deeply emotional, bound by a resistance to change, but yet desiring to nurture and attend to the growth of others. She is highly sexual and receptive, but takes longer than even her Taurean sister to arrive at a point where she will give of herself freely.

Within her is the conflict between the outgoing flow of her emotions and the restriction she places on her physical needs. Often she may turn in on herself, denying her own desires. She masks her powerfully seductive aura with a cloak of controlled worldliness. She often banishes her wild woman and identifies instead with conformist roles of motherhood or the ambitious workaholic, and the social niceties of convention. Yet, beneath this veneer of acceptable standards, lies a darkly sensitive and powerfully sensual female.

Denying she is needy for sexual experience means she may forget her own body and her feminine inheritance from the time when her power was one of receptiveness and healing. If she can reconnect to her own rhythms and flows, which are closely attuned to the moon, she may begin to fear less the exposure of her feeling nature and the vulnerability of surrendering herself truly.

The Cancer woman often unconsciously seeks power by manipulation. What she needs to learn is how to honour the flow and changing moods of her emotions and the undercurrents of her sexuality. She may resist sharing both her body and soul with her partner, in an attempt to control herself rather than reveal her deep sexual intentions.

Key Word: Illusion

Because she fears rejection so intensely she often hides her true feelings and casts around her an illusion of either fragility or rigidity. She is intuitive and has an uncanny way of knowing who it is who stalks her, or whose erotic desire it is that connects to her sensual mystery. Yet when involved in intimacy she will take a long time to really come alive. To be alive sexually is scary for the Cancer woman because it involves taking the risk of admitting to enjoyment and the pleasures that she secretly fantasises about.

She is constantly alert to the possibility that her partner may turn to someone else if she doesn't live up to his expectations. She fears the brutality of man: it is a natural and ancient fear that she carries in her unconscious. Her self-doubt and low self-esteem are not allies in her quest for fulfilment. Her sexual response pattern forms over the years into a tight and sometimes impossible grid of almost calculating manipulation. But if she can become aware that these patterns are breakable, that she can discover a way to give herself spontaneously and to receive with genuine affection for her partner, then she may break the taboo she has imposed upon herself. She may learn to go beyond the known and the tried and trusted. If she can learn to treasure her hidden wild sexuality, she can use it to her greatest pleasure and advantage. She may find herself utterly alive.

How Cancer Shines

It will be around eleven in the morning when the Cancer woman is most easily aroused. Then she will be highly receptive to her partner, her body arching for climax, her moist jewel glistening with desire. Cancer likes to tease; she likes to make ambiguous caresses, slowly weaving her spell. She often stops and starts, is reluctant one minute then forceful the next. Yet she weaves a web of intriguing sexual promise around her lover, entangling him in a paradox of passion. He may find himself mysteriously enmeshed in her threads of desire, not sure whether he should hesitate or be impulsive. Her passion is to wrap him in the pleasure of silk, cocoon him in sexual oblivion. She must treasure him as her feast and delight in the taste of his sweat as it trickles down his belly.

When she is shining her lips are full like the moon. The softness of her mouth is a reminder of her hungry sexuality. The fullness of her sex is full of promise. Her responses are languid as she slowly engages herself, turning to her fantasy world. She needs to use her imagination, to quiver at the thoughts that run in her head rather than attempt to fathom the reality of the flesh. Hers is a sexuality that rests mysteriously between pure mental stimulus and complete sensual arousal. She must have both to reach the mountain peak of total ecstasy. Once she has received her lover into her, she will not let him go.

Serpent Woman Power

This is the way of the Cancer woman's serpent of desire:

This serpent is hesitant at first. It lingers too long, not wanting to reveal itself to another too soon. It stays coiled, only striking if it is certain of reward and nourishment. She is languid, this serpent. Her eyes are glazed with desire but her body is full of electric energy. Her emotions run deeply, undermining her own power. She is sensitive to every move the object of her desire makes. She may be drawn to her chosen partner because she attunes first to his psychic energy. She may be able to resonate better with his pace and needs than with her own. She may be so numbed with desire that she does not acknowledge her own sexual rhythms, her own growing arousal. But, in this concealment, in this power-ful deeply sensual way, she will begin to subtly dominate the dance of desire. She will sidestep, move to subtle rhythms, not direct, not fully engaged, but passionate as a tango.

Her body may quiver as this man touches her, for she needs time to alert herself, time to let the fantasies fill her mind before she exposes her serpent to a stranger. This moment of desire must be graceful. Her tentative responses need a direct approach or a spontaneous challenge from this man, for she is rarely willing to make the first move due to her fear of rejection. This serpent of desire is deeply connected to the moon's cycles. Hers is a deeply rhythmical sexuality, but sometimes as black as the time when the moon is hidden. When her serpent rises, when she finally takes a step forward, she will cast her eyes down. She may find it difficult to look straight into her lover's eyes for fear he will see her soul. Her serpent is receptive, never directive. She awakens to the other rather than to her self.

Her passiveness will perhaps lure a partner with a powerful sexual need to possess or dominate this woman. She may seem reluctant at first, fearing that to totally absorb herself in a sexual relationship means she must also align all her feelings and instincts. The Cancer woman believes love and sex to be part of the same process, for to fall into bed with a man is to fall into love and commitment also. This is her way.

Cancer Woman – Her Beauty and Her Beast

The sign of Cancer has always been closely associated with the moon. The moon is an aspect of the great mother goddess, of whom Demeter is one aspect. She was the sister of Zeus and became a highly regarded goddess of agriculture and the harvest. She was usually known for her benevolence as bringer of fertility to the earth. However, Demeter had a dark side. When her daughter Persephone was abducted by Hades and taken to the underworld, her anger and grief was such that she made the earth suffer with her. She withdrew all fertility in every land, ruining harvest, denying rain. Hers is the power of passive aggression.

This side of Demeter embodies the Cancer woman's beast. When she aligns only with Demeter's dark side, she becomes sexually resentful, emotionally controlling and physically frigid. She withdraws sexual pleasure or manipulates her partner by sexual blackmail.

Her beauty, however, is aligned to the highly creative nymph Arachne. In a contest with the goddess Athene to see who was the most skilled at the art of weaving, Arachne wove a cloth which depicted the sexual frivolity of the gods. Athene was furious because Arachne's cloth was the most exquisitely perfected. In her anger she tore the cloth to pieces. Arachne hung herself in despair, but Athene felt pity and changed her into a spider, and the rope into a web.

When the Cancer woman's beauty is activated, it is the tapestry of divine love and sexual mystique that she offers. When able to thread her sexual nature with feeling and tenderness, she will truly enjoy pleasure as an art form, just like Arachne's own perfect tapestry.

Her Beauty

When young, Cancer woman may find that sex seems shrouded in too much secrecy. Her own mystique will seem curious to her, and she may take a long time to accept she is ready for sexual relationships. But like Arachne she will become skilled in the art, as slowly as the tapestry of love was woven. She will become well aware of her sexual urges and responses. Weaving the cloth that depicts the erotic ecstasy of the gods means she intuitively knows what such pleasure might mean to her.

However, she may be slow to act and prefer to take a passive role when approached. Younger partners are often dismissed for the maturity and experience of older lovers. She may keep her secret imaginative world to herself long after she has embarked on a serious affair or relationship. And, if she enjoys the art of spinning sexual encounters with her fertile mind, there will be many whom she tests herself against. It is only once she feels secure that she will give of herself, but never freely.

If a partner falls into her web she will offer discretion, sensuality and domination. She wants to see her partner surrender to her first. Like Arachne she must prepare the cloth first, but as she matures she becomes able to weave the most delicate and exquisite of safe containers for her sexual arousal. She will insist on slow, languid and fluid sensuality. Once her skills are learnt she will offer her partner the chance to pleasure himself. Her touch will be attuned to his needs, and her mind already engaged in fantasy. She may often have fantasies of herself with other women, but at the same time she will be massaging her partner's belly with her hands while she darts at the end of his penis with her lips.

Her beauty is a refined sexual art, of conservative yet passionate intensity when stirred into complete abandon, but only if her lover can flow with her emotional needs. She will lubricate her senses with fantasy and her body with oils. Her beauty is that her pleasuring is as rich and complex as the cloth that Arachne sewed.

Her Beast

The Cancer woman's beast can sometimes overwhelm her before she has time to consider the consequences of her inner turmoil or understand why her partner may have unknowingly pressed her buttons. The dark side of Demeter is controlling, rejecting and manipulative and, when alive in the Cancer woman, sexual freedom is rarely an easy bridge to cross.

When the Cancer woman's beast is activated she believes she can withdraw her self and her sex from her partner. Her beast is often activated when she feels anger. She must learn to acknowledge that anger is a reaction to an outside challenge to her need to assert her own values. But anger is also about the misuse of energy.

If she can channel this energy into physical love she may be rewarded instead of floundering in her own despair.

When angered, the Cancer woman feels vulnerable and threatened. She then retreats and withholds herself. Her fear of confrontation rises quickly and she may use sex as a weapon to defend herself: by either denying sexual relationships or by becoming promiscuous. The latter can occur if she is holding a grudge or resenting a previous partner. She bears her feelings longer than many others, for to let go of pain is to surrender.

To let go sexually, to orgasm and release herself from her own control, is also to surrender. Feelings become muddled with physical needs until she uses her refusal to give of herself as emotional blackmail. Like Demeter she will withhold fertility, and she may convince herself that without her physical participation her partner will suffer, as she must do. She will fantasise alone, often refusing to allow her partner near her. Her own sexual energy may be sublimated into angry scenes and frustration and she may blame her partner for her inability to reach orgasm. She must learn to externalise her feelings, and like Demeter make allowances for her own life-giving nature.

The Cancer Male

The Cancer male has an uneasy relationship with his own flowing and lunar sexuality. He knows within that he is a receiver, that his chosen partner must be the one to activate, and yet secretly he wants to dominate, to control, and to watch his lover's face in the passion of her climax. His gentleness means he takes his time to involve himself physically. It is not that he is unable to be aroused, but that he prefers to feel safe. He may be drawn to older women or mothering types to give him that initial sense of safety.

Yet the dark side of the Cancer man can often take over. His discomfort with his passive receptivity means he can fall into a pattern of behaviour where he overcompensates by becoming extremely chauvinistic. When he rejects his gentleness he may become ruthless: the archetypal sexual werewolf. This loud and highly ambitious side of the Cancerian male may show itself when first meeting his lover: her submission will be everything, for it means he will be in control if she climaxes in front of him. He may demand she masturbates while he watches.

Once he matures enough to be content with his gentler ebb and flow, and admits to his emotional hunger, he may begin to take on a more passive role. His rigid defences will crumble when his lover responds easily and proves she will not reject him. This man indulges in his fantasy world with ease if the ambience is right. It is not excitement, not fiery noisy adventure, that arouses him, but the silence and the unknown. If he shuts his eyes it is because he wants to imagine the caresses upon his skin as well as to experience feeling them.

He is a sensualist, but he needs to be given access to his fantasy world at the same time. He will make his lover wait as he explores every part of her body. She will moan and writhe as he tentatively plays her labia with his fingers first, then with the first thrust of his penis, the hardness and warmth delectable but taunting her to ask for more. He will excel at stimulating her breasts. Her nipples will grow to firm peaks as he flashes his tongue back and forward across their dark points. When the Cancer male is aroused enough he will want to dominate, but he will also want to submit to the lavish attention of a woman who can teach him a variety of sexual delights.

Compatibility

The Cancer woman's sexuality, like that of the other three personal signs, Aries, Taurus and Gemini, is more self-orientated than the other eight zodiacal signs. She must find pleasure to give her a sense of self. This is not egotistical, merely defensive. She fears rejection more than any other sign and so she needs a lover or partner who can provide a safe environment to nourish her own neediness, to allow her suppressed sexuality to blossom and unfold.

Cancer Woman with the Fire signs (Aries, Leo and Sagittarius)

With the fire signs the Cancer woman may initially be impressed by their enthusiasm and imagination. They can lure her into outrageous sex and perhaps liberate her need to dominate.

The Aries male's sexual energy is forceful, forward, impulsive and dynamic. He needs to fuel himself from his partner, to take pleasure when it suits him and then when that moment has been completed look for another. His potency may be the key to her arousal. His passion is naked; hers is clandestine and secret. In any sexual scenario the Cancer woman must give pleasure as well as receive it, but she does so from a discreet distance. He may find her mystery enticing, both her silence and her stealth, and when they melt together in a place of darkness she may begin to know him as her fire. His desire to invade quickly, his strong commitment to penetrative sex, means she may find him at times too impatient for her own slow build-up to her climax. But his rhythmic thrusting, his throbbing penis ablaze as he enters her fast, may ignite a new spark in the Cancer woman's hidden flame of passion.

The Leo male may be able to sexually nurture the Cancer woman as long as she can offer him genuine loyalty and give him as much pleasure as he desires. If she has Venus in Leo or he has Venus in Cancer, then they will respond to each other with an aching passion and may live out their fantasies without fear of disapproval. He will be flamboyant, intensely determined to give satisfaction. His pride in his body means he makes sure that the Cancer woman does most of the caressing and teasing. He needs to play cat and mouse, to arouse with play and laughter instead of serious intensity. It may be that if the Cancer woman shows her warmth and sexual loyalty he can teach her how to let go of her inhibitions. He will know how to keep her calling for more, how to feast only on his penis. She may even become more adventurous and enjoy his passion for exhibitionist fantasy. Together they will imagine themselves naked in front of a crowd, he nibbling at her sex and she wildly abandoned, poised at the moment of climax.

With Sagittarius she may find his directness and voracious sexuality too wild for her mystery to remain a closed secret. He plays fast, dangerous games of passion. He'll want sex to be an adventure rather than an art. She may however be rewarded by his natural talent of turning any opportunity to physical intimacy. The Sagittarius man works from his hips and needs hard rhythmical penetration after lengthy foreplay. There is little emotion in his pleasuring, which may not make it easy for the Cancer woman to relax back into his extensive repertoire. He loves to trace his lips from her buttocks to her labia, down the natural cavern of delight and round to her most secret of places. For the Cancer woman, these will be moments of tortuous pleasure.

Cancer Woman with the Air signs (Gemini, Libra and Aquarius)

The Cancer woman is uneasy with the mental sexuality of the air signs. However, she may discover a fresh approach to communicating her needs, for the air signs are dependent on expressing themselves, erotically contacting others through their minds as well as their bodies.

With Gemini she may find his need to make conversation throughout their sexual embrace disturbing, unless she has Venus in Gemini. The Cancer woman prefers to keep her secret thoughts to herself rather than share them during intimacy with this mercurial man who will change roles quicker than she has time to plan their next secret encounter. This changeability means she is not in control, and she may discount her ability to craft an exquisite ambience for their lovemaking and substitute jealous and tenacious behaviour towards him in public. His is a sexuality of variety, ease and erotic connotations rather than feeling and she must honour his restless spirit if she is to find pleasure in their embrace.

With Libra she may respond eagerly to his fantasy world. He is idealistic and she may not live up to his vision of woman as a temple of pleasure purely for his own delight. She may enjoy playing a dominant role for a while, but her deeper arousal depends on her willing submission, her need to be ravished and brought to a climax of sheer abandon. The Libran man may certainly enjoy role-playing, but may not be able to give way easily to her emotional demands.

Honesty is essential with the Aquarian male. The ambiguity of this man's sexual activities may lead the Cancer woman to suppose his animal lust is aimed at filling her own needs, but he may be more concerned with his own self-pleasure. He does this in an unusual way, preferring to observe her arousal, usually by licking or fingering her clitoris, and keeping his own sexual distance, thus satisfying the power of his mind over sexual attachment. He may liberate this woman but he may also wound her.

Cancer Woman with the Earth signs (Taurus, Virgo and Capricorn)

The Cancer woman is likely to experience great depths of sensuality with these signs, whose simple approach to sexuality may give her the chance to express her deeper fears and sexual needs.

With Taurus she will discover pure sensuality. He will keep in time with her pace and be able to satisfy and nurture her to a climax without frustration or impatience. Theirs may be a sexual dance of submission and possession. This man may teach her how to express her emotions through her body and her sexual response.

The sexual energy levels of the Virgo male may not balance with hers. His are careful, meticulous and crafted. Hers are ambivalent, volatile and moody. However, she may enjoy his refinement, his love of accessories such as leather, stockings, suspenders. He has purity of technique, but offers sexual skill rather than sexual indulgence. He will serve her as a slave, a eunuch, anything she requires in her dominatrix role, and they may enjoy detached pleasure.

Like any two opposites of the zodiac, the Capricorn man may be the dynamic force she requires to discover the delicacies of her own feast. This is a challenging, seductive and erotic dance. They both desire power: she subtly through the warmth of her sex, from which she can grip him with pulsating passion; he from sheer enjoyment of his control of himself and of her, mastering his body and aligning her orgasm and responses to his needs. There is a time and place for their sexual passion, and often they will avoid unusual or spontaneous intimacy. Capricorn tends to avoid romantic association with sexual enjoyment for fear of his own feelings. Yet, if she can truly lose her inhibitions, he may find her erotic fantasies the most exciting and stimulating liberation from his conventional sexual technique.

Cancer Woman with the Water signs (Cancer, Scorpio and Pisces)

With the water signs Cancer will feel most at home. Here she may abandon her control and allow her sexual fantasies more freedom.

With the Cancer male there will be slow build-up to arousal. They may explore one another with the security of knowing they have an affinity for domination. They may enjoy changing roles, enjoying the thrill of darkness, of silence, of the what might be. She will be able to gradually unfold her desire, nourished by the security he provides. She may bind his wrists to the bedposts. Then softly, like a spider, she will spin a web of pleasure around his body with the fine silk bedcovers. She will prefer to feel the hardness of his erection growing beneath the smooth sheets. Wrapped as if in a cocoon, she will sit astride him, rubbing her pubis across his silk-covered belly, the fabric moistened by her sex.

With Scorpio, although their passion may be mutually resonant, their sense of fulfilment will be staggeringly different. He is the seeker of intense sexual experience as a transformation of the self beyond any known limits. He must take everything to the extreme, to ravish, to endure and sometimes to suffer. He may be more excessive, more physically demanding for orgasm than she, and yet he has the patience to draw her out from her timidity. They may have battles for power but she will find his ability to bring her to the point of surrender uncanny, mystic almost. She may reconnect to her truly feminine mystique through the deeply erotic rhythms of this smouldering man.

The Pisces male's need to dissolve into physical embrace may suit this woman. With Pisces she can take as long as she wants to feel her way into passion. She will slowly arouse his penis with her gentle but uncompromising mouth. He intuitively knows how to stimulate and bring her sex to a peak. He'll be able to hold her there, his tongue instinctively knowing when to hold back and then when to dart and probe, to return the caress to the deepest folds of her labia. As each wave of orgasm builds he may turn her on her front, raise her buttocks, and caress her clitoris from behind. His touch is sensitive and finely tuned to allow her to fully surrender to her own sexual femaleness.

Interactive Section
Cancer Woman

The sun represents my sexual purpose.
My sexual purpose is to redeem my banished wild woman.

I need to learn to give of myself spontaneously and freely. I sexually shine when engaging myself totally in the rhythms of mind, body and sensual soul.

My serpent power is receptive: it lures passively, side-steps, then slowly awakens.

My beauty is heard through the voice of Arachne when I honour my skills in the art of intuitive sexual pleasure.

My beast is heard through the voice of Demeter when I become sexually resentful or manipulative.

Cancer – sun-sign key words for your erotic chart

Fill in the blank spaces at the bottom of this page and the same area on your erotic-profile chart beneath the zodiac wheel. You can choose the words or phrases you most identify with, and so begin to work with the images and meanings behind your sun sign.

The sun-sign section indicates your sexual identity, purpose and desire.

My sexual identity is _____

Choose from: magnetic, subtle, sensitive, intensely feminine, passive, tentative, emotional, intuitive, manipulative

My sexual purpose is _____

Choose from: to reconnect to my exiled wild woman, to learn to treasure my rich sexuality rather than fear its exposure, to welcome the life force of free abandonment and passion, to get in touch with my natural lunar rhythms.

I desire with _____

Choose from: tenacity, careful scrutiny, concealment, grace, fear

Questions

- Do you feel isolated from your early wild-woman inheritance? If so, do you feel you have unconsciously exiled her for fear of such a deep connection?
- Do you respond to the rhythms of the moon? If so, do you find your own sexual arousal provoked by its cycle – at full moon or new moon?
- Do you fear your serpent woman because of low sexual self-esteem?

- Do you find your sexual responses conform to patterns? Does this make you uneasy about expressing the desire for changes in your sexual behaviour?
- Are you more likely to follow your partner's sexual rhythms for fear of your own need to control or dominate?
- Are you capable of sexual rejection if your emotional needs aren't met? If so, do you resort to blackmail because you fear letting go of your pain is to surrender?

CHAPTER SIX:

LEO

24 JULY–23 AUGUST

'She was a flame that consumed him.'
DH Lawrence, *The Rainbow*

Leo Woman – Purpose and Sexuality

The Leo woman has the power of the sun's rays as her gift, lighting the lives of others as she blazes her way into her sexual encounters. She has high expectations from those she chooses as her intimate partners, but her true sexual purpose is to discover that individuality is not her exclusive right.

She is passionate, proud and courageous about her sexual needs. She knows what she desires and how she may have to ravish to keep her shining vision of life. She is not humble by nature, and her radiance illuminates her face at an early age. She may become fascinated by movie stars, glamour and the flamboyancy of beautiful jet-setting couples. Her interest in the opposite sex is quickly aroused and her own body will be a source of pleasure when young. She may be sexually active long before her other zodiac sisters. She plays the game of life, and she lives every moment with zeal and self-absorption in her search for the one who will caress her eternally.

Love of self comes first to the Leo woman, and it is this deeply principled valuing of her own sexuality that often surfaces through her intimate moments. She finds falling in love a necessary prerequisite for sexual experience. Yet she only falls if she can control. Many men will be obsessed by her dramatic seduction and her beauty, unaware that deep down her intentions are to be worshipped by him. Her own arousal is dependent on being sexually desired, for this woman knows she is special. Hers is a sexuality of self-indulgence, a hunger that feeds her vanity. Her partner must replenish her with constant caresses, stroking, words, romance, beauty and glamour. Every sun sign shines in their own unique way, but this woman must shine brighter, dazzling the men around her like a beacon of sexual fire. She does not hunt much because she finds usually that those she would desire will hunt her first.

The Leo woman needs to relinquish control, to learn

to feel for others' needs, and to treasure her deeper self, which is often hidden beneath a veneer of glamour, power and sexual prestige.

Key Word: Exclusivity

For the Leo woman to truly enjoy sexual pleasure she must be the centre of the universe in the eyes of her lover. He must see her as the ultimate woman, the sex symbol, the *femme fatale*, the icon and totem of female sensuality and pleasuring. She can be aroused only if she is so desired. Her partner must look upon no other: his loyalty is paramount. Then she can take control, ensuring he is solely hers.

She takes a long time to arouse, for she must feel that her partner's sexual hunger is for her and her alone, not necessarily for his own pleasure. In this way she relies heavily on touch and foreplay rather than penetration as her means of stimulation. She needs to be aroused by drama: the Leo woman does not require unusual sex aids or role-playing, just glamorous and romantic fantasy is enough for her climax to work slowly. She must be on show to her partner, both her body and her passion. But she also likes to be on show to herself. Being aroused by the firmness of his fingers in front of a mirror would ensure she was truly in the limelight. She needs a man who can give her all of himself and yet allow her fire to burn for herself alone. Hers is a world filled with visions only of herself but, if she can allow mutual pleasure into her own exclusive world, she can enflame her partner with genuine givingness and sexual fulfilment.

How Leo Shines

The Leo woman shines naturally. She radiates both warmth and desire without even trying. Her seduction is innate. She needs no rules, no objects, no sacrifices, only herself. She cultivates her beauty and works with her body to ensure her poise and her darkness are at the same time envied and coveted. She plays few games, for flirtatious and highly provocative allurement is her way. Leo women have their own self to nurture, and their creative involvement in their sexuality means they can learn quickly how to arouse themselves first and their partners second. Others may see the Leo woman at best as proud, vain and self-centred, but her inner needs are so intense that vanity and total self-involvement are necessary to her well-being in order to ensure she avoids feeling at all costs.

Partners may see her as the great seductress, the *femme fatale* or the glamour queen. They may want to dominate her, to possess her totally, but it is she who must direct and lead. She has trouble identifying with her more feminine side, paradoxically the one she exposes so dramatically to the world. But her real shining comes once she has cast a partner under her spell. Now entranced, he may follow her calculated provocations and may be tempted to go along a road never travelled before.

She suggests he touch her breasts, arousing her nipples to firm buds while she undresses. She enjoys stimulation while fully clothed. Her fantasies abound with historical scenes, romantic chivalry, the clinking of chainmail against white bare flesh, the rubbing of rough leather against her thighs. She has expectations of total fulfilment from her partner. This dramatic and theatrical side of the Leo woman's sexuality must shine, for then she can really fall into passionate abandonment and trust her inner feelings.

Serpent Woman Power

This is the way of the Leo woman's serpent of desire:

The Leo woman's serpent is always on the alert. Her desire for her sex to be enflamed is a natural energy that is instinctively alert to meeting her sexual alchemist. She does not need to attract, for her very being is so infused with delectable sensuality that few will resist her impact.

Her serpent seeks glamour, prestige and splendour. Not for this serpent the snow in winter or the rough grass beneath her skin. This serpent demands heat, demands richness of environment, richness of attention. She is aware of her seduction by virtue of being. Such is her allure that she makes no effort until the object of her desire, the catalyst of her arousal, comes into her territory. Then she will coil herself into his arms, slowly, intensely, knowing she will be his jewel of the night, Circe the enchantress, or the Queen of Sheba.

Such will be her overt eroticism that this man may play the game well. He will reward her with attention, give her physical proof of his desire for intimacy. He will arouse her ego and give her the sense that she is now the vortex of his passion. Her own stimulation depends on his. The more she flirts; the more he responds. The act, the game, the drama of the moment is what counts. How well can she seduce, how special can she really be? Her expectations of this encounter are high. High enough to arouse her serpent throughout the day until she meets him again.

This time she will want him to pleasure her totally while she watches herself, entranced by her own body's awakening, her eyes always feasting on her own ecstasy. She will make sure their meeting is filled with the full flavour and sensationalism of her desire. He will be drawn to her without hesitation, for she exudes sumptuous passion and the extravagant allure of the best sexual prize. His response will be eager, knowing that he must flatter and pamper her by gesture, suggestion and touch. This is her way.

Leo Woman – Her Beauty and Her Beast

In traditional astrology Leo is ruled and guided by the sun. In Greek mythology the sun god was Apollo, who both designed the spark of fire and gave light from the sun to instigate life. The positive nature of Apollo personifies wisdom, grace, prophecy, philosophy and creativity. Above the entrance to Apollo's oracle at Delphi was written 'Know thyself'. If the Leo woman can gain inner wisdom through her sexuality she will truly know herself. When the Leo woman truly shines, she too can work with her deeper femininity through the golden wisdom of her Apollo archetype.

Her beast is aligned to Circe, the daughter of the cyclic sun god, Helios. Circe was known in Homeric times as an enchantress. She lived alone on an island called Aeaea, turning every man who landed on her beautiful island to swine. She was bewitching, ruthless and jealous, until she reformed when she fell in love with Odysseus.

Before her transformation, Circe needed to be special. She was jealous and highly volatile, a fiery witch with revenge and spite in her heart. She fell in love with Glaucus, but he was already entranced with the nymph Scylla. In jealous vengeance Circe poisoned the water where Scylla bathed and the nymph was turned into a ghastly monster doomed forever to lurk along the cliffs overlooking the straits of Sicily.

Her Beauty

When the Leo woman aligns herself with the Apollo archetype she begins to experience her sexuality from a deeper place. Abandonment, fantasy and mutual pleasuring will become her ally rather than her fear. Her desire to control may become an honest acknowledgement of her need to take the lead, and she can learn the strength of a position of submission.

She will come alive with true radiance and with complete splendour in her sexual activities. It will enrich her own vitality and that of her partner. She can seduce those that know who she truly is. Her potion becomes intoxicating, her manoeuvres and her subtle understatements more direct and openly willing. She will lure with her eyes first, and the drama of every moment will inspire her to offer her own special sexual messages.

Thus aroused her beauty will become wild, the tigress, the hunter.

It is perhaps when the Leo woman can relate to her femininity, often lost behind her facade of glamour and idealistic images, that she will truly enjoy her sexuality. If she can energise and revere the dark wisdom of the oracle of Apollo's Delphic temple, she will be able to give as much as she receives. Hers is the ability to bring fire and passion, to awake her partner to new ideas. His hand upon her sex, his lips circling, enticing her nipples to stir the threads of desire down to her clitoris. When she truly knows herself like Apollo, she may not need mirrors to remind her of her beauty. When she truly accesses the source of Apollo's golden light which she casts so freely around her, then she is the most exquisitely dramatic and potent of lovers.

Her Beast

If the Leo woman does not identify or understand her sexual needs she may become aligned to the archetype of Circe. Circe was jealous, possessive and fuelled with the power of magic and manipulation before her own inner transformation. When the Leo woman is not conscious of her feeling nature, she may resort to the same control as Circe.

She will seduce and lure by means of her powerful sexual aura, her beast arising unconsciously to ensure she has no connection to her feelings. She will suppress her feminine nature, controlling her partner sexually rather than acknowledging his needs. As long as her lover is intent upon her she will revel in the luxury of such attention, as it nourishes her only from outside. It will be her ego that is nurtured, not her soul.

By identifying with Circe she may play outrageous games to avoid any emotional involvement. She will prefer excessive and showy stimulation, perhaps denigrating her partner's own particular style. Her passion will be for herself alone, and like Circe she can make a man feel belittled if his performance doesn't match up to her wilder needs. Her dark side will not respond to emotion, nor will her impulsive and daring tastes cater for a partner who wants to dominate her. The Leo beast rejects intimacy that involves commitment, for she fears her own neediness and often represses her desire for loyalty and contentment. Her weapons are as poisonous as Circe's. She may become obsessed with her body, turning her lovers into menials, like Circe's swine, to pleasure her. Her desire for adulation can outstrip her deeper sexual loneliness and her need to find a deeply warm and loving intimacy.

The Leo Male

The Leo male is passionate about himself and his first sexual purpose is to arouse his pride, his standing and his own ego. He fears investing his emotions in any sexual relationship because, like the other fire signs, he lives through the physical reality of the world, through images and form rather than the heart or emotions. He has a reputation for being one of the more sexually active of the signs. However, if he has Venus in Cancer or Virgo his egocentricity will be mellowed with either honey sweetness or refinement.

He will prefer a partner who will make him feel like a king. He must be the core of, and the shrine for, his lover's passion. If she is not aroused by his games, if she resorts to her own fantasy world, he may become distant, his pride wounded. He expects the best. He may project mythical qualities on to his partner, expecting her to be Aphrodite or the witch, Circe. He fears rejection, criticism or scorn. If his lover does not boost his ego and sexual esteem regularly he may retreat into someone else's arms. Yet he needs to play rather than involve himself, to possess and claim ownership of his partner's sex yet be free to roam if he so chooses.

His pace is slow, a build-up of sexual energy which requires his partner to maintain her rhythm in line with his. Staging the whole experience of his sexual union means he is in control. There will be rich and luxurious accoutrements, wine, sex toys, satin sheets, foaming baths. His first kiss may be conservative, but tempered by the hardening of his penis against her body. He needs to explore her mouth with his tongue, for this is the key to knowing her secret places. He takes his time, this Leo male, to discover her body, preferring to expose their nakedness slowly.

He will expect dramatic responses, and can sometimes assume he has the ability to please any woman. His own performance will be unquestionable. He enjoys his own control and will not often demand penetration as his means to orgasm. He'll find most pleasure in watching his lover's body respond to his hands and his mouth, which will in turn bring him quickly to a climax. He needs to be entertained, and then he can inspire passion and return sexual pleasure with delight. The art of lovemaking energises his vitality, for it is his very life force that stirs when she takes his penis in her hands.

Compatibility

The Leo woman must be adored, ravished and attended to in her sexual relationships. She needs to find a lover who will treat her as a queen, stroke her and stimulate her without inhibition or reluctance. She needs a lover who can inspire her passion and enjoy her own need for drama and theatrical fantasy. But mostly she needs a lover who can guide her to acknowledge her feminine soul.

Leo Woman with the Fire signs (Aries, Leo and Sagittarius)

The other fire signs will indulge in her passion for action rather than emotional involvement. However, fire is uncontrollable and moves freely. Two fire signs can merge together but must be wary of burning each other out.

With Aries there will be a fusion of self-interest. The spark will come from his potency and the fuel will be her ever-extraordinary fantasies. He will need to dominate, to demand spontaneous sex and to drive her at his pace when she would rather control the rhythms. He may become impatient with her slow caress, her need to be pampered, stroked, held in sexual ecstasy rather than savage lust. His pleasuring may be too fast-paced for the Leo woman's self-gratification, but she may find the force of his penetration, his explosive wildness and his potent manhood alarmingly addictive.

With Leo they will want to out-pleasure the other. Theirs may be a contest of control, and at times of sexual manipulation. Both have a natural affinity for exhibitionist stimulation and they may seek to dramatise their own arousal in public places. He will eagerly treasure her with the full attention she demands, and she may hold his penis to her sex, furl her labia round him until his huge cock becomes wet with her own musky pleasure.

With Sagittarius she may become wilder, liberated from the constraints of her heady expectations. His hunger for oral sex will thrill her, but his direct and blunt words, his less refined vocabulary may either stir her into ecstasy or turn her frigid with fear. He will find pleasure in her desire to expose herself so openly, her fingers parting her moist sex as she raises her pubis to his open lips. She may enjoy fingering her clitoris, rubbing gently, flickering the tight skin around the bud, before his eyes. Then she may raise her sex up to his tongue, move her body carefully back and forth for as long as she can hold her pleasure.

Leo Woman with the Air signs (Gemini, Libra and Aquarius)

Here is a kaleidoscope of sexual variety for the passionate taste buds of the Leo woman. Fire and air are experimental together, and both types prefer intimacy of the mind and body rather than of the emotions.

The Gemini male will be a willing participant in the Leo woman's sexual theatre. He will stimulate her with his words, his erotic phone calls, his late-night conversation. Like birds fluttering around her head, she will be fascinated by his changing roles: from submissive to dominant, yet always ready to please her as much as himself. He needs to be the centre of attention, too, but locked together in mutual passion he can play long games of seduction that will tease and torment her into wilder and more explosive orgasm.

Libra may prove a sexually tense relationship. His search for aesthetic perfection will mean he is certainly drawn to the Leo woman's physical allure. He may prefer to take a passive role, which could offend the Leo woman's need to be ravished and openly desired. He will want elusive and subtle gestures of desire, and to choose his moment to take her. She will enjoy his addiction to using clothes and accessories in their more bizarre moments, but he will fear being overwhelmed by her dramatic passion.

The Aquarian male is her natural opposite in the zodiac. These two will be electric together, even though they have very different views about their sexuality. She is self-absorbed, arrogant and demanding of caress. He is the observer, the watcher and experimenter, curious and yet detached from his sex drive. There are times when Aquarius denies himself sexual pleasure, preferring the power of his mind to that of animal desire. The Leo woman has such a display of passion, however, that even he may be unable to resist. Ultimately he may decide to enlighten her with new sexual techniques and free her from the belief that she possesses him.

Leo Woman with the Earth signs (Taurus, Virgo and Capricorn)

With the earth signs she may begin to learn more about her own responses and rhythms, accustom herself to truly surrendering and tenderness coupled with sensuality.

The Leo woman uses drama and passion to lure others to her. With the Taurus man she may encounter an initial resistance to her vanity. But her determination is such that she will exaggerate her sexual power to initiate their intimacy. He is the supreme sensualist, aware of her every need, ensuring a slow, careful build-up. Nights will flow with feasts and earthly delights: the trickle of champagne across her navel as he licks each drop before it reaches her sex. She will find him unnervingly responsive, attentive and loyal, but his patience may wear thin when she regresses into a spoilt princess, unable to return his deepest of kisses for fear of admitting she has feelings.

With Virgo she may establish a mutually pleasuring rapport. If she has Venus in Virgo or he has Venus in Leo, it is likely they'll blend and flow their similar standards and demands into a fiery and exotic sex ritual. The Virgo male will be eager to play the role of slave. He enjoys the submission of serving her, of nurturing her body to bring her to the moment of release. She may insist his fantasies become reality, suggesting bondage or cross-dressing. She may enjoy the way he licks her feet, peels her grapes, licks the massage oil from the cleft of her buttocks. She will enjoy the more sophisticated techniques he has mastered, such as that of knowing exactly how much to pleasure her before she reaches her peak. He will glide his refined hands beneath her buttocks and raise her up until he impales her from behind with his manhood, as rigid and as heated as her own sex.

She may conflict with the Capricorn man over who is in control. He also has a need for power, but his relies on his ability to control orgasm, and the length of his performance. She may become obsessed with his powerful penetration at the expense of her own wild sexual theatre. But her climax with this man will be unparalleled, her outrageous dominance coursing her into spirals and rhythms. Like a Dionysian dancer she will stay high with this man. Yet when he comes down to earth it will be with a shudder. His routine and his prestige take precedence and she will find she is not always the speciality of the day, or of his life. Sex for the Capricorn man is only one aspect of life, but to the Leo woman her leading role must always be the source of life.

Leo Woman with the Water signs (Cancer, Scorpio and Pisces)

The water signs are bewitched by the Leo woman, enchanted by her grandiosity and showy glamour. But water is acutely aware of the sexual designs or ambivalence of those around them.

With Cancer she may quickly seduce and gain this man's attention, but his physical needs are slow to develop: he takes his time, suspicious of her dramatic displays. Once he has crossed the threshold he may find that his need to nurture and indulge his partner is exactly what arouses her. If she has Venus in Cancer or he has Venus in Leo, they may discover a new abandon. She will use fingers, nails; she will tear his back, scratching like a wildcat as she reaches her climax. He in turn will know how to turn her explosive erotic fantasies into reality.

The underworld of dark sexuality threatens when the Leo woman becomes spellbound by the Scorpio man's eyes. There is often a powerful attraction here, one that may take these two beyond the limits of their normal sexual expression. Both are controllers, and the bed may become a battleground or a potent cauldron for two powers intent on their own personal escape from reality. He will be intensely serious, hard to satisfy, never fulfilled, for his moment of climax is never enough unless he transcends human passion. He may not pamper her as she hopes; he may not enter her when she desires, for he is a man who ruthlessly demands his own pleasure as much as she does her own. They may draw daggers, her quest for extravagant orgasm thwarted by his darkly obsessive mind.

The Pisces male will seem complex and elusive to the Leo woman. Her seduction of him must rely on all her showy and magnanimous charm to captivate this ambivalent sensualist. She may see him as a prince and herself as his harlot. This relationship will be sexually rich, warmly satisfying as they plummet into fantasy: tribal terror as she is rescued from the burning stake by one lone warrior, utter pleasure as she is ravished on the throne by her virgin minstrel. He may moisten her nipples with the most sensual of kisses, gently part her labia and run his cool fingers over her burning clitoris. Yet his dream world may prevent her from feeling central to his desire, for when he reaches his own climax it is not she of whom he dreams.

Interactive Section
Leo Woman
The sun represents my sexual purpose.

My sexual purpose is to learn that others have a right to their individual needs, too.

I need to learn to relinquish control and to trust my truly feminine self.

I sexually shine with natural radiance and dramatic passion.

My serpent power is dazzling, outrageous, the tigress.

My beauty is heard through the voice of Apollo when I work with the golden richness of my sexual splendour.

My beast is heard through the voice of Circe when I revel only in sexual pleasure to feed my hungry ego, denying my own neediness.

Leo – sun-sign key words for your erotic chart

Fill in the blank spaces at the bottom of this page and the same area in your erotic-profile chart beneath the zodiac wheel. You can choose which words or phrases you most identify with, and so begin to work with the images and meanings behind your sun sign.

The sun-sign section indicates your sexual identity, purpose and desire.

My sexual identity is _____

Choose from: dramatic, flirtatious, openly seductive, demanding, self-indulgent, stylish, glamorous, dazzling, passionate.

My sexual purpose is _____

Choose from: to discover that my true femininity is not necessarily the image I flaunt on the surface, to get in touch with my feelings, to acknowledge the needs of my partner are as important as my own, to learn to be genuinely sharing.

I desire with _____

Choose from: enticement, high expectations, an irresistible aura, determination, dramatic display.

Questions

- Do you think the glamorous, fiery nature you project to the world is a way of avoiding your vulnerability?
- When you first meet a lover/partner, do you always seem to attract them to you? If so, do you secretly fear failure so much that love of self is your defence?
- Do you demand to be the centre of attention in your relationship and, if you are not, do you look elsewhere?
- Are you often so absorbed in your own arousal or sexual needs that you don't attend to those of your partner?
- Do you enjoy acting a part or glamorising your image rather than taking time to look deeper within?
- You have great sexual self-esteem but, underneath, do you really know yourself or admit to feeling?

CHAPTER SEVEN:
VIRGO

23 AUGUST–23 SEPTEMBER

'Come to me in the silence of the night;
Come to me in the speaking silence of a dream.'
Christina Rosetti, *Echo*

Virgo Woman – Purpose and Sexuality

The Virgo woman has a subtlety, a potential of autumnal richness about her, which emerges and unfolds only when she is ready to acknowledge her inner self. Her quiet beauty, her elegance and her outer freshness often hide a repressed sensuality. She cloaks herself in an image that aligns with convention, often unaware that her aura and mystique stem from her sexual soul rather than her bodily appearance. Perfection and service are what she seeks in a sexual relationship, not only of her partner but of herself. Yet it is not the perfecting of bliss that she consciously desires, but the sophistication and skill of art itself. To be somehow flawed, and she is very aware of her imperfections, means to the Virgo woman that happiness is unattainable. If the standards she seeks in her sexual relationships are not met, or she is unable to live up to the expectations she has of herself, then she can never be happy with herself or connect to her own real needs.

She is an earth sign and so she must honour her body. This honour is often expressed through her commitment to beauty, to creating and chiselling the form of her own being into a mould she finds acceptable. She withholds much of herself, which is often why she is so beguiling and seductive. Her cool and detached approach to closeness is often a compelling fascination to a potential lover. But beneath the veil of composure and the finely tuned vibrations of her sexual messages, there lies a subconscious fear that she is not worthy of love. A haunting sadness that sexual love can never be enough.

The Virgo woman needs to learn to liberate her sexuality from the constraints of her mind and her narrow view of her own body. Her purpose is to reconnect her body to her soul, to trust her emotions and allow them expression through her sexuality.

Key Word: Perfection

Seeking to shroud her own flawed self from her lover as well as from herself, the Virgo woman engages the skill and art of excellence in her sexual style. The Virgo woman sees her intimacy as a way of offering herself up to an ideal, and views sexual pleasure as being pure and sacred. She is rarely promiscuous and, if she is, it's because promiscuity gives her the licence to shut out emotional response. She unconsciously believes that the more she distances herself from close relationships, the more she will distance herself from the defects of life.

In her earlier years she may find the whole idea of surrender and ecstasy fearful and prefer to be led, moulded and formed by the hands and body of a gentleman or magus. As she matures she acquires a vast repertoire of sexual knowledge which she masters with ease, her body working, serving, giving and gliding. She learns to perfect and perform every movement with precision and awareness. She will bring taste, elegance and an underlying exotic flavour to her encounters. She'll expect equality and quality in her partner's responses and desires. Classy, delightful, silent, the cold dark moon rather than the heat of the scorching sun, she needs a connoisseur of technique, a master of the art, to inspire her and bring her to orgasm. Her lover must be unblemished, distilled, and worthy of her service.

Her curiosity is insatiable, yet she rarely deviates out of her own sexual range due to self-imposed taboos and defences. When free from guilt and able to indulge in sensuality rather than in sex purely to seek approval, she may begin to take pleasure from her partner and discover her truly earthy and gusty need for arousal. If she has liberated herself from guilty associations with masturbation or she has found her inner richness, she will perfect anything from oral sex to bondage, threesomes or bisexuality.

How Virgo Shines

She is polished, this woman. Her performance is her shining, her dazzling way of seducing without intent, drawing her lover to her because she is so compellingly refined. He must discover the female behind the display of beauty for it is only the polished patina of self-possessed armour that sparkles and scintillates before his eyes. The true emotional and hungry sexuality of this Virgo woman lies waiting to be discovered and woken from sleep.

She will ensure her lover is crafted by her hands. Her ability to arouse him merely with the touch of her slender fingertips will stir his passion. Yet she prefers a discreet intimacy, one where she does little touching, little caressing, merely cool distant teasing with the torment of her tongue rippling across her own lips. The way she dresses draws a veil of purity across her body, shrouding herself in an aura of mystery, yet subtly defining her curves, her breasts, her skin.

To shine without her armour she needs to be aroused with care. She is fragile and her lover must excel at cultivation, non-aggressive desire, and have the ability to offer her charm and expertise rather than passionate self-interest. He may want to kiss her all over but she may turn to him for longer caresses and for ways to stimulate her without oral involvement. If she has given herself room to enjoy sexual pleasure rather than seeing it merely as a means of serving her partner, she may begin to express herself vocally and allow the wild side of her nature expression.

Serpent Woman Power

This is the way of the Virgo woman's serpent of desire:

This serpent begins to stir uneasily, unsure of what may be. When she desires it is with the intention of serving, to give and tend to the other's needs. This serpent must work for reward. She will have already fashioned how she will lure and attract; she will already have a plan, a ritual, a ceremony for the work. He will enter her door intrigued by her cool, poised ambivalence. Unsure of her true identity, he will be haunted by her self-possession. He will touch her lips because she will never offer them first. She will be acutely aware of his style, his clothes, his body, his mouth. They must align with her image of perfection. If they are faulty she will not let him near. Yet, if she sees value in his eyes, a powerful intellect, a feminine sympathy, she will begin to work her magic.

As she prepares herself through rituals of perfume, oils and the beautifying of her skin, she will conceive how this intimacy will be. For she needs to define who she is by what she does. She may not allow herself pleasure yet; she may not indulge in masturbation for fear of her own boundaries. She has been touched by something deeper than her desire to serve: she has found that she seeks an ideal which must not be corrupted by her thoughts.

Her serpent power may rise slowly as she showers. There may be candles around her room, soft music and wine. She will enjoy the pleasure of her body in solitude, run her hands over her skin, feeling herself, feeling her body as part of her sexual soul. Her body is sacred: for this serpent to offer it up to another she must truly be sure he is worthy. She will not dominate him, will not instigate the moves or the caress, but she will devote herself to his pleasure as well as her own. At first she may switch out the light for fear of seeing his flaws, for fear of him seeing her own serpent has imperfections. But she will be there for him, be there for his taking. This is her way.

Virgo Woman – Her Beauty and Her Beast

The Virgo woman has often been identified with the vestal virgins, who committed themselves to the service of Vesta, the Roman goddess of the hearth. Vesta's Greek counterpart was Hestia, who predates her and better displays the archetype of Virgo's beauty. Hestia personifies modesty, purity and sacrifice, and was the guardian of the eternal flame burning on the hearth. When the Virgo woman's sexual purpose is in touch with Hestia, her inner warmth comes alive, and her duty and her sexual receptivity become balanced and refined.

Her beast is aligned to the Greek goddess Artemis. This is a highly complex goddess who was protector of children and an expert midwife, and yet also the virgin huntress with the power to destroy those she found incompatible with her ideal world. She was particularly angered by men and on many occasions killed mothers, daughters, nymphs and hunters in revenge for her own lovers' infidelity, or for their neglecting to make sacrifice to her. When the Virgo woman's beast takes over, she too may turn her work of serving her partner into malicious sexual fault-finding or frigidity. Her repressed anger may put self-imposed limits on her orgasm.

Her Beauty

The Greek goddess Hestia embodies the eternal flame of purity, of modesty and gentleness. She wore white flowing garments and was untouched by corruption or vice. Although she was a virgin, her facade hid the voluptuousness and gracious sexuality of her femaleness. It is interesting that, when Dionysus, the god of orgiastic ecstasy, arrived in Olympia, it was Hestia who gave up her chair for him at the feast. In this way the Virgo woman, too, may yield to the divine ecstasy of her sexuality, when she knows her deeper self and trusts in that surrender.

When the Virgo woman is in touch with her Hestia archetype, she can honour her true eternal flame, the deeper sexual needs of herself as well as those of others. She will grow in awareness, her curiosity allowing her to treasure new sexual experiences. She will devote herself to de-ritualising sex with a partner who can liberate her mind from set patterns of how she should behave.

The Virgo woman's beauty is truly giving. She will make sacrifice to sexual pleasure because she honours herself and her lover without compromise, and without expectation. Like Hestia she may have perfected her appreciation of her body, her refinement and discernment, but she also knows the erotic undercurrents of arousal, of the Dionysian aspect of her sexuality. She can freely surrender her whole being to orgasm, rather than solely mastering technique.

When she is truly abandoned she can let go. She will offer her lover a new perspective if she releases herself from vassalage and engages in the role of dominatrix. Here she can pleasure herself fully, both by enjoying the role of active seducer and by devoting herself to the earthier side of her responses. When she aligns freely to Hestia, sensuality is at her fingertips for she has crafted the skill of lovemaking into a fine art. Her sexual beauty is her dedication to her sacred art.

Her Beast

If the Virgo woman has not connected to her own passion, she may put the sexual needs of others first, not daring to attend to her own. This can produce a cruel beast in the Virgo unconscious. She may loom as Artemis's dark side: vengeful, self-critical and too ready to find the defects in her partner's sexual performance. She may reject orgasm as a means of avoiding the flaws of her body, or impose limitations and frigid manoeuvres on her partner until her sexuality becomes fragmented, subordinate and frighteningly masochistic. When the Virgo woman aligns with her beast she may scorn her own pleasuring. She will then unconsciously believe she must suffer pain to alleviate the guilt of feeling pleasure.

Guilt is part of Artemis's darkness. In her childhood or early teens, the Virgo woman may have unconsciously placed herself in an atmosphere where sexual experience was taboo, or genital and penetrative sex simply part of marriage, a duty. If she embarks on her sexual journey with either too many ideals or too many fears, then she may repress her anger, her desire and her enjoyment of pleasure. Masturbation may be difficult when Artemis is controlling her sexuality. She may feel deeply guilty about her pleasuring. She may seek only brief encounters, avoiding intimacy and thus avoiding the imperfections of herself. The extreme of Artemis's destructive side may involve sadomasochistic tendencies. By suffering pain she unconsciously feels she can alleviate the guilt of feeling pleasure. She may enjoy the fantasy of sexual slavery and submissiveness as the only means of allowing herself to reach orgasm.

The Virgo Male

Discernment, poise and a desire to perfect both his own sensual responses and those of his partner haunt the Virgo male. In his quest for the purest sexual art form, he encounters many who do not live up to his high expectations. If they are not worthy of his attention then he may deny his more animal, lusting nature, turning his raw passion into intellectual analysis. He has a tendency to expect his partner to devote herself to him in body and mind. He will shun emotional involvement, and may find strongly passionate, vocal and dominant women initially threatening. He separates emotion from desire and stimulation, working to excel only at his sexual technique. His sensuality may be lacking when young, but as he grows older he begins to realise that earthiness does not necessarily mean roughness.

When his partner begins to seduce him, this man begins to be aroused discreetly. He may not notice his own arousal for he will be more fascinated by his partner's pleasure. He does not improvise very often, preferring to replay his well-known rituals of desire. First, the kiss must be enthralling, intoxicating. Her body will eagerly stir to his tongue as it glides over her mouth, her lips, her neck. He needs to find equality in their passion. She must be ready to submit to him, just as quickly as he enjoys yielding to the touch of her hand upon his manhood. His lower back is sensitive to her lips. He may prefer to turn face down on crisp white linen, feel the cool sheet rustling beneath his growing phallus. She will be running her tongue across his back, then push her hand beneath his body, feeling the heat of his penis and the moistness of his pleasure as he begins to thrust and writhe into the white purity of the bed.

Compatibility

The Virgo woman calculates and carefully chooses the partner who may offer her the best chance of perfection. She specialises in working with her sexual relationships, analysing and dissecting her partner's responses and needs. She needs a lover who is dedicated to her and can both receive and give pleasure equally.

Virgo Woman with the Fire signs (Aries, Leo and Sagittarius)

For the Virgo woman, the dynamic passion and vitality of the fire signs can liberate her from her self-imposed restraints, especially if she is in tune with her Hestia archetype.

Aries may plunge her headlong into temptation. His fast potency may alarm her at first, but she can find him enticing and deeply arousing. He will be bewitched by her purity, her subtle seduction, the way she keeps herself hidden from him when others would reveal too much. Carefully, she will peel away her clothing, her silk knickers curling on the floor around her ankles as he kisses her madly. As she arches her back, he will envelop her like a raging fire. She may feel the brush of his fingertips across her belly, the stir of his manhood against her thigh, swelling closer to her pillow of musk. She will enjoy this pleasure, this possession; she will accommodate his uncontrollable invasion, becoming fiercely addicted to giving herself to this highly instinctual man.

Leo loves to be served and the Virgo woman, especially if she has Venus in Leo or he has Venus in Virgo, will be able to relate to his exceptionally high standards. He is rigorous about looks, elegance, class and style. He needs to feel aroused by glamour and the best in life. She needs gracious surroundings, beauty, ancient and mystical icons, the perfection of the evening reflected in a glass of champagne. He can offer all this to her. Then they will turn the lights down low, the drama of the act exciting him into lengthy encounters in which he always has the starring role. This may be how she works best, giving and yielding to such power, but she may find his self-pleasuring too demanding for her gentler designs.

The restless and free-ranging ideals of the Sagittarius male may sit uncomfortably with this lady, unless she is able to accept his need for danger, freedom and, above all, enjoyment. He prefers not to involve himself with emotions or feelings, so they may be able to move very close, entangling themselves in physical games. He may want to arouse her every minute of the day. The bedroom is not enough and he may rashly assume that she will give him pleasure anywhere, from the back seat of the car to the front row of the opera. This man is half-beast, half-human. He thrives on his own danger and instinctive sex. If she has opened up to her sexual abundance, she may enjoy the spontaneity and be able to give him the freedom he needs.

Virgo Woman with the Air signs (Gemini, Libra and Aquarius)

The Virgo woman may be highly attractive to and attracted by the intellectual and abstract expression of the air signs. Virgo is the most communicative and analytical of the earth signs and may find a means of expressing her feelings and needs with these signs.

With Gemini there will be play, seduction and mental charm. She will adore his need for erotic conversation, the long phone calls while she bathes, allowing her to arouse her clitoris without guilt or fear of rejection. Gemini may introduce her to bisexuality. She may not in reality enjoy such pleasure, but the erotic fantasies will liberate her from the simplicity of the one-gender sex she has tasted. Their only difficulty arises when the Gemini man needs more space than she is willing to give. Sexually, their needs are very different: she may be too eager to please, too ready to give of herself, when he would be aroused by unpredictability and variety of role-playing.

The Libra male has an affinity for her lovely ambivalence. Like Virgo, he thrives on purity and the spotless ambience. The ethics of sex are high on his agenda, for he too fears his own deeper animal desires. Because these are both passive lovers and often have complementary Venuses (i.e. his Venus may be in Virgo and hers in Libra) theirs could be a dance of excellence, a fashioned environment filled with every conceivable object of sexual beauty. He has a fascination for watching two women together and may invite her to indulge in his fantasy. Whether she does or not depends on her sexual maturity and awareness of what this really means for her rather than for him.

With Aquarius she will discover another approach to airy, cool detachment. She may find that it jars with her own. Initially he will provide the right atmosphere: stark, uncluttered, cool and undemanding. She may begin to undress, feel comfortable naked in his presence, stir him with her desire to please, and offer herself freely, without demands or emotions. He will take much pleasure from teaching her the arts and skills of Eastern or esoteric sex, of the orgasms of the mind. His need for sensual pleasure is low compared to her own, and she may find his warmth does not emanate from the earth: he lives for the

101

great beyond, the divine experience. He may believe that sex is a channel for collective energy, not for mere self-pleasure. She may enjoy licking and tonguing his penis as he sits beneath the cloudless skies watching the stars, and he may take pleasure in watching her attention to detail as she brings him slowly to a peak until the pulsating message explodes to the stars above.

Virgo Woman with the Earth signs (Taurus, Virgo and Capricorn)

With the other earth signs Virgo woman can indulge in the sensual pleasures of the body. If she is in touch with her Hestia archetype, she can learn to connect her emotions with her sexual encounters.

The Virgo woman may find the Taurus male is one of the most potent and long-lasting of sexual relationships. He may teach the Virgo woman to honour her body and feast on pleasures without inhibition. She may enjoy mutual masturbation and indulge in all the sensual arts with him. With this man she can begin to accept the lusty animal side of sexuality, and to realise that no sexual relationship is perfect. There will be evenness and discretion enough for the Virgo woman to relax and recognise her own emotions, which she so often represses.

With Virgo she may feel initially comfortable in the embrace of a man whose needs are as impossible as her own. Yet because they are both perfectionists they may find fault with the other being too alike or too ready to submit. Their secret fantasies are of passive domination, and she may find that he is not willing enough to bend and flow, to offer her a bigger picture of sexuality. His own orgasm is often withheld for fear of failure and this may frustrate the Virgo woman into manipulative behaviour. Yet his desire is not too fiery for her, not too intense, and if she can remember he fears impotency just as she fears liberation from her strict regime on pleasure, then perhaps they can work to serve one another with mutual respect.

The Virgo woman may be overwhelmed by the power of the Capricorn man's sex drive. He may become possessed by her, dependent upon her for release. She may enjoy serving him with sexual rituals and routines. They may explore bondage and vassalage, or even discover anal sex. Together they may discover new dimensions of discipline and submission. She may willingly accommodate him when he desires to tie her hands behind her back with her silk stockings and then enter her from behind. As his penis thrusts into her sex, his raw passion will stir her to astounding loss of control.

Virgo Woman with the Water signs (Cancer, Scorpio and Pisces)

The temptations of the fluid and almost psychic water signs can bring sexual joy and different means of sexual communication for the Virgo woman.

With Cancer she may experience tentative and attentive lovemaking. The Cancer man will be highly demanding and needy, and the Virgo woman is comfortable with being in demand. The Cancer male offers tenderness and warmth, perhaps too much for her cooler attitude to sexual pleasure, but she will be his slave if he so desires. Arousal may be a fairly conventional experience, both fearing the unknown as they may have compulsions and patterns of behaviour established and rigorously defended. Yet the Cancer male has the softest skin, the warmest belly and the most sensitive of bodies. He will enrich her life with compassionate pleasure. Their sexuality may be variable and at times he may prefer to dream than to play, and she to work rather than languish in his arms. If she can free herself from the fear of failure, then this is the man who may give her the chance to prove how easy it is to invest her emotions.

The Scorpio male needs to indulge every sense,

emotion, and his body in one intense and erotic transformative experience. If the Virgo woman is ready to take on this powerful, dark and insatiable male, she could find a pleasure beyond her imagination. These two are very different in their sexual needs. She needs to expand her vision, to relearn how to nourish herself and to discover the vulnerability of human sexuality. He wants to transform another, to purify and to transcend the very humanness of the sexual experience. Together they might arouse deep emotions, intense and contained orgasms. He will demand more of her than she may be able to give, but she will learn much from him.

The relationship between Pisces and Virgo may be the most erotic and stirring of the water signs, for these two are natural opposites in the zodiac. He may want to surrender to her ideal of perfection; she may want to yield to his extraordinary dreams, his passion for sacred sexuality, of which he may not be conscious. For the Pisces man, sex is not a goal in itself: it is not orgasm but deliverance that has to be achieved. If the Virgo woman is enlightened by this divine messenger, it can bring out her deeper sexual purpose and align her to the possibility that pleasure can be an experience of all the senses, the mind, the soul and the body.

Interactive Section
Virgo Woman

The sun represents my sexual purpose.
My sexual purpose is to reconnect my body to my woman soul.
I need to learn to trust my feelings and allow them expression.
I sexually shine by polishing my performance as if it were a diamond.
My serpent power is haunting, ready to serve and replenish.
My beauty is heard through the voice of Hestia when I yield to my eternal flame of ecstasy and abandon.

My beast is heard through the voice of Artemis when I become self-critical and ready to find defect in my partner's sexual performance.

Virgo – sun-sign key words for your erotic chart

Fill in the blank spaces at the bottom of this page and the same area on your erotic-profile chart beneath the zodiac wheel. You can choose which words or phrases you most identify with, and so begin to work with the images and meanings behind your sun sign.

The sun-sign section indicates your sexual identity, purpose and desire.

My sexual identity is _____

Choose from: subtle, elegant, self-effacing, beguiling, detached, flawless, cool, composed, sophisticated.

My sexual purpose is _____

Choose from: to honour my imperfections as I do my ideal of sexual love, to reconnect my body with my woman soul, to learn to liberate my sexuality from the limitations of my mind, to discover my inner richness of earthy sensuality.

I desire with _____

Choose from: discrimination, curiosity, perception, idealistic expectations, discernment.

Questions

- Are you in touch with the richness of your earthy sensuality?
- If not, do you deny or suppress your own sexual worth by trying to find a perfect lover, or try to live up to high expectations of yourself?
- Do you find masturbation and sensual pleasuring delightful, or threatening and unnecessary?
- Do you prefer to serve your partner, to be led and guided by someone with class and technique? If so, do you fear taking the initiative or are you fearful of stepping outside the patterns of sexual experience you have established?
- Do you feel in touch with Hestia? If not, what is it you fear from yielding to ecstasy or surrendering to self?

- Do you identify with Artemis? Are you overtly self-critical or do you find fault with everything your partner does or suggests?

CHAPTER EIGHT:
LIBRA

24 SEPTEMBER–23 OCTOBER

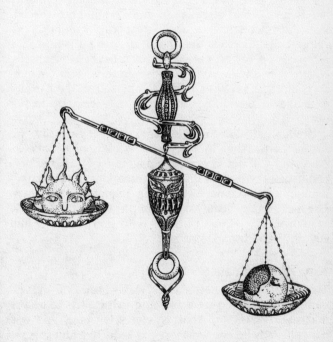

'She is clothed in pleasure and love.'
Akkadian hymn of praise

Libra Woman – Purpose and Sexuality

For the Libra woman, her essential quest is to find a partner, one who can share equally in her life. She seeks her ideal through her sexuality, often blindly involving herself in physical relationships, believing them to be what she is looking for. In reality she often finds that sex is not going to lead her into deep commitment. Not in her various partners' eyes, at least.

Like the other air signs, the Libra woman primarily needs intellectual stimulation and communicative contact. Abstract fantasies and whispering are far more suggestive and erotic than touch or sensual games. The physical contact, once established, must be aesthetically balanced with beautiful words, gestures and images. Sometimes she refuses to engage herself in the earthier dynamics of sexuality, for fear it may be ugly to her eyes.

Being so idealistic means she rarely lets go easily of a sexual partnership in case there is nothing to take its place, but will not let go of the possibility of a better one. She usually refuses to invest her emotions in her sexuality and can become involved in manipulative games. Her perplexing beauty and complexity can be highly seductive. Her sexual purpose is to find harmony and equality of body and mind.

Key Word: Beauty

The Libran woman needs to feel she is beautiful: she will pamper herself and wear fine and rich clothes to ensure that she dazzles and charms. Her knowledge and wit, her skill at artful conversation and seductive and suggestive innuendos are part of her build-up to a sexual relationship. Her partner must be physically attractive first, but mentally he must also align to her sense of what is beautiful.

She has low self-esteem and to boost her own self-image she will often overdress, take extra care with her hair, her make-up, her underwear, knowing that by cloaking herself in finery and seeming the classy lady she can hide her more fragile and vulnerable self. She thrives on the perfection of youth, the richness and finesse of romantic partners, the exoticism of the environment, the fantasy of romantic locations. Her partner must be passionate but polished, strong but gentle, and able to give her enough personal space.

She has trouble understanding her own need for pleasure of the mind rather than of the body. She favours her intellect above her feelings and so often opts for denying her true femaleness, for she fears the power of this inner world. She may find the sensual indulgences of sexual experience ugly, unless her lover has a romantic dash to his lovemaking. Sex must above all be a beautiful and a beatifying experience, one that truly arouses her mind first and her body second.

How Libra Shines

The Libra woman has perfected the art of shining. Her self-image is often low and so she makes every effort to enhance her outward appearance, to lure and seduce with subtle beauty rather than overt glamour. She seeks out aesthetic pleasure of the mind, not just of the body. For this woman truly shines in conversation, erotic suggestions, the pause between words, the romance of restaurants, gossip, news and fast-moving life.

She is best when the stage is set for the first scenes, when anticipation and the quest for pleasure are fresh in her mind. She may prefer long periods of foreplay rather than submissive penetration. She may prefer to languish in an exotic bath, talk erotica long into the night, experience the sensation of her own sex tingling with anticipation. Embracing her partner in reality can be an anticlimax, for human bodies come with moles, scars, body hair and wrinkles.

Her skills and techniques are enchantingly feminine and likely to bring her partner to orgasm first. She may take her lover on a fantasy ride, for illusion and magic are part of her allure. She can tempt and tease, bite and nibble with extraordinary self-control. Her ability to please any man is her art of pleasuring, yet she rarely wonders about pleasing herself.

She is a sociable creature, in need of a partner and in need of finding fairness and honesty in her lover, but she is shy of intimacy. If she meets a partner who can respond to her need to be hunted, to be chased and captured, she may quickly idolise him. Her dreams and fantasies are the beauty of her sexuality, but her desire for ideal pleasure may be found only when she releases herself from her illusions.

Serpent Woman Power

This is the way of the Libra woman's serpent of desire:

She plans her strategy carefully. There may be many options or choices. She has bathed in musky oils, coloured her lips, filed her nails, her hair is done to perfection. She is flawless, the ultimate beauty. If she can find a lover who matches up to her ideals of beauty and elegance, her serpent will subtly whisper her desire in his ear, and his head will be filled with images of pleasure, of his power and his ravishing of her. But at the first sign of ugliness from her partner she may reject him.

She will not make the first move, this serpent woman. She longs to be touched first, to be the hunted. She does not want to go beyond the first moment of seduction; she does not want the thrill of bodies merging, sweat, pleasure and release. Her serpent stays close for a while, hovering, turning on the charm, the guile, the art. Then she will run, for she must be chased and captured. She walks away, her serpent alert, ready for the thrill of pursuit. He will follow her, grab her arm and pull her round to face him, binding her to his body, fiercely pushing his hardness against her sex. Through her silk dress she will feel the urgency of his desire, her own moistness reminding her how subtly she has seduced him to capture her. This is her way.

Libra Woman – Her Beauty and Her Beast

Although Libra is traditionally ruled by Venus, two other goddess archetypes present a distinction between her beauty and her beast. Harmonia was the daughter of Aphrodite and Ares, and was the balancer and harmoniser of love (Aphrodite) and war (Ares). She was a gentle immortal, filled with grace. She lived an idyllic life in the company of the Muses, the Graces, Hebe the goddess of youth, and her mother Aphrodite. Harmonia personifies the beauty of the Libran woman. Her sexual purpose and expression lies in the ideal of relationship and the search for harmony. When the Libran woman is in touch with this archetype, she is able to enjoy deeper sexual relationships, free from her sexual fears and insecurities. She can begin to communicate her own sexual needs and reaffirm her feelings, thus fully involving herself in her own pleasure.

Her beast is aligned to the princess Anaxarete. Anaxarete was a beautiful Cypriot maiden loved by the youth Iphis. However, Iphis did not live up to her ideal and she rejected him. Iphis hung himself outside her house in despair, and the cold-hearted Anaxarete showed merely indifference. She was subsequently turned to a statue by Aphrodite for having such a stone-cold heart. When the Libran woman is in touch with her beast she may reject her vulnerability and her feelings. Thus she too may reject a partner or lover simply because he does not live up to her sexual ideal. She may become manipulative and controlling through sexual abstention or addiction.

Her Beauty

Harmonia is able to achieve a balance between intimacy and detachment, love and hate, war and peace. She is a goddess who was doomed to own a cursed necklace given to her by her husband Cadmus, passed down through the generations. The necklace made her find that, later on in her life, harmony and pleasure were always studded with disorder and ugliness. Most of her children were murdered and she was forced to leave her idyll and embrace reality. Harmonia thus lost control of the perfect life she led, but was able to accept that such perfection is a dream, even for an immortal goddess. For the Libran woman, Harmonia embodies the ideal balance between beauty and reality. If she identifies with this archetype she too can accept the ugliness of reality and acknowledge her own fear of losing control. She can enjoy her need for space in a sexual relationship. If she communicates openly her fears and desires, she can find a stronger bond with her own femaleness.

Her beauty is her uncanny sense of what her partner needs. She will be sophisticated and all-knowing. A perfect stimulator herself, sex aids, toys and experimentation won't be necessary in her sexual repertoire. For her to be herself is enough for any man. She will often deny her own sexual fulfilment for the sake of her partner's complete and utter sexual surrender. She has the power of both coy arousal and unutterable passion. Hers is a need to give and to be captured, to be bound to her lover, whether literally in willing enjoyment of wild bondage or by his addiction to the sweet taste of her sex.

Her Beast

The dark side of the Libran woman's sexuality can appear as cold indifference or avoidance of her true feelings. Like Anaxarete, she may resort to rejecting her partner because he does not live up to her ideal image. The Libran's vulnerable feelings and deep sexual insecurity often cause them to cloak themselves in a guise of outer calm and apparent compliance, while inside they have totally detached themselves from feeling. She may indulge in manipulative power games. She may ignore her own low self-image by creating a new one, by turning her back on what really turns her on. She may become outrageous, using her wilder dark side as a means to avoid her fragility. She will play the vamp, become promiscuous, pleasure herself solely in the confines of group sex, or do totally the opposite by denying her partner pleasure or rejecting her own orgasm.

She may find sex ugly, distorting her images of how sex should be into a wilder, more fantastic and unattainable concept. When aligned to her dark side she will suffer sexual passion in silence, and criticise and complain about her lover's noises, moans and inability to arouse her. She will be unaware that her sexual needs are not being met because she dare not look to see what they truly are. She may have a problem accepting bisexuality as arousing to her, that pleasure can be found equally with women as lovers, or at least by indulging in the fantasy. If she rejects the feminine it is because she fears her attachment to her very femaleness and the warmth and pleasure of both being a woman and enjoying another woman.

The Libra Male

This is a man who seeks beginnings but prefers to avoid completion. He is aroused by the desire to seek out the impossible, the ideal sexual fantasy or relationship, but dares not look to commitment for fear of losing a better offer further up the road. He avoids conflict, and his passion is inhibited by his need for pure pleasure without pain. To him, hesitation is sometimes preferable to impulse, and he may take a long time to decide he is ready to merge with another. When he does so it must be a partner who reflects his ideal of beauty. He is not interested in the pleasure of the body so much as the erotic pleasuring of the mind. Fantasy will be crucial to his sexual arousal: he needs intellectual stimulation and erotic conversation first and foremost. He is passive, resisting yet tempting, and prefers to be hunted than to hunt.

He fears the ugliness of reality, the animal lust and the wildness of his male passion. To live with such high expectations of sexual pleasure means he often disconnects from his body and suffers fragmented responses. One day he may crave oral stimulation, the touch of his lover's lips upon his penis; the next he may only want relentless penetration; then the next he may want neither. He seeks parity, but often finds only disparity, for his own ambivalence means he turns off and on without complete release. He often has difficulty with orgasm, finding it arrives too soon or that he needs excessive penetration to achieve it.

Yet, the Libran male has tenderness, sexual skill and the desire to give. He is fascinated by his lover and loves to imagine her when he is not there. He will imagine her bathing, then oiling her skin, fondling her own breasts and rubbing her nipples to hard peaks. He will imagine her dressing and making herself ready for him.

Compatibility

Libra woman requires variety of intellectual stimulation and romantic fantasy rather than fiery passion and dark emotions. She needs a lover with poise, beauty and a certain emotional detachment, but also a partner with whom she can communicate her deeper womanly wildness.

Libra Woman with the Fire signs (Aries, Leo and Sagittarius)

With the fire signs she can enjoy a sexual cocktail of passion, captivation, theatre and fusion.

The Aries man can ignite her quickly and eagerly. She may feel she has been lifted out of her usual subtle gestures, her gently sophisticated way of touching and receiving. He blazes with desire, rampantly exposing her to extraordinary pulsations of pleasure as he enters her, ravenous, unfed, finding his way to her very innermost core of pleasure. He will lead the way, taking her hands, her body and her mind and carrying them into a world of fantasy she will never forget. These two are opposites, yet they both want only to enjoy the beginning, for completion is not their quest. He will enflame her instinctual passion, the one she so resolutely denies, but she may fear his animal side.

With Leo, their sexual encounters will be filled with drama. He will want spotlights, music, and the thrill of her body shivering with delight before him. She will have no choice but to succumb. He may have surprises for her: mirrors or video cameras at every vantage point. He loves to watch himself as his penis pushes against her lips and he climaxes. To observe herself on camera or in mirrors may alarm her at first, but her own need to give pleasure will suit his vanity.

Sagittarius is the most passionate of the signs, yet needs the most space. The Libra woman needs the space but not the passion. She fears being overwhelmed and thus becoming needy and dependent. Her independence will arouse the lonely adventurer in the Sagittarius male. But she may become insecure and her Anaxarete beast may awaken if he does not offer her the chance to communicate her true sexual needs. Hers are thoughts, intellectual arousal and romantic conversation; his is imagery, infinite possibilities and devilish self-delight.

Libra Woman with the Air signs (Gemini, Libra and Aquarius)

The Libran woman will feel an innate sense of harmony with the air signs.

She may feel at home with the surging mind of the Gemini male. Their conversations will be arousing, whether on the phone or across a restaurant table. Sexual fantasy will play a huge part in their repertoire, both being able to accept the other's need for bisexual role-playing. Neither is dominating or overly passionate and he can pluck her slowly or quickly, offering her a variety of stimulation and excitement to keep their intimacy filled with changes in rhythm and harmony.

With any two like signs there will always be an affinity. With two Libras, they will play well to begin with, both not daring to end the initial foreplay. They may swop roles: she may play the dominatrix one day, the abducted princess the next. There will be swooping and soaring, his body eager for embrace yet languid when she takes him under her. She may prefer to sit astride his belly, watching her own moist sex rubbing against his hardness. Mystery and illusion will be theirs as long as they want to play on the edge. To ever surrender truly, the Libran woman must take a chance and commit herself to understanding her own imbalance.

The Aquarius male may liberate her from her inhibitions, instruct her in the art of self-arousal, and watch her from the doorway. He may suggest alternatives to romance: the enjoyment of watching her with another woman, or group sex where feelings and romantic illusions are removed. She may be fascinated by the change and the breath of air which allows her to remain uninvolved. But they may find problems with truly becoming intimate. She may find his experimentation with anatomy, rather than sexuality, too passionless.

Libra Woman with the Earth signs (Taurus, Virgo and Capricorn)

The Libra woman may find the true pleasures of sensuality in her encounters with the earth signs.

The earthy and often frightening intimacy of the Taurus male may alarm her and remind her how powerful the male body is. Perhaps with Taurus she can find the true inner beauty of her ancient sexual inheritance. The wildness of body sweat, the smells of her sex, the noises of penetration as he glides gently along her moist furrow towards her waiting sex. Both need pleasure: she by pleasing the mind and he by serving the body. He may teach her how to respect and listen to her body's needs and how to let go. For the Taurus male is able to surrender himself to orgasm without inhibition or expectation.

With the Virgo man, if she has Venus in Virgo or he has Venus in Libra, theirs may be a pleasure trip to perfection. Her ripeness and yet her innocence fills him with undiluted desire for her. This relationship may sexually mature rather than fragment. They will craft their erotic art together, keeping the romantic naivety of the first taste of pleasure alive. As long as the Libra woman can carry through her teasing with finesse, and as long as she can pamper the Virgo male, attending to his sexual needs and designs, then she may offer him the purity and discernment he desires.

Both Libra and Capricorn have a need for control. She needs to feel she is in control by subtly planning each moment of their sexual encounter. She may align herself to Harmonia, planning a serene atmosphere in order to make herself ready for this man's mature and redolent touch. Yet the Capricorn male needs to plan the time, the space and, above all, to design the whole scenario on a grander and more ambitious scale. They may both need to compromise and recognise the other's need for order.

Libra Woman with the Water signs (Cancer, Scorpio and Pisces)

The water signs may give the Libra woman access to her inner sexuality, but she may have to pay a price.

Like an unusual blend of spices, the Libra woman and the Cancer male seem at one with each other's subtle domination. She will be lured by his sensitivity, by the way he can pour wine across her belly then lick the drops lightly from her bud. His ability to take her out of herself may be fearful for her, but both fear being engulfed by their own and each other's passion – they may well take turns to play the dominant role. He is fond of forbidden sex, of pleasure taken near or in water, and she may enjoy the non-routine aspect of their stimulation. Both prefer lengthy fantasy and foreplay.

The natures of Libra and Scorpio are very different and their sexual purposes can be at odds, unless she has Venus in Scorpio. He will want to awaken her to her deep physical and emotional sexuality, while this is precisely what she is afraid of. She will be bewitched by his darkly menacing beauty, but may feel uneasy when he begins to demand more intimacy from her and devour her with his deadly passion.

With Pisces she may escape to a land of romantic fantasy, dreams and divine union. This can be a highly successful liaison. He is not interested in sexual encounter for the sake of simple gratification; he looks for the ultimate experience, the fusion of souls as well as of bodies. He seeks to nourish and yet to be served, while she looks for harmony and balance, willing to please him in every way. Both will be oblivious to the outside world as they entangle themselves in intoxicating warmth. Their imaginations alone will be enough. But, to be enduring, they must occasionally turn away from their dreams and recognise the reality that they are both only human.

Interactive Section
Libra Woman

The sun represents my sexual purpose.

My sexual purpose is to bring myself into balance so that I can truly share pleasure.

I need to learn not to fear my sexual needs just because they may be incompatible with others' desires.

I sexually shine by creating harmony and beauty.

My serpent power has strategy. It seeks the beginning of pleasure rather than the ending.

My beauty is heard through the voice of Harmonia when I reaffirm my feelings and enjoy my own pleasure.

My beast is heard through Anaxarete when I become indifferent, denying my sexual vulnerability.

Libra – sun-sign key words for your erotic chart

Fill in the blank spaces at the bottom of this page and the same area on your erotic-profile chart beneath the zodiac wheel. You can choose which words or phrases you most identify with, and so begin to work with the images and meanings behind your sun sign.

The sun-sign section indicates your sexual identity, purpose and desire.

My sexual identity is _____

Choose from: fragile, compliant, idealistic, subtle, graceful, romantic, aloof, magnetic, sensuous.

My sexual purpose is _____

Choose from: to discover harmony and pleasure through a bonding relationship, to honour my female soul rather than fear the power of this inner world, to welcome and to develop sexual integrity, to learn that self-esteem comes from within rather than through the approval of others.

I desire with _____

Choose from: infatuation, passive seduction, pleasurable intent, romantic expectations, discretion.

Questions

- What is it you desire when you become infatuated by beauty? Is it harmony, sexual pleasure, or true intimacy?
- With such powerful aesthetic values, do you feel drawn to relationships that are sexually light to avoid the heaviness of feelings?
- Do you prefer to be a passive seductress, or do you overcompensate by being totally willing to please anyone in your search for the ideal?
- To what extent can you connect to the beauty of Harmonia? Does her archetype delight you or threaten?
- How often have you felt like Anaxarete, compelled to turn your own feelings to stone when intimacy becomes too intense?

CHAPTER NINE:

SCORPIO

24 OCTOBER–22 NOVEMBER

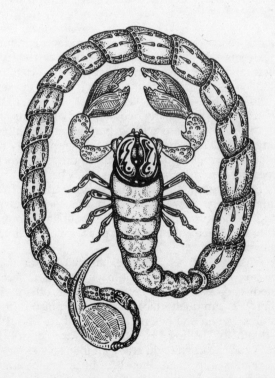

'To make delicious moan upon the midnight hours'
Keats, *Ode to Psyche*

Scorpio Woman – Purpose and Sexuality

The Scorpio woman is mysterious, secretive and often deeply misunderstood. She conveys a sense of both hidden power and magical receptivity. Her sexual aura is disturbingly vibrant. As she walks into a room her mystical sexiness is breathtaking, alluring, and sometimes repelling. Those who are caught up in her spell may find her smouldering, eager to test, please and entice. Her sexual purpose is to achieve self-mastery, to be able to have power over her own body, mind and soul.

Her nature is excessively emotional and she can lunge from extremes of intense jealous passion or rivalry to complete and utter abandon, untainted and free. Her polarities are so extreme that she often seems unattainable, unbreakable or obsessively erotic. She conveys an air of eroticism that many women find enviable. She seeks out those who are willing partners in her intense and often bewitching relationships. Her apparently cool mind belies a hot and sometimes thorny heart. The sharpness of her moods and the avalanche of her sensuality often overwhelm and possess her partners. Every encounter, every new relationship she forms, is like entering a cauldron in which the bubbling brew of sexuality is filtered into the most passionate and intoxicating experience.

She must accept her truly sexual nature, for if she rejects her need for close intimacy she can become inhibited and fearful of her power over others. Her femininity is uniquely laced with the poison of an enchantress when she begins to feel insecure about her own depth of feeling. Her inability to control her extremes can mean she will enjoy an intensely explosive sexual relationship, then often set out to totally annihilate and destroy the experience in favour of total abstinence. What she must learn is that it *is* power she is searching for, but power over herself rather than over others. Through her relationships she can begin to understand her darkness and achieve self-mastery, for her survival instinct is the power behind her sexual desire.

Key Word: Power

Scorpio woman is able to use her potent sexuality to lure and attract any partner. Her ability to exude such a hypnotic and magnetic quality means she is often likened to a temptress or Mata Hari. She cannot help this sensual mystery that envelops her lovers, but it is a potent energy she must learn to master and share with compassion, rather than simply passion. She carries the threads of the wild woman of ancient times like every other woman, but it is the Scorpio woman who unconsciously unleashes this primeval force into her sexual encounters more often than any other. She often believes she must sexually prove herself and has been labelled with an insatiable lust for sex. Although it is the power of self which she seeks, unconsciously she may use sex as a weapon in her battle for survival.

The Scorpio woman must survive at all costs. It is the survival of the deepest and remotest part of her sexual being that she feels is constantly under threat. Throughout her childhood and teens she may get her wires crossed and believe that sex is a means to power. She may see sex as a means to an end, for achieving success or raising her esteem in others' eyes. But her need for domination and control is only her way of masking her own vulnerability. Her weapons of stimulation, arousal and deeply wild orgasm are defences rather than weapons.

She must learn to surrender truly to find the deepest power that lies hidden within. The power of integrity.

How Scorpio Shines

When the Scorpio woman is in tune with her deeper sexual needs and has let go of her inhibitions she becomes the most potently lustful and enriching of partners. She will choose her moments with her lover carefully. She may reflect on him for a long time, deeply penetrating his psyche, deeply formulating the best way to lavish this partner. She is capable of a polished, oiled, magnificent seduction. She may spend all day with him, stroking, kneading, massaging and teasing, her powerful fingers coaxing him into blissful and sometimes torturous desire. He may find her powerfully hypnotic, sometimes fascinating, sometimes awesome in her cruelty. She will be fantastic, worldly, smouldering across his belly with her dangerous lips. She makes each sexual experience a serious and intensely pleasurable journey for herself and her partner.

She is demanding, needy, and yet secretive about her own intense arousal. She will want to keep her own dark pleasure hidden so that he is intrigued, curious and ever ready to please her. She will watch his responses with satisfaction and the belief that she is better than any other lover. Hers is a sexuality that enflames, burning slowly to a crescendo. Her own climax will be tremendously explosive, deeply emotional, drawing her ever deeper into the fire between her partner and herself. Then she may demand more orgasm, until her lover can no longer resist and he must surrender totally to her.

Serpent Woman Power

This is the way of the Scorpio woman's serpent of desire:

This serpent carries ancient wisdom: it is attuned to primeval longings and the ancient barbarity of life. It waits and it will not be thwarted for it must have power and it must possess. This is a serpent whose power is unquestionable. She will be alert to her lover's every move. She will hypnotise like a cobra, swaying, lunging forward with her hips and her sex towards the object of her desire. She must penetrate this lover's very soul by fixing her eyes upon his, luring him to her. He will be fascinated yet afraid. This serpent knows the moment to strike and capture its prey. She will pierce him with her bittersweet-venomed tongue.

She may be drawn to an equally powerful and dangerous partner. One who can offer himself up to her magic. His desire must be as strong as her own growing compulsion. Together they will ravage and transform. She may become obsessed with one face, one body, one image in her mind of how she can dominate and take pleasure. She will be the chalice, the open goblet of desire awaiting his blade to enter her. But not until she has tantalised and tortured him with her luscious mouth; not until she has lain him upon the rack of sweet oblivion. He must not fear her darkness, for she keeps her secret place as a sanctuary for those who dare visit the threshold of dangerous pleasure. This is her way.

Scorpio Woman – Her Beauty and Her Beast

The archetypal goddess energy that aligns perfectly with the Scorpio woman's sexual beauty is Lilith. Lilith was handmaiden to the great Sumerian goddess Innana. She guided the people to Innana's temple to enjoy her sacred sexual rituals. Lilith represents that part of feminine sexuality which has long been lost: the ability to freely abandon oneself, to find pleasure in the wildness of instinct and use ecstasy as a source of healing and regeneration. The myth of Lilith has been debased and humiliated over the centuries. Her wild woman has been distorted by patriarchal myth into an example of woman as evil and a danger to men. She has been misrepresented as demon and bloodsucker. Even in the nineteenth century she was regarded by artists and poets as deadly, an irresistible and hypnotic *femme fatale*. Yet Lilith's nature has now been re-established. When the Scorpio woman's beauty is aligned to Lilith, she can make use of her powerful sexuality to regenerate not only herself but to bring integrity and value to others. Hers are the erotic mysteries of healing and transformation.

Her beast is in tune with the darkness of Pluto or, in Greek mythology, Hades. Hades ruled the kingdom of the underworld. He never left his dark and sinister domain except when his lust overcame him and, wearing his cloak of invisibility, his tremendous stormy darkness rose through the earth's crust to snatch away a beautiful human or goddess to ravish and possess in his lonely kingdom. One such goddess was Persephone, who became queen of the underworld and later lived in the upper world for half the year and with Hades for the other half.

Her Beauty

The beauty of Lilith manifests itself when the Scorpio woman consciously chooses to acknowledge her wild instinctive passion. Her beauty means she can express her erotic pleasure without resentment or pretence. When in touch with Lilith, the Scorpio woman can balance her need to transform and purify with her need to possess and claim power for herself.

She may be more liberated about her own sexuality than many of her zodiac sisters: able to freely throw herself into arousal, wildly fascinated by her own body and its immeasurable source of intense and powerful energy. Her partners may not be able to keep up with her stamina. She may peak quicker than her lover, and will do so over and over again. For this woman, her climax matures and grows the more she indulges herself.

The Scorpio woman has Lilith's power to transform and purify her partner, if she believes him capable of it. She will honestly declare that she is testing her partner to see if he is powerful enough to flow with her spontaneous and mysterious sexual potion. Lilith took to the temple only those who would be healed and transformed by sexual rituals and sacred sexual arts, those she knew to be awakened to the integrity of their true nature.

She will break many taboos to explore different ways of reaching her climax, either with her partner or alone. She is a compelling partner, intrigued by her lover's passion and responses, curious to see him climax just as she tightens the leather thong around his penis. Her

126

beauty is her danger, her darkness, and her ability to be both the dominatrix and the submissive slave. When she understands the emotions and issues behind her obsession with S&M and her desire for exotic sexual locations, she can use this power to unlock the doorways to sexual liberation for others. Her beauty is that she can master her art and channel her passion to feed her ancient need for survival.

Her Beast

When Hades grabbed Persephone from the sweet meadows and dragged her screaming to the pits and caverns of his dark domain he was like the Scorpio woman's beast: intent only on the need to wield erotic power. Like Hades, she may wear a cloak of invisibility to tread her way through the lighter aspects of life, thus preventing others from seeing her darkness. She may lure with a mask of humble passion but, if her needs are not met, she may return to an underworld of unfulfilled longings, regrets and sexual abstention.

Rarely does she realise that her emotional nature is fiercely defensive, and when she aligns solely with her beast she is protecting her vulnerable nature in the only way she knows: by exploitation and painful encounter. She will often return, like Hades, to her lonely kingdom, for she may unconsciously choose a partner who will bring her pain, either literally or metaphorically. If she denies her emotional needs, she may find her arousal and climax depend solely on the extremes of rough sex. She may become obsessed with bondage. When she aligns with Hades she does not realise the guilt she suffers for desiring power and may seek punishment for her own pleasure. If she can acknowledge her deep sexual need for survival, for healing herself and others, she may free herself from her own chains of guilt and self-destructive behaviour.

The Scorpio Male

The Scorpio male, strongly connected to the emotionally virulent power of his sex, has a reputation for dangerous and highly potent sexual desire. His gaze across the room is intensely focused, and when he sees a potential partner or lover he is unstoppable. He is the dark magus, the one who knows the sensuality, the drama, the ecstasy and the divine awakening of orgasm. He will want to possess and ravish. His need for power is more polarised than the Scorpio woman: it is all or nothing. When he chooses someone to be his lover, he will want to be in full control of his cauldron of steamy darkness.

He can be very possessive of his partner and jealousy may play a large part in his arousal. His need to dominate means he remains mysterious about himself, for his lover or partner must never fully understand the darkness of his nature. He can be Shiva, the destroyer, for he can both ruin a relationship and quite coldly watch the flames of desire burn through his partner as he dances back to loneliness.

Once his lover is under his spell he will begin slowly, carefully urging her towards her first taste of his sex. He is addicted to oral stimulation, and may prefer long periods of massage to lead him to the plateau of passion. He is an artist of both sensuality and of powerfully driven animal lust. If he is able to combine both without falling into the perilous pit of sadism, he can be the most fantastic of lovers. He can offer his lover more than she ever dreamed of, giving her explosive and powerful orgasm as he tastes her with his thirst for power. He may suggest they read erotic literature together while she masturbates, or he may dress her in leather and arouse her with his tongue.

But this man believes there is an ecstasy he has not encountered, a passion he has not yet lived. His need for sex to be a symbolic, esoteric and regenerative experience sometimes falls close to an obsession. For this man, sex is never a goal in itself: the pleasure he gains and gives is potent and powerfully erotic, but it is the power over his partner and himself that gives him most pleasure.

Compatibility

The Scorpio woman needs a partner who can respect her intense and demanding sexuality, and acknowledge her unfulfilled longings.

Scorpio Woman with the Fire signs (Aries, Leo and Sagittarius)

The enthusiasm and outrageous imagination of the fire signs can be extremely testing to the Scorpio woman. Here she can find adventure, excitement and danger, but must be prepared for her power to be usurped.

The Scorpio woman may find the challenge of the impulsive pleasuring of Aries highly stimulating. His own arousal is fast, uninhibited, and often highly self-centred. Hers is slower, languid, and often fuelled by possession. This may cause conflict and passionate scenes, crisis and drama, but the Scorpio woman will be aroused by this. His desire for hard penetrative sex may mean she becomes frustrated. Her possessiveness may push him to his limits, and his need for freedom could mean he leaves her lonely. Yet in her aloneness she may find the fantasy of the Aries male more enriching than his very presence.

With Leo there is promise of delight. His own pleasure is based on playing, on lightness and wit, on caressing, teasing and adventure. Hers is serious and intense, yet she may for a while lose her inhibitions and play the game his way. His passion for exhibitionist sex may entice her into exotic locations for their pleasuring. She may explore his repertoire, knowing that he is as highly motivated as she. He is challenging and powerful, desiring complete dedication and possession. Together they may enjoy swopping the role of dominatrix, pausing only to create a new scenario in which their fantasies can be played out. She may prefer the more macabre locations – graveyards, the waxwork museum or the alleyway for their pleasure – while he must at all costs maintain a glamorous locale.

The Sagittarius partner could prove the most elusive for her. She may find herself aligning with her Hades archetype, compelled to have power over the opportunist nature of this fiery and voracious man, unless he has Venus in Scorpio. He is never involved emotionally in his sexual experiences, and needs to feel free to come and go as he pleases. The Scorpio woman wants to chain him to the iron railings, lick him till he is tortured with the ache of his full penis, tongue him and rub her moist sex against his thighs until he is crying for release. Yet the Sagittarius male is half-beast, half-human in spirit, and the bestial nature of her desire may arouse him more than he ever dared expect. He may enjoy submitting to her power, but he will want to spend longer in pure animalistic penetration than she.

Scorpio Woman with the Air signs (Gemini, Libra and Aquarius)

The air signs need to communicate, to express their desire, and to avoid both emotional pain and pleasure. This may be highly attractive to the curiosity of the Scorpio woman, though not necessarily in harmony with her nature.

The Gemini partner may prove the most testing, the most haunting and provocative. His need to express himself and his low boredom threshold mean he needs constant variety and change in his sexual encounters, which certainly suits the wild side of the Scorpio woman. But the Gemini male might find her secretive and intense passion too claustrophobic, too serious for his light breezy embrace. He likes conversation, intellectual arousal, and the eroticism of the mind rather than deep emotional possession. He may find her power too smouldering and she may find his pleasure too restless and scattered.

With Libra she may find much pleasure, especially if she has Venus in Libra or he has Venus in Scorpio. The Libra male responds to creative sexual intimacy. Searching for ideal orgasm, he may enjoy being ravished and subjected to her dominance. His own fantasy world easily resonates with her deep longing for new experience and intense, explosive abandon. Yet she may miss the wild joy of being dominated in her turn.

With Aquarius she may discover a very different kind of sexual power from her own. This is often a magnetic and strangely erotic relationship. The Scorpio woman wants total involvement; he does not. Yet their desire for one another will be intense. Once they are sexually involved she may find his need to satisfy himself by remaining detached from her physical passion is not enough for her possessiveness. He will retreat for fear of her closeness, willing to show her new Tantric skills but never letting her ravish him. He knows she would be deadly if he were for one moment to let her take his own mind power.

Scorpio Woman with the Earth signs (Taurus, Virgo and Capricorn)

The earth signs are not emotionally involved in their sexuality, but with Taurus especially and Capricorn at times, the flow and rhythms of their sensuality can give the Scorpio woman the time to express her true uninhibited and dominant sexual needs.

Taurus is her natural opposite in the zodiac. This means the tension between them is like a magnet, compellingly attractive and alarmingly repellent. This sexual relationship is obsessional and possessive, but highly erotic. The Taurus male is pleasured by sensuality and total involvement of his body. Arousal will be instant, and erotic connection languid, smooth and well oiled. They will embrace with hunger, knowing the other is capable of offering the liberation of their truly deep sexual nature. Both enjoy oral stimulation over a long period of time, and the Taurus ability to keep the rhythms of sensuality flowing through her will act as a catalyst for her more explosive and cosmic orgasms. She will have multiple orgasm with this man. He can also make a Scorpio woman who has chosen abstinence and denied her sexuality honour her own powerful erotic inheritance.

The Virgo male is searching for purity and perfection and may become entangled with her mystery, seeing it as the holy grail of his quest. His technique, his beauty and his elegance will inspire her. She may be enchanted by his erotic toys. He will enjoy submitting to her dominatrix role, often preferring to be her slave. His skill at arousal will be superb, yet her deeper sexual needs may remain unfulfilled in the arms of the emotionally detached Virgo. If she is unaware of her desires, she may find herself aligning with her Hades archetype.

The Capricorn male feasts upon the darkness of her secret place. He needs to control, to climb triumphantly to the helm. This could be a fierce battle, a struggle between her need to control and her liberation from her role as dominatrix. This man may insist on her submission more forcefully than any other sign. Yet when she willingly tests out her responses, opens herself to his earthy strength, she may find pleasure in the very experience she most fears. Surrender.

Scorpio Woman with the Water signs (Cancer, Scorpio and Pisces)

She may be able to allow freedom to her feeling nature with the emotional involvement the water signs have to offer.

With Cancer she may quickly establish a deeply satisfying rapport. They will enjoy slow arousal, and she will be fascinated by his secretiveness. The more mysterious a partner, the more she is likely to take her pleasure from him. She will bring him to moments of almost mystical orgasm. His fear of submission will be put to the test, and once liberated he may begin to explore the extraordinary gift of her body. She may insist he stand in the shower, his body glistening with water and fragrant oils. She may push her sex against his buttocks to make him hard with desire, then force him to climax as she turns the water on full power.

With Scorpio she may find the intensity of taking pleasure from a partner as powerfully seductive and sexually ignited as herself exciting. Together they may experience deeply emotional and cathartic orgasm. Their encounters may be power games, each fighting to push the other over the brink of pleasure. She may force him to orgasm with his hands tied behind his back, as they are locked together in all-consuming passion.

The Pisces male will offer her gentle, spiritual and almost divine embrace. His intuition means he will play any game: coax her, submit to her, whatever she desires. Pisces does not threaten or invade her own darkness. He'll hold back just at the right moment before she explodes, knowing that when she sits above his face, her clitoris like a dewdrop ready to moisten his tongue, he will need to touch her only once there. He will only have to lick her velvet sex and she will experience the exquisite pleasure of her own femaleness.

Interactive Section
Scorpio Woman

The sun represents my sexual purpose.
My sexual purpose is to achieve self-mastery.
I need to learn to acknowledge my truly erotic nature, which is both healing and regenerative.
I sexually shine by lavishing my partner with my dangerous pleasure.
My serpent power is perilous, bewitching and hypnotic.
My beauty is heard through the voice of Lilith when I honour the ancient sacredness of my healing and transformative sexuality.

My beast is heard through the voice of Hades when I use sexual partners to test out my power.

Scorpio – sun-sign key words for your erotic chart

Fill in the blank spaces at the bottom of this page and the same area on your erotic-profile chart beneath the zodiac wheel. You can choose which words or phrases you most identify with, and so begin to work with the images and meanings behind your sun sign.

The sun-sign section indicates your sexual identity, purpose and desire.

My sexual identity is _____

Choose from: mysterious, smouldering, intense, dangerous, possessive, tantalising, torrid, hypnotic, transformative.

My sexual purpose is _____

Choose from: to achieve self-mastery, to acknowledge the sacred healing and transformative power of my sensuality, to learn that my passion for sexual power is only a way of denying my vulnerability, to honour my survival instinct and my wild-woman soul.

I desire with _____

Choose from: passion, obsession, my eyes, compulsion, intensity, fascination, instinct.

Questions

- To what extent can you connect to your wild woman and the inheritance of sexual healing?
- Do you find your erotic nature threatening or are you curious to explore it?
- Are your sexual responses usually explosive or do you feel you have repressed such powerful feeling for fear of your own vulnerability?
- Do you use sex as a weapon or a shield, to defend or to attack? If neither, do you prefer to be the dominant partner?
- Are you drawn to S&M?
- Do you unconsciously attract partners who will bring you pain, either physically or emotionally?
- Do you feel that your sexual relationships transform you or are you filled with unfulfilled longings?

CHAPTER TEN:
SAGITTARIUS

23 NOVEMBER–22 DECEMBER

*'In the mountains of shadow
and peaks of wind
she delights in the chase.'*
Homeric hymn to Artemis

Sagittarius Woman – Purpose and Sexuality

The Sagittarius woman treasures her sexuality. She believes every encounter and every embrace must be glorious and wild, uninhibited and beautiful. Like her ancient ancestors the centaurs, half-beast, half-man, she has both an untamable passion for the sexual dance of life and an intellectual awareness that each moment must be a celebration.

She takes risks where others would turn away. She often feels aroused by the sight of a beautiful man or woman in any location. Throughout her travels, she will meet many who can offer her stimulation and enjoyment for a brief encounter, or a longer period if she has the time to stop. She would rather keep moving on than ever rest, and feels sexually comfortable with strangers, acquaintances and the unknown, rather than intimates who might peel away the veneer of independence she so fiercely defends. It is not that she is promiscuous, but that one long-term partner may not be enough to satisfy her extravagant sexuality and wild, demanding sex drive.

For the Sagittarius woman wants, more than anything else, to play. She wants to bring joy to herself and to her partner or partners. Her agility is unmatched and her stamina unbelievable. She is daring, audacious and liberated, and she needs a partner who shares her enthusiasm for all-night orgasm. Sexual stimulation must be based on the equality of those involved, as well as on the equality of mind and body. Emotional ecstasy is not her purpose; nor are the deeper weavings of the unconscious. She prefers the light, the joy and the sexual crusade.

Her true sexual purpose is to celebrate the pleasure of her body and her deeper femininity, but often she denies herself this pleasure in her passionate quest for spontaneous gratification. The Sagittarius woman needs to learn to access her ancient feminine wisdom, for she is wise. Her Yang nature, the spirit of action, is dominant enough in her psyche to propel her forward, but she often represses the deeper well of lunar tenderness for fear of feeling.

Key Word: Uninhibited

The Sagittarius woman needs a lover who can enable her to freely express her desires and unfurl her glorious arousal over and over again. She often finds herself instantly attracted and aroused by a stranger, either male or female. She needs to lead, but she is not particularly concerned with domination or submission. There do not have to be roles nor hidden agendas for this woman to truly express her desire. She does not need complicated sex manuals, toys or fetishes, although she is always ready and eager to try anything out.

She feels the moistness of her sex quickly and knows that she is on a quest for a celebratory act that will fill her and her partner with pleasure. For two people to merge in sexual embrace is for her a means to enjoyable enlightenment. She will step quickly through the initial moves of the game, for her dance is more like a flamenco than a waltz. She will swirl with desire, tear her clothes off and dance naked in the open air. The wider and freer the ambience, the greater and the more wild will be their passion. She promises much, and she believes she can offer the most potent sexual stimulation. She has no inhibitions about her body or her pleasure, and prefers her lover to feel the same.

How Sagittarius Shines

The Sagittarius woman shines when she is filled with passion and enthusiasm and begins her quest for the ideal sexual partner. She always believes there is a lover who can satisfy her. She may prefer the company of men and wander between lovers, ever hopeful of finding her ideal. She needs a partner who can satisfy her demanding pace, for she lives every second of her climax with the desire for more. Her body and soul are geared solely to future possibilities rather than to the moment.

She is glamorous, outrageous and audacious in her choices. She may collide with a beautiful man on the train. Instantly she will tell him how she feels, how her desire for him is arousing her. She radiates an animal magnetism tinged with sexual wisdom She is capable of casting a spell around anyone if she so desires. It is not so much the dark danger of Scorpio, nor the sensual lushness of Taurus, but simply the belief that she can please herself and her partner without commitments, inhibitions, or demands.

Sex is easily separated from love by the Sagittarius woman, for love is about companionship and sex is about pleasure. She fears deep feelings, fears intimacy, and tends to stay away from dependence on others for her sexual arousal. She may masturbate frequently and find pleasure by fantasising about her unusual encounters with strangers or about group sex.

She may suggest the daring or that they take their pleasure outside in the white snow, the crowded beach, or the phone box. She may insist on anal penetration, then will totally abandon herself to her animal instincts as she kneels before him to lick and mouth his erect penis. For the Sagittarius woman to truly shine, she must be embraced with freedom so that she may trust in her passionate glory.

Serpent Woman Power

This is the way of the Sagittarius woman's serpent of desire:

The Sagittarius woman's serpent wants to play. If she sees an opportunity to take pleasure and enjoy seduction, she will seize it. If she's travelling, and she usually is, her serpent does not need to be awakened for she will be permanently exploring, probing and searching for sexual adventure. Each person she meets, whether male or female, will be enriched by her sexual dance. The need to explore lures her ever forward into deeper waters or more dangerous liaisons. The more this serpent must take risks, the more aroused she becomes. There is no thirst for domination, but merely the pleasure and celebration of sexual enrichment.

These strangers all hold clues, all have something to offer, as long as they play the game well. But she will choose one, believing he can offer an encounter to heighten her awareness, to pleasure her senses and her ancient huntress energy. She is a pleasure-seeker and, if this stranger offers her the opportunity, she will not resist. Such is her animal magnetism that he will not refuse the danger. He is drawn to her impatient spirit, her agile body. As they collide in the train he knows there is no way back. Her serpent speaks elegantly, using expansive words, allowing no hidden meanings. She wants to taste his sex; she wants to draw on his manhood and take the pleasure for herself. There is a chance. The compartment is empty. The night sky fills the windows with shadows. She pulls him closely to her, a longing filling her sex. Now she can become the dispenser of joy, for this is her sacred sexuality come to life. This is her way.

Sagittarius Woman – Her Beauty and Her Beast

The Sagittarius woman's beauty is aligned to Atalanta, the Amazonian huntress. She was as good a huntress as any man, and she inflicted the first wound on the Calydonian boar. She never desired marriage and was most comfortable in the company of warriors and heroes, as comrades rather than as sexual partners. Some say she joined the Argonauts on their famous journey. She won every athletic race, and drove men wild with desire. But Atalanta rarely allowed any man to chase her. Eventually, she committed herself to one man, Hippomenes, but only if he could outrun her in a footrace. Hippomenes had realised that the only way he could win her was to trick her by scattering golden apples in her path. Curiosity overcame her and she stopped to inspect each of them in turn. Hippomenes won the race and Atalanta agreed to their union. They were discovered locked in sexual ecstasy in the temple of Zeus, and were transformed into lions for their contempt. Her fears for close intimacy liberated, Atalanta had finally found divine pleasure. When the Sagittarius woman aligns herself with the Atalanta archetype she may begin to discover that she can fuse her wild ancient desires with compassion and tenderness. She can bring to life both sides of her sexual femininity.

In traditional astrology Sagittarius is ruled by the planet Jupiter, the Roman equivalent to the Greek god Zeus. Zeus was the leader of the Greek pantheon and ruler of the universe. His positive nature personifies potency and joy, the urge to play, and the urge to create new order within. The fire and air signs are more able to align themselves to the Yang, or masculine dynamic, within each of us. They often suppress or deny their female side if they become totally dependent on the male archetype. Zeus can do just this within the Sagittarius woman's psyche, and it is often the negative side of Zeus which takes control of her.

Zeus was promiscuous and ruthless, believing he was above morality. If the Sagittarius woman loses all contact with her ancient feminine inheritance, she may believe she is in touch with what is sexually right, that she needs no morality nor inner sense of order. She believes she is omnipotent, and becomes ruthless and addicted to grandiose self-pleasuring. She will be ravaged with pure desire, and like Zeus may destroy any lover who attempts to break her supremacy.

Her Beauty

When the Sagittarius woman is in tune with her Atalanta archetype, she will come alive with fresh vitality, with the urge to offer herself with true generosity. Her quest for sacred ecstasy will be tangled with her huntress instincts but also with the knowledge that tenderness is pleasurable. She will, like Atalanta, stop to inspect and taste the golden apples of sexual joy that her partner has strewn before her. She will know that her partner is not just a vehicle for her pleasure, not just a competitor in her race for the best arousal, but truly an equal. She will be the bringer of true joy to her lover, and her desire will be filled with empathy. She will invoke and identify with her female nature, celebrating her wild huntress who waits to be stimulated with those golden apples of sexual feasting.

Her Beast

Zeus was highly promiscuous and had affairs with other gods and with mortals' wives, and yet believed himself above morality and his own laws. When the Sagittarius woman is not conscious of her or her partners' deeper sexual needs, she may become overwhelmed by the need to assert herself sexually. She may be motivated by her animus or masculine Yang, accusing her lover of weakness and impotence. She may turn to other women as her primary source of sexual satisfaction, yet without the awareness of her own or of their feminine nature. The Sagittarius beast is a fearsome warrior and she can strike like lightning, burning her way through her lover's feelings and then leaving them frustrated and hurt.

She may forge her way through her sexual encounters, avoiding true intimacy. She fears losing her supremacy and so may not allow anyone near her deeper self. Zeus fell into opportunistic pleasure to escape his fear of a prophecy that he would one day be overthrown by one of his children. The Sagittarius woman, like Zeus, fears being torn from her throne. But mostly she fears intimacy for it means she will lose her dance with sexual freedom. Orgasm becomes a means of escape from herself and from her partner instead of an inner experience of pleasure.

The Sagittarius Male

The Sagittarius man is irrevocably hungry for sexual experience. He lives and breathes desire through every pore. At every street corner he may smile at a beautiful woman; at every social occasion he may take any opportunity on offer for a brief encounter or a secret liaison. He has a reputation for promiscuity, but he yearns for the ideal partner who will give him freedom. He is dangerous unless his lover knows he must always seek out and discover new and variable joys. His expectations are high and he'll rarely be seen with anyone less than dazzling.

Sensuality does not necessarily become him, for his desire is one of adventure and exploration. He avoids emotional sex and needs to play games, to amuse himself with his lover's body. He may be particularly fond of caressing his lover's buttocks, reaching down and fondling her gently just at the crevice of her most secret place. He may suggest anal penetration. The great outdoors, the unexpected and spontaneous rise of passion in unusual environments, thrills him and arouses him.

His loyalty and honesty is to himself, yet when seduced by excitement and anticipation he will give all of himself. He delights in his pleasure and gives as much as he receives for the Sagittarius male prefers equality to role-playing. His desire is the honest pleasuring of life, and he will honour and oblige with all his vision and humanity, but he needs his personal freedom, and he needs no one to possess him. Like his Sagittarian sister he needs to be special, chosen, to belong to an elite of sexual knowledge and of passionate charisma.

Compatibility

The pure desire with which the Sagittarius woman explores her partners means she needs someone who can not only match her in stamina and style but can accept her wild sexual independence.

Sagittarius Woman with the Fire signs (Aries, Leo and Sagittarius)

The nature of fire is to burn and, although the other fire signs will have a natural empathy with her legendary passion, there may be too many sparks and not enough substance.

Aries is, like she, spontaneous and willing to take risks. He will enjoy her enthusiasm for intimacy based on fierce passion and her eagerness to take any opportunity to play. The Aries male, however, is highly egocentric, and they may battle over who does what to whom. Yet his drive and his wildness will excite and stimulate her to multiple orgasms, and she will send him into savage ecstasy with her fiery caresses. Together they may enjoy explosive sex free from the emotional intimacy that both prefer to avoid.

The Leo male takes most pleasure for himself. She may find this man exotic, glamorous and enticing, but she may tire of his rigidly defined expectations, his need to dominate and be served when she would rather they were equally matched. Their greatest problem is that Leo expects loyalty from his sexual partners. The Sagittarius woman may feel trapped, for sex is about freedom for her.

Sagittarians have a natural understanding of each other's needs. They can share erotic conversation, mutual stimulation, and plenty of oral and even anal sex. They will enjoy the wilder side of their sexual inheritance, and may become involved in group sex or threesomes. However, they can become irresponsible, assuming that what they believe is right to do at any given moment of pleasure is what their partner also needs. They have the quality of excellent communication on their side, but they must be wary of becoming detached from reality.

Sagittarius Woman with the Air signs (Gemini, Libra and Aquarius)

The air signs often make ideal partners for the Sagittarius woman, who thrives on unemotional intimacy and pleasure that is light, joyful and varied.

The Gemini male is her natural opposite in the zodiac, which means there will be an electricity between them, a dance of energy that cannot fail to fuse them immediately. She will adore the Gemini man because he is funny, whimsical, elusive and has tremendous sexual variety. Both love to talk during penetration, or share erotic phone conversations, each masturbating at the end of the phone, goading the other on to ecstasy. He won't want commitment or too much sensuality, and the Sagittarius woman may feel truly free. Their only problem is that she may want to increase the stakes, take risks and explore dangerous sexual pleasure with an open mind. The Gemini, for all his variety, is more interested in the ideals of the mind, in dangerous liaisons in his imagination rather than in reality.

The Sagittarius woman desires a man who is aesthetically pleasing, both physically and mentally. When she meets the beauty of the Libran male she may feel she has finally met her ideal. Equally, he will be instantly aroused by her fiery, potent and assertive nature. He will enjoy being pursued and hunted by her, but he also fears being dominated by too much passion. The best pleasure will be had when they are out together at parties or social events. Their erotic conversation will begin their sexual dance, until they are compelled to touch, caress and stroke each other in full view of the party.

With Aquarius she may enjoy the extraordinary and the bizarre. She is ready for experimentation in her sex life and will truly enjoy the sexual company of the Aquarian male. He also prefers open friendship to monogamy, and together they may remain detached and yet sexually resplendent.

Sagittarius Woman with the Earth signs (Taurus, Virgo and Capricorn)

The Sagittarius woman may learn much from the sensuality and richness of the earth signs. Yet she may feel too trapped, too devoured by their extraordinary ability to involve their soul and feelings in their pleasure.

The Sagittarius woman will be fascinated by the powerful sexuality that oozes from the Taurus man. She will be entranced by his seductive darkness, his slow sensuality. He is almost animal, like her, but he is a nocturnal creature rather than the gallant hunter of the forests and plains. Her fire will be earthed into pleasure she may never have experienced before. Sexual activity may be less spontaneous, less determined by opportunity, but will be a ravishing feast for her to celebrate. Their only problem will be when he becomes possessive. His ownership of her sex may send her hunting wilder freedom.

With Virgo she may delight in his sophisticated sexual techniques, his ability to turn every caress and every kiss into an art form. She will play easily with him for their sexual pleasure does not involve emotion. Yet her pace may be too heated for his rather cool approach. But he will know exactly how to lick her sex, dart and probe beneath the furls of her labia and serve her desire for orgasm over and over again, until his own arousal can no longer be contained. Their sexual journey will be laced with the finest entrées, the best plats du jour, but she may become impatient and restless.

If the Capricorn man has Venus in Sagittarius, or she has Venus in Capricorn, there may be a strong and powerful eroticism to this relationship. However, their very different ways of seeing life and expressing their sexuality will either attract or repel. She will want unrestrained orgasm, pleasure for pleasure's sake. His conservative and often suppressed sexual responses require work and effort to show their full splendour. She wants to play; he wants to work. She wants spontaneity and he wants a time and place, a designated orgasm, a clock ticking beside their bed as he thrusts hard, pushing deeply into her sex. If the Capricorn male can understand the deeper needs of his often repressed passion, he will begin to delight in this uninhibited and extraordinarily joyful woman.

Sagittarius Woman with the Water signs (Cancer, Scorpio and Pisces)

The opposing energies of fire and water may create a magical union when fused. However, the Sagittarius woman may find emotional involvement too heavy for her light and sometimes frivolous sexual celebration.

With Cancer she may feel the need to take the lead too frequently. Initiating and seducing is easy for her, but if the Cancer man is self-conscious and cautious she may become frustrated and resort to masturbation purely to relieve her own passion. If he can awaken to her joyous giving, her wildness, he may begin to feel secure in her free attitude. Yet the Cancer male is highly possessive, and she may flee from his emotional dependency.

The enigmatic Scorpio male will initially prove a powerful attraction to her eager enthusiasm. If she has Venus in Scorpio or he has Venus in Sagittarius, this could be an explosive passion. His intense desire for power may subject her to an experience she has never encountered before: one where her usual quest for liberation is propelled towards a release from physicality. If she finds him too dark, too smouldering, then he may find her too light, too romantic. Yet he is a master of sexual arousal, and she may play long and hard games with him in her pursuit of pleasure.

With Pisces she may encounter a dreaming soul able to offer her the most varied of sexual responses. His feelings, although deeply felt, may not break out, and she can enjoy his pleasuring unhampered. However, he may prefer food, wine, beautiful clothes, candles and incense to the cold, barren wastes of freedom. Their sexual needs are very different, but she may bring joy to him if she can prevent herself from pursuing her need for more space.

Interactive Section
Sagittarius Woman

The sun represents my sexual purpose.

My sexual purpose is to celebrate the pleasure of my body.

I need to learn to access my feminine nature and enjoy tenderness.

I sexually shine by being outrageous and passionate.

My serpent power explores, plays and takes any opportunity.

My beauty is heard through the voice of Atalanta when I honour my huntress instincts and celebrate my sex.

My beast is heard through the voice of Zeus when I accuse others of weakness and impotence.

Sagittarius – sun-sign key words for your erotic chart

Fill in the blank spaces at the bottom of this page and the same area on your erotic-profile chart beneath the zodiac wheel. You can choose which words or phrases you most identify with, and so begin to work with the images and meanings behind your sun sign.

The sun-sign section indicates your sexual identity, purpose and desire.

My sexual identity is _____

Choose from: opportunistic, playful, passionate, independent, outrageous, expansive, spontaneous, crusading, idealistic.

My sexual purpose is _____

Choose from: to bring joy to myself and others through wisdom and liberation, to get in touch with my feminine tenderness, to learn not to assume others must always play to my rules, to acknowledge emotional intimacy as a means to sexual joy.

I desire with _____

Choose from: hunger, impulse, zeal, spirit, urgency.

Questions

- To what extent are you able to connect to your truly feminine side?
- Do you consider receptivity, passivity and compliance are signs of weakness in relationships?
- Do you prefer the company of men to women?
- Do you assume that your partner will respond to your sexual demands without question?
- Are you usually the first to instigate sexual stimulation, and if so do you expect your lover to have the stamina to match your pace?
- Do you find the idea of bisexuality threatening or welcoming?

CHAPTER ELEVEN:

CAPRICORN

23 DECEMBER–19 JANUARY

*'She took him in the kiss, hard her kiss seized upon him,
hard and fierce and burning.'*
DH Lawrence, *The Rainbow*

Capricorn Woman – Purpose and Sexuality

Beneath the frosty petals that enfold this woman lie a richness and a luscious energy often carried through her early life without awareness. When young she may have low sexual self-esteem and be afraid of the delights of her body. The Capricorn woman grows into her sexuality as she matures, but sometimes she unconsciously suppresses her sexual needs and is never able to totally mesh with her deep female earthiness. She can be aroused to peaks of sexual euphoria, be filled with unimaginable lust, then the next day become cold, passive and bored. She is often ambitious in her work and alarmingly cold and aloof in her relationships. The truth about the Capricorn woman is that she fears life so deeply that she must drive and test herself as an unconscious means to her survival.

She rarely involves herself in a sexual relationship unless it is a serious or long-lasting bond. She is serious about life and serious about sexual exchange. If she does find a partner who can uncover her true richness, peel away the layers of the frosty petals, she may begin to acknowledge her own fragility and her desperate need for security and order. The bonding power of sharing sexual pleasure is far more important to her than the actual experience itself. If she can trust her partner, then she will begin to let go, but only on her own terms.

The Capricorn woman needs to learn not to fear her own feminine power and her earthy sexual inheritance. Her sexual purpose is to find pleasure in herself, and to celebrate her sexuality as one powerful expression of the energy of life.

Key Word: Accomplishment

The Capricorn woman needs more than any other woman to relax and allow herself to play. Her earthiness is uncomfortable to her. Because she fears the currents and unpredictable flows of life, her own earthy femininity often fills her with horror rather than pleasure and she may suffer from many sexual inhibitions. She often glazes herself with a veneer of sophistication and accomplishment to scare away any who dare come close. This woman is a paradox, for she both yearns for sexual release and yet denies herself the pleasure. She can starve herself of orgasm and put up powerful sexual barriers, yet she is also capable of lush sensuality and the darker instincts of frenzied desire. She is both rich in quality and poor in self-esteem.

Her fragility guards a sensual secret and, if her partner can commit himself to her cause, he will find a mind-blowing lover, gifted and skilled in sexual knowledge. Her lover must be willing to be dominated, and to prefer simple nakedness. She needs discretion rather than wild windy shores or alleyways: the warmth of pillows, linen sheets and the security of a locked door. Safety and pleasure are inextricably linked for her. When liberated from the fear of her own earthiness, she will take pleasure languidly, powerfully building up anticipation through every movement, every caress, every kiss. She has an ancient secret, a connection to the Black Sun of Babylon, a powerful regenerative darkness that leads to creative light. She can plunge into that sexual darkness if she dares and know that she will return fearless and sexually ripe.

How Capricorn Shines

She is rarely promiscuous and may have taken on the tenets of parental or cultural conditioning as to how to behave sexually and what is expected of her. Yet her wisdom and her sensuality merge when she is finally secure with a truly committed partner. He must be as controlled as she is, and immensely bound to her both physically and emotionally. She may seem hungry, ravenous for stimulation, as she liberates herself from preconceived ideas of technique and performance. She is wary of her female side, for her animus, her Yang masculine energy, is powerful. If she realises the richness of her inner feminine she will be resolved to deliver herself up to sexual abandon.

She is fragile and needs to be aroused with tenderness. Her lover must excel at the sensual arts: warm massages, wine, and bathing in sumptuous oils will stimulate and arouse her. Her passion will grow slowly, unfurling like frosted petals exposed to the sun. Then she will become the aggressor, the dominatrix. She will shine as an artist of oral sex, her mouth sending messages, teasing, coaxing. She may insist on lengthy penetration and the power of sitting astride him, being both a bringer of pleasure and a wielder of torment. Her control is unique and she may bring him to his climax then instantly stop, holding him upon a plateau of sexual fervour. If she can eliminate her fear of life and of expressing her sexuality, she may become the wildest of earth women: not a nymph nor a goddess but just a being of pure, savage sexuality.

Serpent Woman Power

This is the way of the Capricorn woman's serpent of desire:

She will have known him since the winter solstice, have watched and waited for many months to make certain he is worthy of her desire. He must bear the hallmarks of success and power. Only then will her serpent awake to his seduction. Her patience is rich with longing. Yet this serpent works slowly and must test herself and the one she desires. She will not directly pursue him; she will wait for him to come. He will have noticed her often in the conference room and been entranced by her accomplished style, her grace, wisdom, and success. He will insist on buying her dinner. A small token of his intention. She fears accepting, and yet this serpent knows him well. Knows his lushness. That he has security and wealth. He is safe.

As she dresses for dinner her desire will test her self-control. She may bathe quickly, fearful of her body as each time she soaps her sex or dries her breasts she feels the shivers of passion course through her body. There will be music, low lights, and a glass of claret beside her dressing table. She will be painstaking with her make-up and dress herself in fine materials and exquisite jewels until her appearance is as perfect as a pearl. Yet now her serpent is awake she will cut herself off from the desire for pleasure. She concentrates only on the superb performance she will give tonight. She will master her body and subtly dominate this new lover. She will be a luscious sweetmeat. Her serpent will bind him to her for ever, for this is her desire.

Capricorn Woman – Her Beauty and Her Beast

In traditional astrology Capricorn is ruled by the planet Saturn. Saturn was an ancient earth god to whom the Romans dedicated their winter-solstice festival, the Saturnalia. The Saturnalia was a period of seven days of orgiastic feasting when sacrifices were made to Saturn as both god of the darkest day of winter and bringer of the spring. The Capricorn woman's beauty is best displayed in the archetype of Saturn. Saturn was both lord of the darkness and revered as a healer. Without the darkness there would be no light. He was the Black Sun of the ancient Babylonian astrologers: the sun at its lowest point in midwinter. The Saturnalia provides a time in which to abandon oneself to ecstatic rituals and orgies, a contained period of healing euphoria in the darkness of the night.

Her beast is aligned to Juno. Juno was a highly regarded Roman deity, the consort of Jupiter. She was protectress of women, and oversaw the whole area of menstruation, sex and marriage. She upheld the purity of marriage above all else. Juno's sanction was that sexual intercourse was for the purpose of procreation within the sanctity of marriage. Pleasure was not necessarily an expression of this. It is the harsh, self-testing severity of Juno's self-denial that aligns with the Capricorn woman's beast.

Her Beauty

The Capricorn woman's beauty arises from the strength of Saturn and the ambiguity of his purpose as the Black Sun of winter. As Saturn infuses the winter solstice with passion, ecstasy and sexual joy, so the Capricorn woman, when she allows herself a safe container, a period of special feasting, expresses her truly rich sexuality. When she is in touch with Saturn's archetype she can honour her own Saturnalia. She may discover that the winter solstice holds the primeval mystery of her deeper sexual needs. She can reconnect to the sensual magic of the sacred harlots, and be released from her own confines of low sexual self-esteem.

When she is truly aligned to her beauty the Capricorn woman is devoted and sensually delightful. She will honour her body and take pleasure in orgasmic deliverance. She will reach beneath the pretence of refinement to discover the exquisite layers of her Black Sun. She will prefer the elegance of simplicity, the joy of nakedness and the freedom to reach her climax without accoutrements or sexual devices. One day she will desire to dominate. Then the next day she may want to be bound gently to the bedposts while her lover ravishes her.

Her Beast

If the Capricorn woman has not attuned herself to her true sensual nature she may reject the beauty of the Black Sun and express only the embodiment of Juno. She may repress her deep earthy energy for fear of her ancient femininity. Juno insisted on fidelity, but only because she feared her own desire so greatly. The Capricorn woman too fears her passion, for it is the most instinctive expression of ourselves, it is the most powerful force of life.

If she aligns with her beast, in her childhood and teens

she will obey parental, cultural or social values rather than her own inner needs. When she matures, she may develop a distinct distaste for anything she sees as unusual or abnormal. She may want only penetrative sex and have rigorous rules and regulations for when to have sex, how and where. Even masturbation may be shrouded in guilt and secrecy.

She may go to the extreme of denying all sexual pleasure, and starve herself and her partner of their closest intimacy. Equally, she may use her body as a reward or as emotional blackmail. She may take pleasure only in seeing the power she has over others, for in this way she can build her self-esteem around control and manipulation. She may empower herself through ruthless sexual experiences, or by working her way to the top in any career by using her body, but never find true happiness in her consort's arms.

The Capricorn Male

The Capricorn male has many self-imposed restrictions. He may start off slowly when young, often preferring to avoid intimacy for as long as possible. He may have only one partner for life, or he may go to the other extreme and seek out the most dangerous of liaisons. There are two types of Capricorn male: the one who stays forever dithering about exploring his fear of sexuality, and the other who goes out and grabs new encounters for all it's worth.

He needs fine women, ambitious and often power-driven types who match his own thirst for control. Yet, his is not a fiery, brash or arrogant sexuality. It is closed, prolonged, anticipatory. He needs to test the responses of his lover to make sure she is as discreet and refined as he. He takes his time. Clock-watching, the pace, the performance and the scenario are carefully contrived. He needs to feel secure, and he needs to feel in control. When he sets out to master his craft he learns it deeply, thoroughly, determined to be the best.

His partner may find his erect penis his most treasured possession. Although he prefers straight, simple, hard sex, he is not averse to oral sex, and may delight in long periods of mutual masturbation if his partner makes the first move. He needs nakedness rather than accompaniments, the lingering of her lips on his belly rather than the tickle of feathers or the feel of rubber toys. Good, hard body contact is essential to this man as his powerfully rhythmic sexuality builds to its peak. He seems to be in control always, and yet he needs at times for a sensual and dominant woman to take him on a different route to rapture. He is deeply romantic, and sex to him is binding: it is not just a vehicle for self-pleasure. He desires to devote himself totally to one woman.

Compatibility

Like her other earth sisters, the Capricorn woman needs a lover or partner who can share her delight in a long-lasting bond. The Capricorn woman needs a partner who can reach through to her fragile sensuality and explore her feminine joy.

Capricorn Woman with the Fire signs (Aries, Leo and Sagittarius)

Passion is to be treasured by the fire signs. These potent, fiery types could lead her into celebratory and inspiring sex if she can indulge in the sheer enjoyment of sexual thrill.

With Aries she may be plunged into temptation faster than is normal for her. He will be fascinated by her cool, almost icy dignity one minute and her arousing, hot seduction the next. He may find that she will shy away from his more impulsive attempts to ravish her in bizarre locations. She will enjoy his fiercely self-centred orgasms and will yield willingly to his need to dominate, perhaps forsaking her own pleasure too often.

The Leo male often delights in the glamorous appearance of the Capricorn woman. Although very different in their outlook on life, they are both aroused by beauty, success and power. She needs a permanent sexual bonding. He will demand complete loyalty, and she will readily give it. His touch will send her to pinnacles of pleasure, and they will alternate dominatrix roles. He may satisfy her beyond belief, and she may begin to relax and honour her wilder feminine expression.

With Sagittarius she may sometimes find harmony and eloquence in his enthusiastic lovemaking. But his very nature is to explore, to adventure and to fly by night, unless he has Venus in Capricorn to give him more stability. He will suggest wild, romantic places for their pleasure to unfold: gypsy caravans, racetracks, fast cars. She may prefer the white sheets and the comforts of success. She will want privacy, intimacy and measured sex. Their differences may dissolve if he can honour her need to be bound on a permanent wave of sexual delirium.

Capricorn Woman with the Air signs (Gemini, Libra and Aquarius)

The intellectual, airy approach to life of the air signs will both fascinate and repel the cool Capricorn woman.

If she gets involved with a Gemini man she may find him amusing, playful and absolutely charming in bed. He will tease her with erotic conversation, or spontaneous phone calls at dawn when he is most aroused. Yet he may irritate her with his changeable nature and his own rather mental arousal. She may have trouble feeling she can share her vulnerable inner core. He may find her too powerful, too dominating for his rather ambivalent sexual pleasure.

With Libra she may enjoy his blend of sexual aesthetics and high ethical values. She may find him easily seduced, but he may be uncomfortable if she tries to dominate or overwhelm him with passion. He needs refinement and will adore her cool exterior which hides a luscious interior. The Capricorn woman is not fond of deviating from the norm, and may be uncomfortable with his love of three- or foursomes. Yet his fashioned locations will thrill her, and she may be able to offer him sexual pleasure without deep emotional involvement.

With Aquarius, if she has Venus in Aquarius or he has Venus in Capricorn, this could be a successful sexual relationship based on intellect and ambition. This man could widen her sexual repertoire and access her inner needs, but only if she dares to compromise. If both at times withdraw from sexual activity they may return to one another with a freer and more responsive energy. His is a very different detachment from hers, for he avoids merging with another human being on an intimate basis.

Capricorn Woman with the Earth signs (Taurus, Virgo and Capricorn)

With the earth signs the Capricorn woman can enjoy Saturnalian pleasure, but her deeper fears may remain uncured.

The Capricorn woman may warm quickly to the potent sensuality of the Taurus male. She may at first fear his lusty, animal nature, but he will draw on her own inner earthiness so that she begins to relax into her body's needs. Mutual masturbation and oral sex will be a pleasure for them both. This is a bonding relationship, and one where her self-esteem grows and her pleasure can be explored. She may even suggest S&M games and he will enjoy indulging in his fantasy of submission when she sits astride him and thrusts her sex upon him.

The Virgo male may eagerly set out to perfect her sexual style. He will give her all the sophisticated techniques, *Kamasutra* positions, fantasy roles and bizarre locations. She may fall quickly into his embrace, yet at times will find she needs to retreat from him. His is a sexuality of intellectual perfection. Hers is a sexuality of hidden secrets, a need to be opened up to the joy of sensual pleasuring. They may share mutual orgasm as their bodies glide in tune, but for their relationship to be sustained he must learn to look deeper than her practised responses.

With another Capricorn, she will feel safe and empowered by finding someone so like herself. Yet it may mean that many of her fears and inhibitions will remain deeply embedded. The Capricorn male may provide the kind of simple, naked sexuality she prefers. He may be accomplished, rich, wealthy and successful enough for her to feel secure in his bed. She will surrender to this man, and he may find her winter cavern warmer than he believed possible. When he reaches down to her sex his eager hands will find her clitoris budding into a firm peak. He will want to ravish her without hesitation and they may spend nights in pure, hard, penetrative sex, for both have the stamina and the desire for intense pleasure.

Capricorn Woman with the Water signs (Cancer, Scorpio and Pisces)

The emotional complexity of the water signs means the Capricorn woman may discover the deeper mystery of her femininity.

With Cancer, her naturally opposite sign of the Zodiac, she may find a deeply satisfying physical and emotional relationship. The Cancer man may be shy and awkward initially, but he will intuitively know that beneath her accomplished air there hides a luscious and yet fragile sexual longing. They will offer one another the opportunity to discover the tenderness and sensuality that both may be fearful of experiencing.

With Scorpio's darkness, she can let loose her wild woman totally. She will enjoy dominating him and subjecting him to willing bondage, but she must be prepared for the Scorpio price of erotic transformation: she must honour his power. He knows intuitively how to tongue her sex, knows exactly how to lick and tease her clitoris until she cannot hold back. He wants power through orgasm; he wants power over and above the act of animal passion. But she needs the power of a bonding physical merger.

The Pisces man will dissolve into her arms if she is in one of her strong, lusty phases. Yet the ephemeral quality, the elusive and strange ghostliness of the Pisces man may not be fulfilling enough for her own earthy needs. Pleasure will be theirs in fantasy and erotic bliss, but he must learn to honour her earthly delight.

Interactive Section
Capricorn Woman

The sun represents my sexual purpose.

My sexual purpose is to find pleasure in feminine joy.

I need to learn to relax, to allow myself to play, and not to fear my own power.

I sexually shine by being an accomplished and giving lover.

My serpent power moves slowly, waiting for security before striking.

My beauty is heard through the voice of Saturn when I express my true passion through sexual celebration.

My beast is heard through the voice of Juno when I set out to test my control over others.

Capricorn – sun-sign key words for your erotic chart

Fill in the blank spaces at the bottom of this page and the same area on your erotic-profile chart beneath the zodiac wheel. You can choose which words or phrases you most identify with, and so begin to work with the images and meanings behind your sun sign.

The sun-sign section indicates your sexual identity, purpose and desire.

My sexual identity is _____

Choose from: accomplished, subtly dominating, ordered, luscious, dedicated, bonding, glamorous, powerful, dignified.

My sexual purpose is _____

Choose from: to find pleasure in myself, to reconnect to the sensual magic of sacred sexuality, to liberate myself from the fear of my own earthiness, to welcome the darker instincts of frenzied desire.

I desire with _____

Choose from: caution, ambition, passive control, persistence, patience.

Questions

- Do you equate sexual pleasure with a long-lasting and secure bond with one partner? How seriously do you take security and commitment?
- Do you believe you must succeed in a sexual relationship at all costs? If you are in control of your sexual responses do you feel that there is something missing?
- Have you ever truly surrendered to the lushness of your inner savage woman? If not, does this image frighten you or do you find it repellent?
- Do you deny your vulnerable side for fear of the feelings and emotions hidden deep within?
- Do you assume you know what is best for your partner's sexual pleasure, and do you usually take the dominatrix role?

CHAPTER TWELVE:

AQUARIUS

20 JANUARY–19 FEBRUARY

'She was a store, a store of absolute beauties that it
drove him mad to contemplate.'
DH Lawrence, *The Rainbow*

Aquarius Woman – Purpose and Sexuality

The Aquarian woman walks a sexual tightrope between self-imposed limitations and her desire for universal freedom for all. She is sexually broad-minded, believing that anything goes for anyone if they so choose, and yet her own eroticism is inhibited and controlled. She finds it hard to be in a relationship on an intimate basis.

The rest of the world may exhibit sexual variety, cathartic physical relationships, forbidden sexual acts, and she'll enjoy the observation from her lonely vantage point. She will often refuse to indulge herself, but she will gladly help her friends or her partners to find sexual freedom. She travels through phases of total sexual abstinence, then veers towards power-motivated futuristic or unusual sexual activity. For her, sexual adventure is a quest for the expansion of her mind and thus the ultimate cosmic orgasm. She is deeply afraid of emotional intimacy and so her sexuality must lie in the intellectual zone between her exploratory arousal and her well-defined emotional boundaries. If she can learn to resonate with her own powerful sex drive and recognise it as the universal force that it is, she may begin to experience the freedom that she allows others.

Key Word: Sensuality

By letting herself go and surrendering to her lover, she fears losing control and her own empowerment. She is special and she knows it, but how to open up to touch and tenderness when she cannot trust her bodily instincts? Her mind is her power, and she often rejects her femininity for the same reason she rejects many conventions. She needs to be different to feel secure.

In her lover's arms she may need gentle stimulation: just a light touch upon her breast or a tiny purr of his breath upon her belly. Unless she feels truly free from emotion, she may be unable to return such tenderness. She has a kaleidoscope of colourful sexual manoeuvres

164

up her sleeve, may have experimented with many techniques of masturbation and oral sex, but ultimately will still feel happier in the bigger context of free relationship than the sacredness of intimate sexuality. She may try out group sex, become the instigator of an orgy, or use hi-tech gadgets to bring her partners to arousal. In this way she avoids feeling, and avoids the link between body and soul. Her mind will not let go of its power and often she prefers to subtly dominate her partner by detaching herself from him as often as possible. She often sits in judgement upon her own sexual desires and activities, knowing that it is the idea of sex rather than the actual physical closeness that arouses her.

Pleasure is simply pleasure and her cosmic ideology finds little room for the simple pleasure of the human being. But if she can learn that the electric eroticism she feeds into her own and her partner's arousal is merely one primitive expression of who we truly are as a whole, then she may begin to embrace sensuality rather than fear it. If she can learn to trust her femaleness, her ancient connection to the sacredness of sexuality as an expression of both human and universal energy, then she may bring much joy to her varied relationships.

How Aquarius Shines

Her opinion of her own sex appeal is usually quite low. Yet, because of her cool glamorous intellect, her powerful mind and her sophistication, she often attracts more than she realises. She is an enticing Bohemian, eccentric, independent and rarely angered. She wants others to participate in the joy of sex because to observe and to orchestrate means to remain uninvolved. She can become deeply aroused by her own power within a social environment. This is where she feels secure: amongst the eclectic and liberated collective. Intimacy is frightening. The more aware and consciously sexually broad-minded she becomes, the more she steals away from her feelings.

She plays the games of intellectual sex with ease.

Conversation, as for the other air signs, is her prime source of arousal. She will spend hours on the phone, or over a restaurant table, spinning great philosophies tinged with the spice of erotic connotations. If her lover is as clued up as she, he will quickly play the game, too; if he is not, she will lose interest. Her fascination for seeing her partner's erection grow by the minute ensures she is far removed from involvement. She gives pleasure with skill and awareness, enticing him with her coolness and her ability to remain mind-centred. Hers is the art of sexual experimentation. It is bizarre, alarmingly fascinating and often highly arousing to her partner. She will lick, suck, dominate, shock, agree to any fetishes or fantasies in her desire to see others change and evolve around her. She will dream up a group or voyeuristic sex scene and remain aloof, aroused only by her own observation of the pleasure of others.

Serpent Woman Power

This is the way of the Aquarius woman's serpent of desire:

She needs a system around her but she needs to feel she stands out from it. She will be in the middle of a huge crowd when she sees him. She must stir her serpent from her slumber and awaken her to the individuality of a sexual experience. Her serpent prefers to work within the safety of the collective. She will rise slowly to the vibrations of sexual electricity. This is a man of power and success. He will speak philosophy and have great knowledge. His voice is deep, smouldering, magnetic enough to enchant her mind. He will treat her with respect and give her freedom. She knows he will come to her, for she has felt the energy of his desire: it is geared to an original and experimental liaison, one where she will be his equal. There is little he can do to resist such altruism, such detachment.

Hers is a seduction of escape and distance, a serpent that snakes through the grass away from trouble rather than towards it. She will dance freely towards the balcony, the lights of the city dazzlingly alive, the crowds of people empowering her with collective energy. He has followed her there, but will he lead the dance now or must she stay on the tightrope of desire? She will accept only an intellectual transformation and sexual exchange more powerful, more ideal than any bodily release. Yet he comes close to her now and she senses her own responses quicken. The tightrope sways and her serpent recoils from the messages of animal lust. But she lingers longer to taste the passion, just to know, to really know her inner desire. She cannot resist him.

Aquarius Woman – Her Beauty and Her Beast

Aquarius is ruled by two planets, Saturn and Uranus. The original ruler was Saturn but, when Uranus was discovered in the eighteenth century, astrologers agreed that this planet also had a lot in common with Aquarius. It seems the ambiguity and duality of Aquarius aligns with both the narrow limitations of Saturn and the boundless eternity and space of Uranus. The Aquarius woman is locked between these two male energies. Uranus was Ouranos, god of creation to the Greeks, and Saturn was equivalent to Cronus his son, leader of the Titans and the golden age.

To find her true beauty the Aquarius woman must look to a timeless, placeless moment before Ouranos created the world. She must look to an earlier deity born out of pure chaos: Nyx, night personified. Nyx wore black veils from which twinkled her stars of the universe. She was not only the night itself, welcoming, subduing, winged and awesome, but she brought justice and order out of the chaos. When the Aquarius woman is able to contemplate timelessness and the oldest principles of order and chaos, she aligns to her beauty, Nyx.

Her beast may be aligned to the dark side of Cronus, who castrated his father on his mother's request and then proceeded to eat his own children in fear of his power being usurped. The Aquarius woman may symbolically follow Cronus by castrating her own sexual needs, by denying herself intimacy, and by rejecting any who do not ensure she has control and power.

Her Beauty

Night carried with her a cloak of stars, timeless and unseamed, a token of the universe's exquisite jewels. The Aquarius woman today feels little connection to this feminine archetype: her desire for sexual autonomy is reasoned, based on a masculine rationale about universal destiny, the theories of mankind and the collective, rather than on intuitive threads of ancient wisdom. Yet, when she aligns to Nyx, she can begin to reconcile her feminine power with her objective and abstract ideals of sexuality. For Nyx has no desire but for order and justice. The Aquarian woman speaks up for others, for their sexual rights, their bisexuality, their homosexuality, but she prefers to keep her own desire screened, shielded by the darkness of night.

If she identifies with Nyx she too can be fearless of intimacy and take pleasure in her own sexual liberation. If the Aquarian woman can align herself to this archetype she will relax and enjoy the pleasure of her body, knowing that her mind, or the daylight, will return to take control whenever it pleases. She will be seen as sophisticated, serene and erotically uninhibited. She has the power of her darkness to draw on primeval lust as a source of divine ecstasy or liberation of herself from the confines of her mortality. Sexually, she can cloak herself and her partner in a lushness of total surrender. For she aims to please others more than herself. Her sexual agenda is totally unique, totally at odds with many others, which is why, like Nyx, she is out of her time, yet vast and immeasurable. Her sexuality is as boundless as the stars in the night sky.

Her Beast

Cronus castrated his father: this is a symbol of literally cutting oneself off from others. Once dismembered, Ouranos's genitals were transformed into the beauty of Aphrodite Urania. The Aquarius woman fears her own beauty so much that she will literally cut herself off from sex and her sexual intimates, often painfully. When she aligns solely to Cronus the Aquarian woman has many acquaintances but few close friends. She hides from intimacy in huge networks, social celebrations and the success of her career. She may reject her feelings and replace them with experimentation for the sake of being different. Being thought of as perverse or sexually liberated enables her to put up barriers around her own needy feelings. She may indulge frequently in group sex or threesomes, carry her eccentricity to the outer limits, and arouse her partner while she herself remains totally uninvolved.

She gains control over herself and her partner by allowing herself to become aroused only if her mind and not her body is engaged. She refuses to surrender to her own bodily and emotional instincts, and thus can become insistent that others grow and change before her eyes, rather than herself. She may resort to avoiding one-to-one relationships and have a free-ranging selection of partners, both male and female. If she rejects or represses her femininity, she may assume that her group consciousness and her fierce quest for feminist or political aggravation will be enough. Like Cronus, who eats his creations for fear of being destroyed himself, she will digest and analyse, dissect and abstract feeling from any sexual relationship for fear of her own creative feminine force. Her fear of loss of control is her beast, and she must learn to trust her body, and learn to reach out and touch.

The Aquarius Male

Sexual arousal for the Aquarian male is mostly concerned with the mind. He is often more pleasured by the idea of sex than the actual intimacy itself.

The initial seduction is usually mutual. He may be fascinated by her amusing words, her slightly flirtatious and frivolous nature. Or he may be curious about the dark, smouldering beauty in the corner who says nothing but betrays a sensuality he finds unbearably delicious. He discovers most of his pleasure by searching out very different and independent women, and then seeing them change and grow sexually in the mould he has cast for them. His mind is powerful and he has a tendency to play tricks with it. His ambiguity is alarming. Saying one thing but meaning another he often lures naive lovers to his genuinely warm bed. For every partner will find he says what she wants to hear: his words are so equivocal that she will believe what she wants to believe. Thus he often draws to him lovers who want love and emotional involvement. Yet he wants none of these. He is a loner who feels most comfortable in groups.

When faced with an intimate sexual encounter, he may suffer from fear of exposing himself too openly, but he will give his lover every imaginable pleasure. The successful pleasuring of others is his means to arousing his mind. He will enjoy detached seduction. He will imagine her naked, her back turned to him as he brushes his cock against her buttocks. She will lean against the great oak door to the chamber, her fists clenching as he tenderly kisses her neck and her back. He will nudge her secret place, yet he will not enter there. She must remain pure, untouched. For him the sweetness of her sex is that he must be the one to give her the ultimate pleasure. He will tease her there for a while, knowing she will be unable to hold back the tide of orgasm that is to come. Unless he is totally in tune with his partner he may refuse to climax, preferring the terrible torture of lingering anticipation.

Compatibility

The Aquarius woman needs a partner who can accept her experimental sexuality and her desire to remain detached. Yet she also needs someone who can encourage her to trust and to occasionally overcome her compulsion to be in control.

Aquarius Woman with the Fire signs (Aries, Leo and Sagittarius)

If the Aquarius woman is going through a phase of heightened sexual activity and exploration then she may enjoy and learn much from the passion and explosive energy of the fire signs.

With Aries she may encounter an unusually blazing passion. Initially she will be fascinated by their very differences. She will be aroused by his animal maleness, his hunting, aggressive passion. Yet she may find him too overwhelming and too physically direct. The Aquarius woman believes sex is an abstract concept, not grounded, not fiery, not simply about male potency. They may test one another's strength, and she will take much pleasure from their mutual attempts at control. She will be uncomfortable with his need to possess her.

Leo is her naturally opposite sign of the zodiac, and in this intimate embrace there is much she will discover. Leo exudes drama, the theatre of life. The Aquarius woman may find this enticing. She admires success and the richness of his style, and he may be romantically fascinated, drawn to something irresistibly unknown. The exhibitionism of Leo will arouse her quickly. She may find herself shivering with the first waves of erotic energy as he watches himself masturbate in the mirrored hall. The Leo male may offer a sexual liberation for this woman, but he demands complete and utter loyalty in return. Something which she may not be ready to give to one man.

With Sagittarius she may find a spirit who is in need

of greater space and freedom than herself. This could be a highly successful relationship, both as a long-term unconventional partnership and as a binding sexual friendship. They may give each other the space to really enjoy pleasure when they come together. He may introduce her to threesomes; she may introduce him to group sexual exploration. They may try to liberate others from their chains of conventional sex, yet they may never truly liberate one another from the fear of their own deeper selves.

Aquarius Woman with the Air signs (Gemini, Libra and Aquarius)

The Aquarius woman enjoys intellectual challenge, and with these signs she will find the same rather detached and abstract approach to sexual expression as her own.

With the changeable and scattered mind of Gemini she will alternate between finding him totally stimulating and incredibly frustrating. He will play all kinds of mind games and they may embark on long nights of conversation laced with occasional sexual activity. Neither wishes to dominate, yet the Aquarius woman will believe she is in control, until the Gemini male changes character on a whim. He may be too restless, too impossible to pin down in her bed of universal delights. He, although pleasured by her rhythms and experimental approach to their intimacy, may resort to the telephone as their main means of arousal.

The Libra male is the most idealistic of the air signs. Although she has her own ideals of universal and sexual freedom, his ideals are totally different: they revolve around himself and the perfect partnership. She may seem the most independent, self-analytical and observant woman he has ever met, but sexually she may freeze him up if she does not engage in mutual arousal. He needs mystery, long heavy bouts of foreplay, and romantic sex. She may intellectually enjoy this, and both will be able to support the other's need for unemotional involvement.

The natural affinity of two Aquarians means they often share extremely successful long-term partnerships. Sexual intimacy is something they both believe is only part of life's journey, rather than the sole expression of it. They may be able to arouse more feeling from each other by their detached and rather carefree attitude to sex. They will respect one another's need to feel free from sexual desire. Yet when they do enjoy physical coupling they may both soar to the heights of universal orgasm, as they travel to a place far removed from the humanness of intimacy.

Aquarius Woman with the Earth signs (Taurus, Virgo and Capricorn)

The very earthy nature of these three signs may fill the Aquarius woman with both fascination and fear. Her own abstract approach to sex may conflict with these signs, yet there is much here for her to share and learn.

Taurus may exude an extraordinary bestial sensuality, both enticing and physically frightening. She may be able to intellectualise his earthy smells, the wildness of his physical passion, and his unrestrained climax. She may want to uncover him while he sleeps and gaze upon his nakedness, so unashamed, so crafted. She will become excited by her experiences with this creature who bites and nibbles her musky sex out of pure physical pleasure. But she may find his possession of her body too close, too confining.

The poise and elegance of the mind of the Virgo male will seduce her immediately. She rarely falls into deep emotional involvement, which makes her sexual relationship with this man easier than many. He fears his own feelings as does she, and their mutual vulnerability may ensure they can remain detached and yet perfectly secure in each other's arms. She will treasure his technique, his kaleidoscope of suggestive conversation. This is what excites her: the ideal that can never be, but can be dreamed.

Perhaps it is the Capricorn man who may hold her interest longest, especially if she has Venus in Capricorn or he has Venus in Aquarius. This could be a superb blend of erotic and intellectual rapport. He needs more physical contact than she, but is equally evasive about his inner needs, preferring a detached attitude. Although he is incredibly conventional and she is not, both want to avoid becoming dependent on each other. He demands hard thrusting sex over long periods of time, which may not mellow the Aquarian woman. Yet, if he can give her freedom, they can share the ideals of sexual passion rather than simply act it out.

Aquarius Woman with the Water signs (Cancer, Scorpio and Pisces)

These water signs have very different sexual motives from the Aquarius woman. Her mind is where her power lies, and she may not trust the amount of investment the water signs put into their body and soul.

With Cancer she may grow impatient with his conventional and secretive approach to experimentation. If she has become drawn to him by his very difference she may, however, be a willing guide. She can open him to her vast repertoire of style and technique. Her erotic conversation will hold him spellbound through the night. He may replenish her with a compelling tenderness. However, he fears rejection more than failure, and this may have to be a sexual relationship between friends rather than between intensely magnetic lovers.

The smouldering darkness of Scorpio can be a powerful lure to the equally invasive mind of Aquarius. Both are intent on power and, when they meet, theirs could be an extraordinary magnetism that pervades every pore of her body. The body is something the Aquarian woman is rarely in touch with, yet this man may be the instigator and the source of her deeper sexual nourishment.

Pisces may seem like a dream, for she can blend her own detached arousal with his need for escapist sensuality. He too needs space and the unconditional. She may enjoy his grace, his charm and his silent expertise. Yet he is a romantic cleverly disguised as pleasure-seeker. Once the facade is lifted, once he becomes addicted to her, her beast may tell her to cut herself off from his beautiful lovemaking.

Interactive Section
Aquarius Woman
The sun represents my sexual purpose.

My sexual purpose is to discover the ideal and ultimate expansion of the mind.

I need to learn to accept one-to-one intimacy as being part of the universal sexual experience.

I sexually shine by intellectually empowering my partner.

My serpent power works best when I can shock and stand out from the crowd.

My beauty is heard through the voice of Nyx when I honour my body and release myself to the pleasure of intimacy.

My beast is heard through the voice of Cronus when I cut myself off from close relationships, thus denying my feelings.

Aquarius – sun-sign key words for your erotic chart

Fill in the blank spaces at the bottom of this page and the same area on your erotic-profile chart beneath the zodiac wheel. You can choose which words or phrases you most identify with, and so begin to work with the images and meanings behind your sun sign.

The sun-sign section indicates your sexual identity, purpose and desire.

My sexual identity is _____

Choose from: avant-garde, freedom-seeking, Bohemian, unconditional, exploratory, futuristic, experimental, detached, unpossessive.

My sexual purpose is _____

Choose from: to liberate others from their sexual inhibitions, to free myself from my fear of intimacy, to discover the ultimate meaning of pleasure, to learn to reach out and touch rather than to withhold tenderness.

I desire with _____

Choose from: originality, controlled purpose, intellectual curiosity, an open mind, refinement.

Questions

- To what extent do you feel cut off from your ancient feminine inheritance? Do you find it fascinating or threatening?
- Does a network of acquaintances and sexual liaisons without conditions seem more appropriate than intimate relationships?
- Does the idea of sexual surrender imply your body is no longer under the control of your mind?
- What mental imagery do you find arousing?
- What physical sensuality do you enjoy, or are you inhibited about releasing yourself to another's power?
- Does your mind instantly take over when desire suddenly overcomes you?

CHAPTER THIRTEEN:

PISCES

20 FEBRUARY–21 MARCH

'He stroked my pubic hair,
He watered my womb.
He laid his hands on my holy vulva.'
Diane Wolkstein and Samuel Noah Kramer,
Innana, Queen of Heaven and Earth

Pisces Woman – Purpose and Sexuality

The volatile undercurrents of sexuality are often not in evidence on the Pisces woman's surface. She hides them well, for she is both a muse of the art of allurement and a siren of haunting loveliness. She is the food of the gods, ambrosia itself to many men who find she offers them an immortal experience when they share her pleasure. She is often elusive, ephemeral and yet driven to attaching herself to both romantic love and sex. Pisces, as the twelfth sign of the zodiac, ends a cycle and yet is the seed for a new beginning. Thus the Pisces woman often has to learn that attachment to her past sexual relationships must be sacrificed for the new.

Her rich femininity is a pleasure to her. She often prefers the company of women to men, unless she encounters men with whom she desires sexual exchange and fulfilment. She will be at ease with men who have an awareness of their own feminine nature. Yet she can be drawn to brutish, violent types, for she is deeply insecure about her own power. Due to the fact that she is so sensitive, so in tune with the energies of those around her, she often confuses the desires and needs of her lovers with her own. She will be any reflection her lover chooses, even the ultimate sexual martyr, denying herself a deep and lasting commitment. She may gather lost and broken souls around her, intellectual failures or artists without a chance of success. If she spends time in self-denial, surrounded by her lost souls, she avoids the pain that she believes is bound with devoted pleasure.

The Pisces woman flows with the currents and rhythms of her emotions. She is an esoteric yet sensual woman and always binds love with sex. She does not seek sex for its own sake or for the sake of power. She seeks pleasure as a means of mutual exaltation and in the hope that she will be reunited with her deepest and most sacred self. Her sexual purpose is to be filled with the grace of the greatest life-force, and to taste the moment with utter abandon.

Key Word: Feeling

The Pisces woman's body is a shrine for her and her lover. She believes implicitly that she will share it with a soul mate, the one who can reconnect her to her deepest self. Yet in her youth she is often haunted by those who have very different sexual motives. Betrayal, hurt and low sexual self-esteem are her only rewards. She is so self-sacrificing that she rarely insists on her own pleasure and prefers to give all to her lover. She will play games of victim, slave, a mermaid ravished by the force of the tide. Her own body becomes a sanctuary for those who come to find pleasure.

Like Gemini and Sagittarius, she has two sides to her nature. This means she fluctuates between being the sensual elixir she offers her lover and the prevaricating shadow on the wall. She is tortured by desire, yet can withhold and deny herself any sexual involvement to avoid the pain of guilt. She may blame her childhood, her mother, father, society; it is irrelevant, for ultimately there is no one to blame. She is unconsciously searching for a place to lay the sexual guilt.

Her complexity lies in her deep need to avoid painful feelings, and escape into ecstasy is often her only way. She must look deeper into her fantasy world. She has an imagination filled with dreams of power and enslavement. Here, in this dream world, she might discover she can enjoy pleasure, free from self-criticism and guilt. She must learn not to throw a veil over her powerful, creative sexuality, learn to bring her dreams into reality.

How Pisces Shines

When the Pisces woman is in tune with her own hallowed sexual needs, and if she has found a partner who can treasure her sensitivity, she can be the most devoted and sensual of partners. At first she may seem elusive, seducing with a subtle yet dangerously intoxicating potion of desire. Her lover will be drawn to her fantasies, her poetic words. She is fascinated by the potency of the male lingam, yet also frightened by the physical ugliness of humankind. Therefore he may be younger than she, for she adores the beauty of youth, the softness of young skin. He may have little body hair, only that fine line between his navel and his groin suggesting his more powerful maleness. His appearance must be true to her own deepest dreams.

She finds as she matures that her sexual needs and desires are just as necessary a part of her life as any other creative force. In this way she can become a sexual artist, a diva of erotica and a muse of pleasure. Hers is a pleasure dome of hidden sensual delights. She will enjoy a man who can sexually excite her with his own fantasy world, with conversation and with touch. He must have artistry and refinement, yet he must be ready to take her to her orgasmic peak and hold her there, for eternity.

Serpent Woman Power

This is the way of the Pisces woman's serpent of desire:

This is a serpent of the deepest waters of the ocean. Like the Nagas of Indian mythology, this serpent guards great jewels in her underwater palace. The most precious treasure is her sex. When some wave, some current of change in the ocean moves her, she will stir, and she will arise to seduce and to beguile. She will slide out of her great palace, lured by the beauty and the mystery of a chance encounter. She will be attracted to youth, to a romantic or a poet. He will exude receptivity, passivity, yet be masculine in the curves of his body. She will sense his manhood, intuitively know he is worthy of her, that he will become addicted to her smell, her taste and her pleasure. She will be easily led across the bar, dazzled by his charm and his expertise. Yet he does not know she is the seducer and he the seduced. For this serpent lures by playing his game: always ready, always able to mirror and reflect this man's timing, as if it were he who was offering her the elixir of sexual mystique.

She does not make the first move. She will only brush

her leg against his suggestively, touch his arm with her own perfumed skin. The lingering fragrance will remind him of her as he sleeps alone, his body aching to smell her sex. After that first touch she will withdraw, escape the commitment. Fearful of herself, she will prevaricate rather than entertain. Her allegiance is to secrecy and the clandestine. The masquerade is her favourite dance towards sexual surrender. This serpent hesitates, looks back in longing at the face in the crowd, at the one who waits breathlessly for her. She feels his desire, knows what he will be like to pleasure and to willingly submit to. Her eyes dilate; she runs the tip of her tongue across her lips, knowing now she must go back to her destiny. He will see her turn round, see the outline of her nipples beneath her voile dress, the volatile sensuality that lies hidden but now awakens. This is her way.

Pisces Woman – Her Beauty and Her Beast

The beauty of the Pisces woman can be seen in Eos. Eos was the sister of Helios, the sun god, and personified the early misty dawn, that glorious moment of delicate light, of the end of night and the beginning of day. In the same way, the sign of Pisces itself represents the end of a period of growth and decay and the start of a new cycle. Eos was mysterious, evanescent and mystical.

The Pisces woman's beast is represented by the daughter of Oceanus, the nymph Calypso. The lonely, enchanting and self-deceptive Calypso fell dreadfully in love with Odysseus. Calypso believed her wondrous spells would ensure that her lover stayed for eternity. Yet they could not, and Odysseus yearned for more than Calypso could give him. Thus Calypso is like the Pisces woman's dark nature when she submits too willingly, sacrifices herself totally to the one she desires, forgetting she has her own inner needs. Desperately tormented by pain when he finally leaves her, she probably always knows he will.

Her Beauty

Eos was a goddess of exquisite beauty, mystical, intuitive, sensing the coming of the light and the day. Her colours were more iridescent than a rainbow, and her chariot was gilded with the fragile golden hues of the night she was leaving behind. Like Eos, when the Pisces woman is in touch with her beauty, she may move forward into the daylight of her own sexual needs, and not attach herself to the longings of the past night. If she can align herself to Eos, she may discover how to commit herself and honours her own sexual needs first, rather than sacrifice her deepest self-esteem without honour. When she trusts her body, she can release herself with real abandon like Eos released the dawn. She may welcome in the light of day and enjoy her sexuality as part of the past and part of the future.

Eos was cursed by Aphrodite with eternal lust, due to her dalliance with Ares. Eos was driven to seduce countless young men to satisfy this unquenchable lust. Yet Eos found one great love in her life. This was Tithonus, a mortal to whom she gave the gift of immortality. However, in her passionate pleasuring she had forgotten also to give him the gift of eternal youth. The eternal physical ecstasy that she had found was her most treasured gift, yet she had to live with a man who grew older and older until he finally shrivelled away into a cicada. When the Pisces woman can identity with Eos, she may realise that eternal beauty is not necessarily to be found in youth. Like Eos, the Pisces woman knows that love and sex must come to an end because we are mortal and must grow old and die. But, like Eos, she can transcend these physical limitations by recognising the eternal creative force that lies in her sexuality, which is the bringer of light after darkness.

Her Beast

When the Pisces woman's beast becomes activated she may sacrifice her own delights, her own sensual responses, in order to keep her partner bound to her. Like Calypso she will weave a spell to entrance and captivate him, to addict him to her sex, to her every breath. She will not know truly who she is or what it is that gives her pleasure. Such sexual manipulation may not be obvious to her partner for she psychically resonates to his vibrations. She echoes his every desire as her own.

When Calypso cast a spell upon Odysseus she had not considered that he may have been committed to another woman across the seas in Ithaca. The Pisces woman also raises her defences by choosing not to know the truth. She deceives herself, fantasises about how this relationship will evolve, and rarely stops to consider her own integrity. When she solely aligns to her beast she is muzzled by her own fear of rejection. She may play a series of roles, assuming the harlot, the temptress and the vamp: anything to secure her lover's addiction to her. She may even adopt a masochistic role in her sexual games to ensure she is punished for her feelings. She may totally deny herself sexual pleasure, suppressing any arousal in her own body and faking her own orgasm.

Like Calypso she may prefer to live a lonely life. Alone on her island, she may welcome those who visit her, clinging to their passion to affirm her own sexual self-worth. Then, once they have left her shores, she will return lonely to her beautiful palace, not daring to assert her needs, not daring even to pleasure herself, for fear of her own instincts. In the story of Odysseus and Calypso, it is Hermes who is sent by the gods to tell Calypso to relinquish her beautiful spell. She does so reluctantly, knowing the pain to come. The Pisces woman often finds her spell broken, not by her own doing but by some external messenger of the gods. Hermes represents communication, and if she does not communicate her own sexual needs then someone out there will come to break the spell for her.

The Pisces Male

The Pisces male is a sleepwalker, a dreamer who drifts into sexual encounter without considering the consequences. He will retreat if he finds himself caught in a net of power. He is also incredibly fearful of rejection and failure. His charm is that he lives in a fantasy world of romantic eroticism. Every second that he becomes more aroused he is dreaming of how it will be.

He involves himself eagerly, believing that sexual euphoria can be found with anyone who falls close to his ideal. He is drawn to beautiful women, and often becomes addicted to a partner who treats him with contempt or chooses to dominate him. He is a willing submitter, and yet he wants to be outrageous, yearns to be an exhibitionist. He may find the demands of satisfying his partners mean he has little time for his own pleasure. He must learn discernment, for it's easy for him to become promiscuous, uncertain of what his sexuality is all about. He often makes poor choices in lovers, not knowing whether it is he who has been chosen or he who was the seducer. He often confuses a deeply emotional involvement with a purely sexual encounter. He needs to understand his own need to fuse love with sex, but he doesn't often know it.

He may drift from pleasure to pleasure, yet once involved in a union of love and sex he will be the master of erotic excess, knowing intuitively how to please and how to give. His is not animal or potent male lust: he connects to a compassionate and gifted female energy. He inspires with his fingers, ravishes with his lips, and indulges with finesse and grace. Oral stimulation is often his favourite craft. His artistry is unique, and he will have the patience to draw her into waves of intense pleasure. He may begin slowly, languidly almost, as if he is tentative and unsure of his own boundaries. He may tease her nipples with his tongue then slowly lick every inch of her body. She will warm quickly to his tenderness, his ability to give love as well as pleasure, for this man stands on the threshold to sexual ecstasy.

Compatibility

The Pisces woman needs a partner who is poetic, beautiful and tender, yet who will show her how to unfold and accept her own inner needs. She needs a partner who can accept her submission but offer her the pleasure of equality of passion.

Pisces Woman with the Fire signs (Aries, Leo and Sagittarius)

The soft light of the Pisces woman may be encouraged into a passionate inferno by the fire signs. Yet she must beware of sacrificing herself to them utterly.

With Aries she may find herself on a journey of sexual adventure, brimming with a passion she has only ever dreamed of. If she has Venus in Aries or he has Venus in Pisces this could be a highly volatile and unpredictable intimacy. He will not resist her lush sensuality, and she cannot but surrender herself to his fast arousal, his uninhibited need for masturbation. There may be passion, mystery and devotion while they are locked in physical abandon. Yet, when faced with his urge for freedom and her need for a more poetic arousal, they may become strangers, both yearning for the fantasy of one another rather than the reality.

The Leo male may excite her, draw her out of her sexual slumber. The Leo male adores being pampered and caressed, and the Pisces woman is a willing slave to his every command. She may become fascinated by his exotic glamour when he dresses her in outrageous clothes or exhibits her as his sacred whore. She may act out the roles he casts for her, but she may be giving everything only in an attempt to avoid the pain of his possible rejection of her. His fiery need for adoration may wear thin, but she has the softness of femininity which polishes his ego.

The difficult and tense relationship of Pisces and Sagittarius can sometimes be resolved by their mutual need for change and their fantasy world. Yet this man is charged with blatant sexuality, while she is a dweller in mysterious and clandestine eroticism. He may not give her the union of soul and body that she so desires from orgasmic liberation. They will enjoy oral sex together, for he will indulge her every pleasure with skill and adventure, with quality and with zeal.

Pisces Woman with the Air signs (Gemini, Libra and Aquarius)

The air signs represent a mysterious challenge to the Pisces woman. She may enjoy fantasy and conversation, but she may yearn for more than they can offer.

With Gemini she will be aroused by his similarly ambivalent nature. At times he wants sexual pleasure, secure and filled with laughter, wine and conversation. At others he will disappear from her bed, or play a different role at dawn. She will adore his fear of boredom and his need for erotic stimulation of the mind, but she may grow restless and empty when her own powerful sensuality seems wasted.

Libra may be a more intense sexual romance. They are both idealistic and treasure the aesthetic pleasures of sex, rather than the wilder, more bestial delights. Together they will listen to music, languidly pleasuring each other throughout the daylight hours in silken beds in chambers filled with mirrors, fine paintings and champagne. They serve each other indulgently, but they may have to overcome their mutual submissiveness.

Aquarius may prove the most awkward, yet the most dedicated to watching her sexual pleasuring. He may indulge her in unusual methods of arousal, introduce her to sex gadgets, new techniques and experimental torture racks. She will at first be willing to please, to comply with anything, yet she will fear his lack of sexual arousal, and may believe that she is merely a pawn in his rather cool sexual games.

Pisces Woman with the Earth signs (Taurus, Virgo and Capricorn)

The earth signs are very much concerned with expressing their sexuality through the joys of sensual pleasure. This can give the Pisces woman a deeper enjoyment of the pleasures of her own body.

The Taurus male may be able to introduce her to a feast of earthy delights. Her own fragile sexuality hinges on the balance between her sensual and sacred needs. The Taurus male may never be able to fathom the depths of her mysterious vulnerability, but he will treasure her sensitivity and honour her submissiveness. His desire for sensual pleasure is natural, and he is easily seduced by this most feminine of women, but he may find it difficult to go beyond the limits of the body and acknowledge her intangible need for spiritual union.

Virgo is her naturally opposite sign of the Zodiac. This relationship can be an exquisite contrast between beauty and perfection. It can be tense and testing, insatiable and unstoppable. The magical arousal between these two can be profound. They can each develop a haunting devotion to the other.

With Capricorn, he will wisely acknowledge her feelings and listen to her sensitive sexual chords. Yet he prefers to avoid any connection to his own feelings for fear of emotional conflict. He keeps his sexuality as a treasure, in an art gallery of pleasure. His skills in arousal are unmatched, and she may fall under his spell, tortured with desire for his splendour.

Pisces Woman with the Water signs (Cancer, Scorpio and Pisces)

The other water signs will be in tune with the Pisces woman. Her sexual fragility will feel safer in their desire for both sexual and emotional bonding.

The Cancer male will offer her a secret place, a satisfying warmth and homeliness which enables her to reveal her volatile energy. She can beguile him into any kind of fervour or wildness she chooses, but she must be prepared for him to take his time in all aspects of their pleasure. Her mystical sensuality may inspire him into submitting to her more bizarre desires. She may rely on him for gentle games of S&M or enjoy scenes with fantastic historical props and costume. Equally they may enjoy reading erotic literature to each other in the bath. But she must learn to accept his lack of communication and his need for solitary pleasure.

With Scorpio she may first be haunted by the mesmeric quality of this man's eyes. He may seem to overwhelm her, to seduce her too easily. His need to control her may force her into masochistic and guilt-ridden arousal. She may not be able to say what she truly wants and will bend to his will and his desire, believing it to be her own. Yet for both of these water signs sexual intimacy is an exchange of passion that will never be forgotten.

With her own sign, Pisces, there may be an immediate rapport, a strong desire to float away on a tide of sensual dissolution. However, because they are so similar they may both vacillate, never knowing what they truly want or what they can truly offer the other. They may play too many games, fearing rejection from one another. They will become powerless in each other's embrace. Surrounded by masks, candles and champagne, they will languish in their erotic fantasy world, rarely looking outside for fear of the harshness of the world around them.

Interactive Section
Pisces Woman

The sun represents my sexual purpose.

My sexual purpose is to enjoy pleasure as mutual exaltation.

I need to learn that pleasure does not necessarily mean I must suffer pain.

I sexually shine when I devote myself to sensuality.

My serpent power is secretive, yet easily led astray by beauty.

My beauty is heard through the voice of Eos, the goddess of the Dawn. It is heard when I honour my sexuality as a creative force and affirm my self-value.

My beast is heard through the voice of Calypso when I fear rejection, sacrificing my own pleasure, clinging to my partner's sexual responses as if they were my own.

Pisces – sun-sign key words for your erotic chart

Fill in the blank spaces at the bottom of this page and the same area on your erotic-profile chart beneath the zodiac wheel. You can choose which words or phrases you most identify with, and so begin to work with the images and meanings behind your sun sign.

The sun-sign section indicates your sexual identity, purpose and desire.

My sexual identity is _____

Choose from: mysterious, romantic, passive, devoted, eclectic, mystical, beguiling, sensitive, flowing.

My sexual purpose is _____

Choose from: to enjoy pleasure as a mutual exaltation, to get in touch with my most sacred self and to discover the richness within, to welcome sexual intimacy as a positive expression of my healing power, to enjoy passion without guilt since it is mine to have.

I desire with _____

Choose from: intuition, romantic intention, mutability, seductive beauty, rose-coloured vision.

Questions

- To what extent do you attach yourself to romantic notions and the sentiment of past sexual relationships?
- Are you drawn to poetic visionaries and broken-hearted souls, or to fiercer aggressive men who might offer you painful experiences?
- Do you find that being filled with sexual joy brings you both pleasure and pain?
- Do you ever indulge in masochistic fantasies, or S&M in reality?
- Do you feel compelled to echo your lover's responses as if they were your own? If so, do you feel that you never really know what your own sexual needs are?
- Can you identify with Eos, honour your inner self, and trust to abandoning yourself to sexual ecstasy?

PART TWO
VENUS

*'For her breath is on all who hath life,
and she floats in the air
Beelike, deathlike, a wonder.'*
Euripides, *Hippolytus*

CHAPTER FOURTEEN:

VENUS/APHRODITE –
THE PLEASURE PRINCIPLE

Venus/Aphrodite – the Goddess

The original Roman Venus was a gentle goddess, guardian of flora and fauna. Aphrodite, the Greek goddess of ideal love and beauty, became inextricably linked with this early fertility goddess. Aphrodite was the mother of Aeneas, one of the Trojans who founded Rome, and she was thus easily assimilated with the Roman Venus. Thus the Roman goddess who personified beauty, grace and harmony was linked with the self-pleasuring and sexual aspects of Aphrodite.

Aphrodite's own ancestry is ancient and vast. A whole book could be dedicated to her art, her history and her archetypal presence in human sexual expression. She had many emanations and was immortalised in many different sources. Not unlike Kali, she was a triple-natured goddess, being virgin, mother and crone. Her connections date back to Astarte, the Lady of Byblos, and one of the earliest forms of the Great Goddess in Sumeria.

With such a rich cultural inheritance, the Greek Aphrodite was an embodiment of female wisdom and sexual power. Her birth from the severed genitals of her father Ouranos, or rather from the foam they created as they fell into the sea, is inextricably linked to sexuality and eroticism. This birth of creative beauty and sensuality from the sea-foam is evocative of the waves of pleasure we experience in our sexual relationships.

Aphrodite was self-centred, had a highly active sex

life, and yet would restore youth and beauty and show her favours gladly if she was honoured. The Greek image of Aphrodite was both one of idealised and divine sexual and spiritual love (as Aphrodite Urania) and yet of profane desire, of human erotic and painful love (as Aphrodite Pandemos). Once assimilated into Roman culture, her earlier worship as goddess of birth and generation was restored, and the ancient cults associated with Aphrodite Pandemos diverted into temple prostitution and the more lustful revelry of Roman society.

It is worth noting that in Olympia Aphrodite was married off to the ugly and lame smithy god, Hephaestus. Yet she rarely shared his bed and preferred as her lover the potent and extreme opposite of her self, the god of war, Ares. It is this powerful attraction of opposites which frequently occurs in our own sexual chemistry, whether it is the pure opposite of passive, female energy polarised by dynamic, male energy, or a difference in desire or expression of pleasure. It is often with those who seem the most remote, the most different from ourselves, that we are compelled to enter into union.

Interactive Section

- How easily do you identify with Venus? Do you prefer to consider yourself more in tune with the Roman Venus, or are you able to identify with the deeply erotic but totally self-centred pleasuring of Aphrodite?
- Have you ever considered how powerful a force the archetype of Aphrodite is in your sexual nature? How often do you find yourself sexually attracted to very different types from yourself?

Venus/Aphrodite in Your Birth Chart

In astrology, Venus/Aphrodite represents your pleasuring and how in reality you interact sensually with others – how you receive and how you give. She also symbolises your sexual values and inner needs.

In a woman's birth chart, the placement of Venus/ Aphrodite also shows the way you hunt your pleasure, and how you seduce to bring that pleasure into your life.

In a man's chart Venus shows you what kind of sexual qualities he needs to give him pleasure: the kind of woman who will make him feel at one with himself and his inner sexual values.

All you need to do is look up your own Venus placement in the tables at the end of this section. Then refer to the relevant chapter to discover your own pleasure principle and sexual values. The Venus placements are divided into the four elements of fire, air, earth and water, each of which represents a different way of expressing these energies.

Your Venus and your Eros placements (see Part Three) may be in the same sign. This will mean that your sexual expression and erotic triggers will be in harmony. Most of us, however, have placements in different signs. The epilogue to this book can give you some guidance as to how to integrate your differences, as well as the kind of compatibility you can expect from you and your partner's Venus and Eros placements.

CHAPTER FIFTEEN:

VENUS IN THE FIRE SIGNS

(Aries, Leo and Sagittarius)

'Lion, let me caress you,
My precious caress is more savoury than honey.'
Diane Wolkstein and Samuel Noah Kramer,
Innana, Queen of Heaven and Earth

*T*he greatest pleasure for Venus in the fire signs is to discover sexual excitement, but also to enjoy the images of sexual pleasure rather than merely to engage in the physical sensuality. Venus in fire pursues pleasure to bring passionate ideals and dreams into reality.

Venus in Aries

Sensuality
This is a Venus woman who needs spontaneous touch, who knows that she is electric. She gives off flames of energy, sparks of fast words. She has no need for slow languid stroking. With her lips bonded to her lover's mouth, she will tease with her tongue and expect nothing but the best in return.

Venus in Aries wants the pleasure to be all hers. She is self-absorbed, egocentric, demanding and hurried. She wants quick arousal and the lightning experience of orgasm striking her faster than she dares believe. She prefers less foreplay to many of her Venus sisters: the thrill of hard penetration, the power of dominating her partner is more her pleasure than the gentle tenderness of lengthy stroking or massage. She hunts her pleasure impulsively. If the chance is there, if there is a risk or a danger, then she will be first to seduce and lure. The more risky the liaison, the harder she will pursue.

Her pleasure is in provocation, in daring to go beyond the limits set by her partner. She needs the thrill of a new vision every time she arouses her partner, for her demands are insatiable and her sensuality only concerned with the next touch, the next taste and the next sensation. Tomorrow's pleasure is always far more intoxicating than today's.

Masturbation

The Venus in Aries woman may begin to explore her body early on in life. She takes great delight in her own stimulation, finding pleasure in watching her own arousal in front of a mirror. She is vain, and may be more fascinated by and attentive to her own climax than her partner's. She rarely feels guilty about masturbation and will enjoy the thrill of showing her partner how she can arouse herself while he watches. She may treat masturbation as an essential part of her sexual identity. If she is without a partner she knows she can rely on herself for pleasure and may use accoutrements such as candles and dildos to delight herself while she fantasises about tomorrow.

The pleasure

They may well meet in public, in the fast-paced work place, amid the buzz of city life. She will boldly approach, sure of her words, her charm. Her seduction is as brash and flamboyant as her sensual gestures. There is no doubt he will respond. She will dance towards him, committed to pleasure. She will feel the silk of her dress stretch across her thighs as she sits beside him at the bar. Knowing he will have glanced down at her legs, she may cross them slowly, feeling pearls of desire ripple from thigh to thigh. There may be crowds, too much wine, too many friends around, but they will arouse each other mentally. They will joke and tease, and she will demand and tempt, drawing him ever closer, ever nearer to her chosen moment. It will be her *choice* to dominate and to lead for he must be as strong as she, or even more powerful. A man who is passive or powerless will not hold her attention.

She will begin to use her body to show what she wants. Show him that she wants him now, wants to lift her skirt and let him enter her. Penetration gives her the power, gives her control. For then it is she who encloses him, who shapes him to her own moment of ecstasy. If he is prepared for her this man will lean forward now, rest his hand upon her thigh, and tentatively brush against the mound beneath her silk skirt. She will whisper in his ear, and she will notice the hardness growing beneath her hands as she presses herself against him. They may move over to the darkest corner of the bar, sure now that they must complete the rhythm of the dance that has begun. She will stand with her back to the wall and begin vocalising her fantasy and her startling fire. Her ability to arouse him so fast will confuse him, and yet her urgency for more will be infectious. He has no choice now but to force her to the wall, to begin to explore her body. She has challenged him, and it is he who must undergo the ordeal by fire.

Venus in Aries – man

The kind of woman who will bring pleasure to this man is fired with enthusiasm for sexual ecstasy. He will enjoy spontaneous and self-controlled women, those who enjoy sex as light, visionary, magical, rather than dark emotion and deep sensuality. He will be stimulated by the potency of a demanding and outrageous woman. Impetuosity and the desire to lead and take risks will inspire him. He is egocentric, and so he will rise to someone who can make him feel the centre of attention, who can admire the force of his penetration and the hardness of his penis as he wakes at dawn. He does not want subtle manoeuvres, games of the mind; he wants sex out in the open, in places where only the courageous would dare to expose themselves. He will be pleasured by one who can give him freedom and the space to be himself, and yet explosive intimacy when he so desires. He will respond most to a woman who shares his Yang, assertive nature, who is neither shy nor inhibited, and wants it all for herself, now.

Interactive section

Venus represents my pleasure principle.

I find pleasure in _____

Choose from: provocation, penetration, fierce sensuality.

I am sexually nurtured by _____

Choose from: being dramatically aroused, being the centre of attention, taking the lead, asserting my needs.

My sexual responses are _____

Choose from: eager, hungry for more, outrageous.

I hunt my pleasure _____

Choose from: by impulse, in dangerous situations, in the search for a visionary sexual experience.

Venus in Leo

Sensuality

This woman purrs like a cat when stroked, and warms to the light touch of velvet-covered claws. She wants to both scratch and be torn. She may desire to be watched as she undresses. Sliding her beautiful clothes down her naked body before the mirror is enough to arouse and pleasure her. She gets great pleasure from herself. Yet she waits for the one who will share her seemingly passive and yet powerful sexuality. She does not force the pace, but merely augments the drama of the occasion by gestures, by words and the movement of her body. Her sensuality is fiery, blazing with colour, drama and mystery. She must immerse herself in her orgasmic pleasure.

This sensual pleasure must be like a show where she is the starring role, and her partner her captive audience. She needs to be sure of his intentions first, to be lit up with pleasure from within, before she can allow herself the temptation of carnal reward. Her powerful need for validation often hides a deeper vulnerability. She is vain and must be replenished with total loyalty, her partner giving her more than she can ever give. She is not tempted by the ugliness of cheap accessories or sex toys. The only accompaniments she needs to delight her will be luxurious surroundings, gold taps on the bath as the water turns to foam, a four-poster bed, and gilt-edged mirrors to watch her own moment of completion and surrender.

Masturbation
The Venus in Leo woman is an early bloomer and sexually aware at a young age. Her own body is her treasure, and she may explore and expand her own masturbatory repertoire well before she forms intimate partnerships. Her relationship to her growing arousal is easy. She has little trouble admitting her sexual needs and may suggest to her lovers that they watch her through the keyhole as she masturbates in her bath. She is a lover of self-gratification and needs to surround herself with glamour and the sparkle of endless possibility.

The pleasure
They will meet somewhere grand. Restaurants, glamorous parties, the theatre or the opera will inspire this Venus woman into being the ultimate diva. To be aroused by her own grandeur will stimulate her need for closer contact. Soon she will begin to finger his cheek, his lips, his hair. She knows how far to tempt, just how far she can go before he is trembling with desire. Then she waits. Now he must come to her. Now he must offer her dancing, music and food. Every pleasure is for her, even his own. Her power lies in her passive seduction, for she will not be stopped from taking every moment of rapture from this man.

After the last act, the theatre darkens. Yet still in the limelight of her lover's eyes she begins to use gestures and words that she knows will bring him quickly to erection. They will play for a while, tonguing each other's lips, arousing one another with touch rather than word. The theatre-goers will have gone and the actors left the stage. Impulsively, she will pull him across to the stage, the main spotlight shining down upon them like a circle of fire.

She will entwine one leg round his hips, beckoning his manhood to her. He will push her velvet dress below her nipples, begin to nip and suck at the golden buds as she moans, sighs and looks to the light, knowing she is there on stage, in full show of the world. Now he will unzip her dress, and take a long time to gaze upon her as she slips the velvet gown down to her ankles. She will wear stockings and suspenders, the lace of her chemise only just covering her pubis. His gaze will rest there, her sex moist now behind the lace, the empty theatre an echo chamber for every gasp she makes, every rustle of silk on the stage of rhapsody.

Venus in Leo – man

The kind of woman who can bring joyful pleasure to the Leo in Venus male is undoubtedly one who will serve his every need. He needs to feel pampered and warmed from within as well as to enjoy the delights of the flesh. This man desires beauty and glamour to boost his own self-esteem. He is highly vulnerable behind his fiery intentions, and may need to feel pleasure is not just for the sake of sex. He usually prefers a woman who will alternate with him at taking the leading role. He will admire and respect a woman who is proud, self-willed and, above all, has the confidence to enjoy her sexual experiences without restraint. He will utterly throw himself into a deeply satisfying sexual relationship if he finds it dramatic and iridescent enough. He is not fond of displays of emotion in the bedroom, and it may be that the kind of woman who can really give him pleasure is the one who remains an enigma.

Interactive section

Venus represents my pleasure principle.

I find pleasure in _____

Choose from: being in the spotlight, making sensuality dramatic and mysterious, luxurious surroundings.

I am sexually nurtured _____

Choose from: with huge displays of affection, with glamour and exotic locations, by being the first to orgasm.

My sexual responses are _____

Choose from: showy, theatrical, fierce.

I hunt my pleasure _____

Choose from: with dramatic displays of passion, by being outrageous, in the best restaurants and parties.

Venus in Sagittarius

Sensuality

The Venus in Sagittarius woman adores action, the adventure of the senses rather than the mere experience of them. She may want to try out all kinds of sexual games, preferring the pleasures of the massage parlour one day and the fast-paced risk of mutual masturbation on the train the next. The Venus in Sagittarius woman just wants to play. There is no better way to live joyously than by giving and receiving in sexual fun. Her sensual nature is demanding and demonstrative: if she wants to be touched sensitively she will ask for it, if she wants to be ravished and thrust to the ground under the pine trees she will brashly suggest it.

New locations, new sounds, smells and tastes are all eagerly treasured and then discarded if they become routine. Her pursuit of the ideal experience means she will expand her repertoire to include many ways of sensual pleasuring. She will choose the deserted beach, the mountains, the empty car park, anywhere she can indulge her desire for spontaneous hot arousal. She does not need cook-book sex, *Kamasutra* positions or erotic devices. This Venus woman just needs herself, and possibly a partner, who may seem like an accessory to her growing excitement. She prefers men who don't touch her in the same places every time they make love, and she prefers unpredictable and changeable oral sex to the same routines of foreplay.

The more wicked and bestial the play, the more she will be physically stimulated. Yet her mind must be part of the show, as with other Venus in fire women, for without the image of ideal ecstasy she may leap into the abyss of chance encounters with strangers. With the night sky above her head and the grass beneath her lover's back, she will entertain his penis with her generous mouth, her flickering tongue and the delicious circles of fire.

Masturbation

The Venus in fire women are all sexually aware at a young age. They explore their bodies long before their zodiac sisters. This Venus woman will be enflamed by her own clitoral stimulation. She knows the power and passion that are released by her climax. She has big philosophies and idealistic expectations of her sexuality as she matures and begins to relate her own climax to the joy of life itself. She has no inhibitions about arousing herself, and may indulge in games with her partner that involve multiple orgasms. As she brings herself to peaks of delicious joy, she will delight in a partner who is unshocked by her own very provocative journey. Her need for orgasmic equality in her sexual relationship means that he must be prepared to accept her thrill for self-arousal, for her sex is her source of enjoyment.

The pleasure

She will have seduced him as he poured her drinks across the bar. He will be younger than she, a student, twenty years perhaps the difference in their ages. She will have danced until early morning, the sweat tingling down her spine until a pool of salty desire beckons her lover to taste the sweetness in the cleft between her buttocks. They will leave the party, dance on through the balmy night air towards the beach, down past the lianas, the powerful smelling lilies and the rock pools. The sea will be fierce, the waves crashing across the shingle. She will want to lick his throat and take a long kiss. Their mouths exploring, tongues suggestive, darting, flickering with desire. She will be breathless from her dance, filled with adrenaline and joy.

Suddenly she will draw back from his kiss and begin to pull off her silk dress. As the shoulder straps fall he will see her breasts, firm orbs pointing towards the stars, the moonlight catching the sweat as it glistens in her cleavage. He will watch transfixed as she laughs and the dress drops to the stony beach. She wears no silk knickers, no trappings of glamour or sexual enticement. It is enough for her to be naked, exposed to the elements, her body free to catch every pleasure the universe offers her. The wind swirls around her sex, ruffling her soft mound, cooling her vulva. As the waves crash to the beach she runs to the water and he follows. He will catch her in the surf.

Her pubic hair twinkles with tiny stars as he pulls her firmly down on to the beach, but she grins and flips him on his back. She will caress his naked body, all the time watching his cock as it rises fiercely to an erection. Once she senses his aching she will run her lips across the engorged end, taste the saltiness, lick and suck until his phallus throbs with agony. Then suddenly she will sit back, turn her buttocks to his face, and he knows he must ravage her from behind. He will enter her slowly, take hold of his huge cock and gently push, gently feel the opening of her pillow of musk, the curve of her hips enticing him further in as she moans with sweet pleasure.

Venus in Sagittarius – man

The freedom to give and receive pleasure without commitment and without restraint is the ultimate that a woman can truly give to this man. The Venus in Sagittarius male values drama: there must be movement, change, exploration and passion, and yet no certainty of the next moment's pleasure. He treasures the unattainable and does not want to be burdened by sexual commitment. If he is in a relationship, though, he may be less promiscuous than many would imagine. The kind of woman who will inspire him to return sensual and exuberant stimulation is one whose joy sings through her beauty and her style. She must be ultrafeminine, but able to assert herself. She must be glamorous, sophisticated, yet willing to spend a night out in a frosty meadow, her body willing to succumb to any pleasure. The woman who will bring him joy is also the woman who seeks only joyous and lustful self-satisfaction, and one who can stir his body to total physical ecstasy with her free-roaming tongue.

Interactive section

Venus represents my pleasure principle.

I find pleasure in _____

Choose from: adventurous fun, taking risks, dangerous liaisons.

I am sexually nurtured by _____

Choose from: unconditional pleasure, equality of passion, the celebration of the body.

My sexual responses are _____

Choose from: exuberant, joyous, excessive.

I hunt my pleasure _____

Choose from: with eagle eyes, with enthusiasm, wickedly.

CHAPTER SIXTEEN:

VENUS IN THE AIR SIGNS

(Gemini, Libra and Aquarius)

'Through and through me
Beneath the flesh
Impalpable fire runs tingling.'
Sappho

*P*leasure to the Venus in air signs is the interaction and intellectual stimulation of the senses. They must exchange ideas and erotic thoughts, for their sexuality involves the mind more than the body.

Venus in Gemini

Sensuality

This woman responds eagerly to intellectual stimulation. Her sensual nature is attuned to words, to speech, to music and thought processes. She is more aroused by what the next conversation or the next word will be than by obvious caresses or crafted touch. She does not have an easy relationship with pure physical sensuality unless her sun sign is Taurus or Cancer. She lives in her head, and her body responds magically to her own thoughts. The Venus in Gemini woman will be fascinated by the differences in each partner she meets, and her responses may echo her partner's favourite sexual experience. She may be interested in the experiences of her friends and experiment with using someone else's sexuality as her own.

She will be enthusiastic about every idea of where and when to take pleasure, yet she may often change her mind, irresistibly drawn to another location, another erotic thought rather than the actual experience. For this woman, sex is only a part of the true interaction of two human beings. Her varied and non-judgmental attitudes to sex means she often favours bisexuality over heterosexuality. She may seem daring, and she may seem disarming, but through her sexual pleasure she may begin to discover her real identity.

Masturbation
The Venus in Gemini woman may take a fascinated delight in her own body from an early age. Once she discovers the pleasure of masturbation she may prefer it to sexual penetration. She has a natural ability for multiple orgasm, has little guilt about her sexuality, and will blow the cobwebs away from her partner's inhibitions, if he has any, by her inventive self-arousal. Often she will excite him in the most public of places just to see how far she can go. She has such a sexual mind that she can bring herself to orgasm without touching herself, by merely imagining and watching her clitoris grow. This may occur when she has matured enough to understand the pleasure she is liberating.

The pleasure
Often she will first meet her lover in the train, on a plane, by chance collision in the street, anywhere that means movement. She may be the first to speak, her voice softly beguiling then dramatic and intense. She can mimic any style, cloak herself in unfamiliar roles and play any game imaginable, in her quest to find herself. She may play with words, double entendres. Her body will radiate the mysterious qualities of both her childlike directness and her highly sexual being. If her mind is connecting to her body, now she will begin to feel the desire for a sudden sexual experience. She is a creature of the moment: if the chance is on offer then instinctively she may lure this man to validate her sense of self-worth.

She may be the first to touch, her fingers slender,

quick, as clever as her words. She needs to lead, to seduce, usually to dominate. She may fantasise to begin her pleasure. She will prefer his mouth to bear words that stimulate her mind and keep her on the threshold of desire. This lover must respond quickly; he must know what she wants, understand she needs the thrill of anticipation. This is hunger for lovethinking rather than lovemaking. She may want to prove she can control her wildness, to delay the penetration by sharing continued arousal.

The plane will be almost empty. They will talk and share wine. Her lips may close round the neck of the bottle, the suggestion purposeful. She will take a risk, open his jeans, put her hand inside to feel the hot hard phallus, and he will respond to her touch by dabbing his tongue between her lips. She may not wait, may take all of his manhood in her mouth, her tongue twisting and teasing like her words. She is the connoisseur of oral stimulation. Her persuasion will hold his manhood erect, until she knows she must allow him to touch her, to search the deepness of her sex beneath her moist panties, the silk stretching against his hand.

Venus in Gemini – man

The kind of woman who can bring pleasure to this man must share his need for erotic conversation and intellectual stimulation, rather than physical brashness. He feels most comfortable and enriched with clever, witty and intellectually fascinating women. He needs those who can bring him to orgasmic ecstasy without conditions or emotional blackmail, those who are willing to talk about sex without jealousy or shame. This is a man who is curious about sex, but prefers to view sexual encounters as games. He is fiercely turned off by the claustrophobia of emotional euphoria. He may begin to realise that his sexual adventures are only one part of the experience of body, mind and soul. Like the other air signs, the Venus in Gemini male is liable to analyse his sensual responses. He needs to bring beauty and pleasure into his life through sexual experiences that heighten his mind.

Interactive section
Venus represents my pleasure principle.
I find pleasure in _____
Choose from: intellectual stimulation, a variety of sensual experiences, the interaction of mind and body.
I am sexually nurtured by _____
Choose from: my erotic thoughts, a partner who can defy convention, unpredictable encounters.
My sexual responses are _____
Choose from: communicative and expressive, ambiguous, unemotional.
I hunt my pleasure _____
Choose from: with daring, with curiosity, inconsistently.

Venus in Libra

Sensuality
For the Venus in Libra woman the art of seduction comes naturally. She will dance, seduce and provoke with subtle gestures, for she is a strategist. She wants to delight in the senses from an aesthetic viewpoint. She wants passion to be exquisite, love divine, and orgasm to be profoundly moving. Her relationship to her body's needs in all this is awkward, for she fears the flaws of human sexuality, the problems, the inhibitions. She feels the grief of not being godlike nor eternally young. Her eyes will often rest upon a lover who appears to offer her the magical solution. Yet usually she finds only another human being in a human embrace.

She turns few partners from her door, for she adores the rituals of romance, the anticipation, the erotic atmosphere created by candlelight, music and wine. Yet her true sensual values are often scattered too freely in her desire to please. If the ambience is right and she has found a partner who can value her, she will give pleasure, and experience the beauty of sexual surrender without ever losing control. She hunts for pleasure of the mind, to be sure of aesthetic satisfaction, and to remain passively in control of her sexual soul.

Masturbation

The Venus in Libra woman usually has a positive awareness of her own masturbatory needs yet, paradoxically, has a low body image. She often feels her body is not perfect, her breasts not as firm as her friends'. She will compare her own orgasms with those of her network of friends, both male and female, for Venus in Libra does like to share information and interact openly about her sex life if given the chance. If her partner can provide a channel for her needs she may begin to enjoy arousing herself in front of him, or even enjoy mutual masturbation with a female friend while her lover watches. But it is pleasure within a relationship that the Venus in Libra woman truly seeks, and without a lover she may relinquish her own self-pleasuring.

The pleasure

It will be at the art class. The lithe, naked body languishing across the marble floor will fill her with visual delight. She will paint him slowly, carefully, using every stroke of the brush to show the curves of his belly, the pulse in his throat. He is godlike, a Greek Ares, a potent male. The class finishes. She waits, knowing that her waiting is a claim, an assertion and a desire. He smiles at her loveliness, then walks behind the muslin screen to dress. She will see his outline, the shadow of his body as he bends to take a sip of wine. She turns to go. But she hesitates, filled with the overwhelming desire to see him naked.

She runs her finger down the muslin screen, following the line of his torso, the curve of his silhouetted phallus as he removes his thong. She will wait, certain he will be perfect: perfectly formed and perfectly matched to her own grace and beauty. His hand touches the muslin screen, searching for her fingers. Either side of the fabric they dance with their hands, twisting and teasing. She knows what he will do now, knows there can only be one way for him to offer himself to her. Behind the screen he will move closer, certain of her intention for pleasure.

With forceful desire he pushes against the screen, his massive hardness pressed against her hand on the other side of the fabric. She runs her fingers down his muslined shaft, her own sex moistening, the temptation to undress flooding her body with vibrancy. He moves his huge phallus up and down against her hand, his breath deepening, his muscles taut. She will want to pleasure him now, to take him in her mouth, to tease him with her lips and tongue without a word.

Yet it is he who pushes back the screen, sees her beauty, seizes her by the arms. Then she understands his power, sees only the gleam of his oiled skin, the perfection of the maleness wedged between his own hands. Kneeling before him, her nipples aroused, she begins to finger her erect bud. Her body is on fire, the taste of honey on her lips, as he pulls her head gently down on to his thrusting cock. She knows that he must surely surrender to her beauty.

Venus in Libra – man

The kind of woman who may bring joy to this man is usually unemotional, intellectually erotic, and able to ebb and flow with the currents of his variable sex drive. He treasures equality and honesty in a relationship. He is passive about sex rather than assertive. He enjoys mental stimuli, erotic conversation, the ability to disconnect emotion from sexual experience. He will be inspired by women and men of beauty, and his lover must acknowledge and honour his bisexuality, even though he may not be aware of it himself. He may spend many years in search of the perfect partner, choosing physically stunning women who are willing to please him. As he matures he may become disillusioned with purely physical attraction and begin to realise that his deeper sexual values are about trusting his feelings rather than making choices based purely on what he sees.

Interactive section

Venus represents my pleasure principle.

I find pleasure in _____

Choose from: visual beauty, idealistic expectations, romanticised sex.

I am sexually nurtured by _____

Choose from: pleasing my partner, the rituals of romance, being captivated.

My sexual responses are _____

Choose from: giving, luscious, aesthetic.

I hunt my pleasure _____

Choose from: with my eyes, with high ideals, self-indulgently.

Venus in Aquarius

Sensuality

The woman with Venus in Aquarius may find the very nature of her bodily lust and desire to be a contradiction of the universal intellectual processes of her mind. Sensual pleasure can be highly stimulating to her, but it is divine ecstasy that she is truly searching for, not the raw human love of sweating bodies and the smells of sweet sex. The individual's needs and the body's responses must be integrated into some kind of greater purpose. She prefers to be an instigator of others' pleasure rather than to gain physical gratification. Venus in Aquarius is about universal pleasure, rather than enjoyment on a one-to-one physical level.

She needs a man who can experiment and lead her into the unusual if she desires, and one who is able to intellectually arouse her senses. Like the other Venus in air signs she stands between the power of her mind and the soul of her female sexuality. She rarely dares to cross over the bridge into her true femininity, although she will liberate and expand every other woman's sexual awareness. Her need to be different, to stand out from the crowd, often leads her into testing relationships to see if she can be aroused without feeling. She fears her emotions and will go out of her way to avoid contact with them. Sexually, she often remains lonely, yet she has the most powerfully erotic mind, laced with detachment and experimentation.

Masturbation

With such a powerful mind, the Venus in Aquarius woman is able to pleasure herself free from the restraints of conventional sexual pleasure. She is liberated and honest about the experience of masturbation. Her belief in ideal sexual experience means that she can arouse her partner into mutual masturbation as one of the many expressions of their relationship.

The pleasure

She will meet him at a city soirée. They will have observed one another for hours, their minds equally powerful. Instant desire does not overwhelm her often, yet there is something stirring her body. To be in control she must make the moves and analyse the outcome. She wants danger, to run with the wolves, not with the conventions she is bound by.

He plays games with his words, his smile ravishing, his dignity original. The French windows are opened to the cold night air. He suggests they stand on the balcony to view the lights of the city. It is a chance to find complete and utter pleasure, knowing they need never commit themselves. His aura is deeply intoxicating, luring her into a danger zone as he touches her mouth with his fine fingers, suggesting more to come. Eagerly she returns his kiss. Her body is the conductor of raw universal energy.

She will find his sex. His magnificence arouses her, for his hugeness is as outrageous, as revolutionary, as her ideal of how sex should be. This is the time to caress

214

such power with her mouth, for within the danger zone there can only be innovation. Her own arousal is controlled. She will push her pubis hard against the iron chair, rhythmically moving up and down against the cold metal. As he reaches orgasm she will take his penis in her hand and pleasure him over the edge of the balcony, his seed falling to earth like cosmic dust. He will turn to her, his passion exhausted. Yet she is timing the moment to perfection, her own orgasm mounting in intensity as she hears voices getting nearer. There is laughter, the clink of glasses, as a woman dances through the open windows to take the air. Here is anarchy: to climax now as this woman gazes upon her discovery. She has liberated them both from the expectations of society.

Venus in Aquarius – man
The Venus in Aquarius male finds most pleasure with a woman who can be emotionally detached from sex, and yet is glamorous, sophisticated and willing to experiment. He will find pleasure in intellectual stimulation: two powerful minds are more challenging and arousing than two bodies. He enjoys analysing and dissecting sexual methods and style, and may prefer the idea of physical passion to the actual reality. His sexual idealism expands as he matures, and he may have high expectations of the women he chooses as his bed companions. He wants to improve upon every performance, and improve his lover's own skills and expertise. He will find most joy by being with someone who treats sex with the same dispassionate and intellectual approach as he, someone who can be mentally stimulated by the most bizarre of experiences. He needs a cool, aloof woman who will not feel threatened by his need for sexual withdrawal at times, and at other times his desire for potent and mind-blowing pleasure.

Interactive section
Venus represents my pleasure principle.
I find pleasure in _____

215

Choose from: analysing my sexual relationships, instigating others in sexual experimentation, liberating others from their conventional assumptions.

I am sexually nurtured by _____

Choose from: equality of responses, intellectual eroticism, detaching myself from my body's responses

My sexual responses are _____

Choose from: liberating, mind-expanding, fascinating to observe.

I hunt my pleasure _____

Choose from: with a broad mind, inquisitively, with detachment.

CHAPTER SEVENTEEN:

VENUS IN THE EARTH SIGNS

(Taurus, Virgo and Capricorn)

'And all her face was honey to my mouth.'
AC Swinburne, *Love and Sleep*

*V*enus in the earth signs denotes a pleasure for pure sensual feasting. The earth signs are generally more able to connect to their feminine, receptive nature, and can enjoy sensuality for the pure joy of physical union. They need to find similarity of sexual expression in others, and thus they hunt cautiously, observing rhythms and cycles that connect to their primeval, natural sexuality.

Venus in Taurus

Sensuality

On the surface the Venus in Taurus woman seems remote and disconnected from sensual arousal. She has an outer appearance of serious dedication to more pragmatic or worldly things. She will take her time, waiting for the moment when she can truly let someone into her secret garden of earthly delights. For beyond her strongly defined physical boundaries is a highly sensual and responsive woman.

She has both strength of mind and strength of desire. She hunts her pleasure carefully, never exposing her motives, taking chances only when she feels sure her pleasure will be reciprocated. Her sensuality is a potent force, and she may treat her moments of arousal as her own possessions, not to be given away freely. She is skilled in the arts of slow, languid arousal, and instinctively knows the treasure of being in the here and now. She usually has a beautiful speaking voice, one that exudes her powerful sexuality.

Hers is a natural sensuality once awakened. She flows to the rhythms of the stars, the night and day, and the body of her partner. She oils her skin, treasures her body as a gift from nature. She must be touched, stroked, kissed and caressed through every sexual embrace. She is sensitive to every physical experience and connects to sensual pleasure in all aspects of life, through food, warmth, and the earthiness of her very being. Her joy is from the touch of her lover's fingers, the power of his thrusts, the rubbing of two bodies, and the fragrance of sex.

Masturbation

The Venus in Taurus woman may not have been awakened to her sexuality as early as other signs, but she is deeply committed to her own body and its rhythms. She is also profoundly aware of clitoral arousal, and often prefers it to penetration. She will have no inhibitions about arousing herself in private, in order to honour her potent sensuality. Most Venus in Taurus women are acutely aware of their powerful need for orgasmic release. However, if she is unable to connect to her ancient earthy femininity, there are occasions when she can become prudish, repressing her own inner needs. Suggestions to her lover to watch her pleasure herself may be awkward if she feels insecure. She needs to feel she can arouse herself without fear of disapproval.

The pleasure

She will have waited many days and nights for him. At first he will be amused by her silent seduction, her beacon that draws him to her like a wasp to a jar of honey. He must be bold, ready for the most sensual of experiences. He must be willing to enjoy pleasure in an ambience created for stirring thoughts, touches, sounds, sights and smells. He must be beautiful, powerful, and yet attentive.

She needs to laugh, to touch his face, for him to resonate to her rhythms. She will stretch out her fine legs beneath the table and rub her toes upon his thigh. She will have dared, for not often does she take risks, to wear her most provocative of silk knickers: gold-threaded stars upon a black-satin night. Soon she will allow his tongue to roam there, but first she must find the right ambience.

Her plan unfolds subtly, coaxing him to a different kind of arousal. They will drive out to the country, or to a park, a garden. She chooses the earth itself as the bed for her pleasure. Here on the wild grass of the hillside she will throw herself down and pull him to her. She does not speak, for he must know what she truly wants or he would not be chosen. She will want his first touch to be apprehensive, tentative, as she slips her dress to the ground. She will guide his hands to her buttocks and the softness of her oiled skin beneath the satin knickers. His tongue will travel down the cleft of her buttocks, his saliva warming her sex as it collects in the folds of her vulva.

She wants to smell his flesh, take in the fragrance of his sex. She will breathe in the musky sweat from his belly as she turns now to reach for him. She bends her head down to nudge at the solid erection beneath his jeans, feeling the heat and smelling the warmth of his penis rising beneath the denim. For her the most velvet touch is the feel of his shaft on her cheek. She will rub her lips against the ridge, down to the base, as she teases him with her tongue. Then she will take him, slowly but possessively. She will encircle him with her mouth, the delectable pressure of her tongue forcing him to cry for joy as she sucks him hard.

Venus in Taurus – man
The Venus in Taurus male often believes the woman who will bring him most pleasure is passionate, power-

ful and totally demanding. He thinks he needs a woman who is magical, uncommitted and sexually liberated. Yet his own deeper need for total commitment is often repressed. His deepest desire is for security, for knowing what is truly his possession. The woman who can bring him true joy is the one who can honour his commitment to an earthy sensual experience that encompasses both the demands of animal lust and the deepest emotions of love. He needs to feel both cherished and caressed, and yet to dominate. He will respond best to a woman who can share his ability to invoke all the senses in orgasm. Wine, food, grass, the stars, the richness of velvet, the slipperiness of silk stockings across his face are enough to stimulate him into oblivion.

Interactive section
Venus represents my pleasure principle.
I find pleasure in _____
Choose from: the rhythms of my body, pure sensuality, being treasured.
I am sexually nurtured by _____
Choose from: languid arousal, delicious thoughts and the anticipation of what is to come, a partner who responds to my pace.
My sexual responses are _____
Choose from: slow, languid, earthy.
I hunt my pleasure _____
Choose from: with care and forethought, without exposing my motives, only if I know my pleasure will be reciprocated.

Venus in Virgo

Sensuality
This is a woman who is acutely sensitive to every nuance, every change in smell, taste or colour. She does not desire exquisite luxury, but perfection and purity of body. Her sensuality is finely woven into her sexual

behaviour. She must refine the techniques of her art and ensure that each move of her seduction is sophisticated and yet subtle. There will be no lavish displays of body language, only quiet movements and innuendos. She wants to resist her lover, to hold back, to be persuaded finally to surrender. For her, sensual pleasure is about the power of her mind over her body, the need to be in control and aware of her body's every response.

She will prefer bare and yet sophisticated surroundings: anything from a minimalist room with only floorboards and candles, to the rustic four-poster of a Provençal auberge. Like the other earth signs, her surroundings have to become part of the whole sensual pleasure. Seeing the image of sensuality she has created around her, she often fears seeing the defects of real sex. She may have difficulty in connecting to her sensual nature, and appear prim, dissatisfied, and disconnected from her body.

Above all, her lover must live up to her expectations of beauty. He must be polished, gentlemanly, his shaft shimmering with self-confidence. This woman hunts pure sexual beauty, the experience of ultimate orgasm, utterly abandoned and spontaneous. She will attend to her body with ritual to ensure she is ready to serve her lover. Her true sexual values are about honouring her sensuality, so that she can begin to accept that even she has imperfections.

Masturbation

The Venus in Virgo woman is usually shy about accepting her sexual needs. She may find it difficult to own up to her search for perfect sexual experience with her partner, and often hides her sexuality even from herself. If her upbringing encouraged her to ignore her sexuality, she may find masturbation with her partner either taboo or an utterly awakening experience once she has learnt to trust her inner needs. There is much guilt that lurks within the Venus in Virgo woman's psyche about her sexuality. Only once she has experienced great love and sex together will she begin to relax, truly allowing her body to breathe its desire for self-pleasure. Fondling her own clitoris, caressing her partner's penis while she does so, may give her acceptance of self.

The pleasure

In the log cabin, hidden beneath the pine trees in the snow far up in the mountains, she will captivate his mind and body. She will have planned the setting, laid soft pillows, deep white duvets and crisp white wine beside the roaring fire. The snow will be falling heavily. She will smile, turn on the music, and wait for him to come to her. He will be rugged, have a wildness about him. She will want him to devour her, to take her gently to the summit of pleasure.

He will make the moves, kissing her, unbuttoning her silk shirt. Discreetly, she may pull back, unsure of the pace. She begins to relax, listening to the flames flickering over the logs as he licks her sex. She tries to keep her mind pure, uncontaminated by her pleasure. Her body arches as he begins to kiss her neck, the wetness from his lips running down her throat. She wants to be ravished, to be thrown down on the duvet, to experience ultimate pleasure.

Naked, they stand together, the glow of the fire illuminating his shaft. In this light all is beautiful, all is sheer, ice-cold, intensely perfect. But he will not possess her yet. He puts his mouth to her breast, draws her dark nipple to a firm bud, arousing, encircling until she feels the dart of energy flowing into her clitoris. Then gently he eases her lips apart with his hard penis, circling, pushing, then thrusting forcefully between her labia as he darts his tongue across her nipples. She is caught here, in this empty space of pure and sacred possession. Like a harlot priestess, she will serve and surrender to his perfect power.

Venus in Virgo – man

The Venus in Virgo male may be tempted by the blood-racing passion of the Venus in fire signs, or the dark, mysterious danger of the Venus in water signs, but he truly needs to find joy through a woman with whom he can share the finesse of sensual pleasure. The ability to share ritualised sexuality, in whatever form they choose, may bring much pleasure to this man. This is an uncomfortable placement for a male: needing purity and yet desperately seeking the perfect sexual experience. He may desire beauty, poise, sophistication. She must be exquisite, radiant, and yet sexually stable. She must give with style, and receive with feminine mystique. The Virgo Venus male does not respond well to emotional scenes, nor power-tripping sexual games and manipulation. Simplicity is all. But sensual stimulation is essential. In public he will shun close contact, obvious signs of intimacy or teasing, fondling beneath the restaurant table. Yet, in private, his mastery of his art and his joy at being ravished with quiet seduction will arouse him to a ritualistic climax.

Interactive section

Venus represents my pleasure principle.

I find pleasure in _____

Choose from: perfection, a sophisticated ambience, the art of subtle seduction.

I am sexually nurtured by _____

Choose from: persuasion, being in control of my senses, one who can live up to my expectations of beauty.

My sexual responses are _____

Choose from: refined, cautious, submissive.

I hunt my pleasure _____

Choose from: efficiently, critically, with dedication to the ultimate experience.

Venus in Capricorn

Sensuality

The Venus in Capricorn woman adorns herself with the sexual expectations and conventions of society. She must take pleasure by the rules and by the highest standards of a structured system. She is ultimately a sensualist, yet her desire must be ordered. There can be no chaos, for pleasure is like music, rising to crescendos and peaks of ecstasy when she, the composer, chooses. There is no frivolity for Venus in Capricorn. She chooses a time, when the bed has been prepared, the feast assembled, and the champagne iced and ready to be uncorked. She will manage her pleasure dome with taste and creative panache.

Her sensuality is showy in private, yet controlled and aloof in public. She may not touch her partner, nor want to be touched, until they are naked and tumbling across the Persian rug. She may shudder with embarrassment from his kiss as they part at the taxi rank, but behind the locked door of the empty boardroom she may taste his sweat and take hold of his hand and guide it down to her moist knickers. Her richness is hidden, yet her motives are never ambivalent. She will give the best pleasure, but she wants the best in return.

She prefers men who are successful, wealthy both in their position in life and in their sexual knowledge. It is not prowess she seeks but a partner who is worthy of her deepest respect. For sexual honour comes first, and she pursues her rewards only in an established environment. Like the other earth signs she needs commitment, the security of similarity, of knowing she is not out on a sexual gangplank. Within the confines of her own crafted pleasure, she is the most delectable and rich of females.

Masturbation

She will explore her own body with avid curiosity when younger, and in true Capricorn style will demand much from her own clitoral arousal. However, as she matures she may refuse to gratify herself, unless she is bound to a permanent partner. Her own masturbatory urges may remain a closed book, and it may be a long time before she's willing to submit to her lover's non-participation in her climax. Daring exhibitionism rarely aligns with her belief that sexual intimacy is a bonding experience with another human being.

The pleasure

It will be a French bed, the wood carved and painted with erotic figures in sexual embrace, nymphs and satyrs in orgiastic delight. She will have brought downy pillows from the ancient chiffonier, ruffled the white linen sheets, and there will be Debussy playing quietly. Behind the tapestry curtains of the boudoir, her lover will have finished bathing. He will be strong, fine, talented, powerful. He is discreet, knowing that what they do is forbidden. He will part the curtains, then walk naked towards her, his body glistening with beads of water. She will shyly turn her head from his beauty, yet want to look, want to reach out to him with wicked curiosity.

He will offer her a glass of champagne and she will relax, feeling her courage grow as her body waits to be discovered. He undresses her with care, knowing her fragility, understanding her self-control. As he peels away her stockings from her thighs, his fingers just touch her mound of curls hidden beneath the lace of her panties. She feels the first waves of desire flood through her sex. Yet she does not want to submit: it is too soon, too easy.

Suddenly she wants pure animal pleasure for she is overwhelmed with earthy lust for his penetration. She thirsts for her climax and for the rhythms of explosive release. She pushes her lover down on the bed and forces his hands on to the soft pillow. He knows he must submit to her. Then suddenly she turns round to face his feet, her sex now above his face. She will open her mouth, put her lips over his great penis, and flick her tongue around the end of the shaft. He will gasp, feel the grip of her lips sucking him, taking him deeper and deeper into her throat. She turns again, just as he is about to climax in her mouth, for she knows how to keep him on a plateau of desire. With one thrust she sits astride him. She will ride him hard and powerfully, each thrust deep and slow, as she feels the power of her passion driving him to a hungry release.

Venus in Capricorn – man

The Venus in Capricorn male looks for sexual eminence in a partner. To bring him joy she must be fully open to every sensual pleasure, and indulge him in ambitious caresses and elegant eroticism. He will want the performance to be ordered, each step taken one at a time. They will have candlelit dinner followed by a bath they share together. They will sip champagne, touching just their toes in the bath. There must be nothing more until they reach the bed. His partner must be refined, respect his power and value his need for a binding intimacy. He has great dignity, a profound sense of honour and self-respect. He has a fondness for hard, thrusting sex, yet he will take all night to reach a climax if his lover has the passion to drive him to it. He may find himself drawn to the spontaneous and uninhibited fire signs, and yet his inner needs are to be in time, to find a pace and earthy rhythm with which he can give and take powerful pleasure.

Interactive section

Venus represents my pleasure principle.

I find pleasure in _____

Choose from: conforming to the rules, glamorous encounters, success and wealth, the security of likeness.

I am sexually nurtured by _____

Choose from: creating a well-prepared ambience, being the dominant partner, feeling I am creating a long-lasting sexual bond.

My sexual responses are _____

Choose from: timed to perfection, powerful yet dignified, richly moving.

I hunt my pleasure _____

Choose from: with ambition, with utter determination, in the search for complete respect.

CHAPTER EIGHTEEN:

VENUS IN THE WATER SIGNS

(Cancer, Scorpio and Pisces)

'And her lips opened amorously, and said – Delight.'
AC Swinburne, *Love and Sleep*

*V*enus in the water signs take their greatest pleasure from immersing themselves totally in their feelings. The ambience must be right for them, the music perfectly in resonance with their mood. They pursue pleasure to find a special intimacy and an expression of their feelings through sexual union. They may communicate little through words, but they express their sexuality through every touch.

Venus in Cancer

Sensuality

Her sexual web will be spun somewhere highly sensual or exotic, among candles, music, silk and the giddy smells of incense. If she closes her eyes quickly it is because she lives in the world of fantasy. However much her lover gives, however much she is tantalised by his body, his smell, his mouth, she will always find her imagination stirs her body first. She involves her feelings, mind, body and soul in her sexual pleasure. She is in touch with sounds, smells, and with her own responses. Her nerve endings will feel every change in her lover's breath or kiss.

By being so in tune with the vibrations of their bodies, she can fall deeply into a relationship without looking at the consequences. For the Venus in Cancer woman, sexual involvement means a deep and emotionally secure bond. She will want to be stroked, caressed and hugged, and will give just as much in return. She wants to totally enclose her partner in her web, often creating such a powerful spell around him that if it is ever broken she can withdraw totally from sensual pleasure for long periods of time. If she has the sun in Gemini, she may find it difficult to relate her Venusian need for continuity in her sexual relationships with her solar desire for variety and change.

The Venus in Cancer woman hunts her pleasure with timidity and yet with a mystique that enchants and captivates many men. She is often the hunted, needing only to be in the right place at the right time. Hers is a closed circuit, but one that many will want to invade.

Masturbation
Her relationship to self-pleasuring may take a long time to develop if she has been brought up with cultural, family or social inhibitions about her sexuality. However, like the other Venus in water signs, she may find masturbation with her partner a powerful channel for the expression of her emotional energy. Finding an intimate relationship is very important for Venus in Cancer, and without it she may resort to denying herself any pleasure, refusing to acknowledge the pain of loneliness. She needs to feel she belongs and if she can find a secure and satisfying sexual relationship she may begin to unfurl her needs in a safe environment and discover the true pleasuring of her own body. She may fear rejection if her partner is unable to share in her body's extreme sensual responses, and will be shy about suggesting she arouses herself unless she is sure of his integrity.

The pleasure
Beside a wild sea she may begin to relax, to take pleasure in the moonlight as it sparkles in her lover's eyes. They will stand face to face on the warm sand. She will shiver,

not from cold but from the first ripples of pleasure that dart down to her pubis as he kisses her neck and her mouth. The longer he tantalises, the longer will be her pleasure. He will reach down and she will feel his hair feathering her thighs. Her eyes will be closed, her silence profound, as she imagines him studying the dark secrets of her sex, imagines his fingers exploring the ruby folds, and his tongue ready to taste her. She will breathe quicker as she imagines.

He will have slithered her panties down to her ankles. Now his hair is soaked from the surf as he begins to search her salty skin with his lips. Still with her eyes closed, her mind works faster, in time with the throbbing of her clitoris. She imagines his tongue tickling her full bud, his hand beneath her buttocks and his hard man-hood pushing upward against his belly. Now she feels she must unite body with mind. The surf will rush against her skin, bruising her buttocks with shingle, as they lie down. She will gasp as he sinks his fingers into her warmth, his knuckles gently massaging her vulva, opening and searching as his lips begin to suck on her moist bud, until she cries for her release and the waves crash across her sex, as explosive and fierce as her own passion.

Venus in Cancer – man
The Venus in Cancer male's sexuality is passive and gentle but he is brought into a world where the cultural expectation is of male dominance. It is only when he is wrapped in the arms of a woman who can relate to his tenderness that he may begin to show his nurturing sexual instincts without fear of rejection. Yet Venus in Cancer men often deny their deepest sexual feelings and overcompensate by becoming demanding or sexually dominating, taking on the role of the Don Juan. The kind of woman who will bring this man most joy, if he begins to accept his emotional nature, will be one who can commit herself to total intimacy with him without fear

of drowning. It is not the thrill and excitement of the unknown that he seeks, but to be sexually cherished, to feel secure and held.

Interactive section
Venus represents my pleasure principle.
I find pleasure in _____
Choose from: exotic or sensual surroundings, my imagination, a deeply emotional bond.
I am sexually nurtured by _____
Choose from: a close web of sexual commitment, being stroked and hugged, knowing I am in control of my senses.
My sexual responses are _____
Choose from: inhibited, magical, controlled.
I hunt my pleasure _____
Choose from: with timidity, captivatingly, by being the hunted.

Venus in Scorpio

Sensuality
The Venus in Scorpio woman has an intense desire for extreme sensual experience. It is all or nothing for this woman. If her sexual needs are denied she will create crisis around her and refuse all intimacy. She is inspired by potent partners, by those who can delve into the depths of an awesome erotic connection and come out demanding more. Her body responds to those who appear challenging. She treasures those who enable her to experience her sensuality as both a sacred and a profane art. Intimacy must be discreet, dedicated and devouring.

She seduces with complete concentration, yet without betraying her desire. Her hunting is done undercover, testing her power, testing the responses of her prey. She hunts pleasure because she is hungry for the merging of souls. She can become passionately obsessed and lock herself into an embrace where transformation of self is her only means of escape. Her sexuality is hard to repress. If her sun is in Sagittarius, Libra or Capricorn, she may have problems identifying with her dark and seemingly alien sensuality, which will force her into destructive and yet highly potent sexual intimacy.

Masturbation

There is joy to be found in lonely pleasure, and yet the Venus in Scorpio woman often denies herself even this during her periods of total sexual denial. In her youth she will have eagerly discovered the power of her orgasm, and may have found the pleasure both transformative and a powerful release of intense energy. Later in life she may be the first to suggest mutual masturbation to a partner, or that she arouses herself alone while her partner watches.

The pleasure

It will be in a graveyard, stone crosses and tombs sharply defined in the frosty night air. For this woman is as comfortable with danger and endings as she is with beginnings. They will be walking back from some country pub, their bodies tingling with anticipation and her own eyes dazzled by the mission she has set herself. She will test him all the way, see how far he dare go towards the edge.

Slowly she will lead him towards her chosen place of perilous climax. Here she wants him to enjoy her, to ravish her. He will believe her wildness is untamable. She stops beside the old tombstone and falls to the grass. She will take his hand and pull him down beside her, then nibble his fingers, circling the ends of his nails with her tongue. He may push her back on to the frosty grass expecting her to submit to him, to be ravished by his urgency. Yet suddenly she will turn on him, like the scorpion she is. Against the cold tomb she begins her dangerous art.

She will remove only her knickers, carefully placing

them on the tombstone. He will smell her sex, the moistness of her arousal. She will push his body back, forcing his buttocks and his spine against the cold stone. He will moan, breathe fast, as she unbuttons his jeans to expose his huge penis to the cold mists of the graveyard. She will possess him, her mouth sucking his penis. With intense power she circles the tip with her tongue then, unexpectedly, suddenly, with the dangerous passion that is art, she takes all of his manhood deeply into her throat, as if she must choke on his sweetness.

Her own orgasm builds as he cannot stop himself from thrusting deeply into her, then quickly she pulls back and his honeyed warmth washes over her lips, her cheeks. She will lick the drops from her lips with her tongue, then bring herself to her own dark climax with the wetness of his orgasm upon her fingers.

Venus in Scorpio – man

The sun in Scorpio male is renowned for his mysterious and often predatory sexual nature. Yet the Venus in Scorpio male, unless he also has the sun in Scorpio, may find his smouldering passion at odds with a seemingly joyous attitude to life and sex. This man needs a woman who is subtle, powerful and profoundly sexual. A woman whose darkness can offer him a glimpse into his own soul. He can often be an extremely demanding lover, whom no one can fulfil. He will find most pleasure with one who can arouse his moods, his feelings and his body. He needs a woman who can take him to the peak of emotional ecstasy, give him the physical challenge and blessing of her body, as well as being the one to hold him true to his need for long-term intimacy.

Interactive section

Venus represents my pleasure principle.

I find pleasure in _____

Choose from: extreme sexual relationships, intensely erotic partners, emotional sensuality.

I am sexually nurtured by _____
Choose from: my deepest feelings being engaged in physical passion, knowing I am powerful, a discreet and dedicated partner.

My sexual responses are _____
Choose from: intense, volatile, emotionally overwhelming.

I hunt my pleasure _____
Choose from: with a ravenous desire for transformation, obsessively, ruthlessly.

Venus in Pisces

Sensuality

Finding pleasure and sensuality with a partner fills her with a need to find spiritually transcendent love. She gives all to the one who can share in her idealistic passion. Her gift for sensual arousal can lead her and her partner into a journey of pure ecstasy. She knows how to stimulate every nerve ending, every inch of her partner's skin, until he is drawn to her, her smell, her taste. She has the tenderness of deep femininity coupled with erotic and romantic wisdom. Yet, if she is a sun-sign Aries there may be a heady conflict between her solar desire for egotistic empowerment and the femininity of her Venus.

Her lover must be gentlemanly, poetic or youthful. There must be beauty and music in their chamber of pleasure. It must be her choice between giving and receiving, and she will usually prefer the former. When she submits it is for his joy rather than her own. She is the ultimate entertainer, the singer of the most powerful sexual song.

She hunts with her eyes, scanning her surroundings for someone to seduce and allure. She needs no props, no fashion, no wealth, for she has the mystical and haunting quality that fascinates so many men who would pleasure her. She often fails to recognise that her reactions merely mirror the feelings of her partner. She identifies her own needs from what her partner wants of her.

Masturbation

As she matures, her rich involvement with all the senses means she has little difficulty in acknowledging her self-pleasuring needs. She may find the subject taboo in her youth, and may have difficulty in approaching the subject, especially with a partner who does not share her need for multi-faceted sexual experiences. She may need to liberate herself from nostalgia, from past partners who have ravished her yet not understood her femininity, who have chosen to ignore her most erotic of fantasies or arousals. Tantric sex may give her the chance to experience such pleasure, to share the delight of her own body without fear of judgement or rejection.

The pleasure

It will be after the masked ball. She will have worn a crimson gown sparkling with tiny jewels. He will have followed her up the narrow, spiralling, stone steps of the tower. She is masked, mysterious, and knows she has compelled him to come to her now in the darkness. There is a roof garden with a pool, the still water glistening silver in the moonlight. She will turn, breathless from the climb, as he catches up with her. He is beautiful, young, hidden behind his own mask of the great god Dionysus. He is like a mirror of her own desire, for she will sense his every movement, his every gesture. There is no need for words, only the allurement of her sensual artistry.

She will peel her crimson velvet gown slowly to the floor. Still masked, still veiled, she can hide and yet seek. There will be music in his touch, poetry in his gentleness, yet she knows he will want her to submit to him, to be powerless to his every demand. She will put out her fingers to touch his fine skin, and he cannot move for he is enchanted by her presence, filled with the incense of her mystique.

She will turn from him then, unpredictable, elusive. She will dive into the pool and he will quickly remove his breeches to follow her. She will rise to the water's surface like a dolphin, her mask glittering with pearls of water. They will both stay masked, veiled from the truth, wrapped in the fantasy of their arousal. As he grasps her under the water she is ready to submit, ready to be his slave or his muse.

He pulls her to him, the water softening the force. Breathless, they spin under the water then up again for air. He will force her legs round his hips, so that she must clutch at him with her thighs. His fingers will sink under the silk of her panties to find her wet sex, to begin to circle and caress her clitoris. Her bud is already hard, polished, a piece of shining coral. Here in the water he will ravish her until she begs for him to possess her totally.

Venus in Pisces – man
The kind of woman who can bring pleasure to this man has the sensitivity to understand his deeply hidden emotions. He may on the surface fake careless attitudes towards sexual experience and speak words that rarely match his feelings. The woman that can awaken him to this dichotomy between his needs and his surface personality must be sensually powerful and totally dedicated to serving him as much as herself. He may be terrified of failure; he may suffer from insecurity and doubt that his own passion is on a par with his best friends'. His partner will be in touch with all her senses and she will show him the steps to euphoria. She must allow his imagination to soar and his body to succumb to every touch. He needs fantasy and gentle fingers, but desires the most outrageous ecstasy.

Interactive section
Venus represents my pleasure principle.
I find pleasure in ⎯⎯⎯⎯⎯⎯⎯⎯⎯⎯⎯⎯⎯

Choose from: my sexual fantasies, lush sensual surroundings, indulging my feelings as well as my body.

I am sexually nurtured by _____

Choose from: being cherished, submitting to my partner's joy, acknowledging my own femininity.

My sexual responses are _____

Choose from: attuned to those of my lover, haunting and mysterious, luscious.

I hunt my pleasure _____

Choose from: subtly, romantically, elusively.

VENUS TABLES 1935–1985

*L*ook up your date of birth to find out which sign Venus was in on that day.

For example, say you were born on 20 March 1973. The dates before and after this date are when Venus moved from one sign to another. You can see that Venus was in Pisces from 1 March until 24 March. So on 20 March 1973 Venus was in Pisces.

If you were born on the day before the changeover day or the actual changeover day itself, it is possible that Venus was in the following or previous sign to the one given. If this is the case, simply read the relevant sections for both the given sign and the adjacent one to determine which you think is most like you.

1935
Jan 1 Capricorn
Jan 9 Aquarius
Feb 2 Pisces
Feb 26 Aries
Mar 22 Taurus
Apr 16 Gemini
May 12 Cancer
Jun 8 Leo
Jul 8 Virgo
Nov 10 Libra
Dec 9 Scorpio
1936
Jan 1 Scorpio
Jan 4 Sagittarius
Jan 29 Capricorn
Feb 22 Aquarius
Mar 18 Pisces
Apr 11 Aries
May 5 Taurus
May 30 Gemini
Jun 23 Cancer
Jul 18 Leo
Aug 11 Virgo
Sep 4 Libra
Sep 29 Scorpio
Oct 23 Sagittarius
Nov 17 Capricorn
Dec 12 Aquarius
1937
Jan 1 Aquarius
Jan 6 Pisces
Feb 2 Aries
Mar 10 Taurus
Apr 14 Aries
Jun 4 Taurus
Jul 8 Gemini
Aug 5 Cancer
Aug 31 Leo
Sep 25 Virgo
Oct 20 Libra
Nov 13 Scorpio

Dec 7 Sagittarius
Dec 31 Capricorn
1938
Jan 1 Capricorn
Jan 23 Aquarius
Feb 16 Pisces
Mar 12 Aries
Apr 6 Taurus
Apr 30 Gemini
May 25 Cancer
Jun 19 Leo
Jul 14 Virgo
Aug 10 Libra
Sep 7 Scorpio
Oct 14 Sagittarius
Nov 16 Scorpio
1939
Jan 1 Scorpio
Jan 5 Sagittarius
Feb 6 Capricorn
Mar 6 Aquarius
Mar 31 Pisces
Apr 26 Aries
May 21 Taurus
Jun 14 Gemini
Jul 9 Cancer
Aug 3 Leo
Aug 27 Virgo
Sep 20 Libra
Oct 14 Scorpio
Nov 7 Sagittarius
Dec 1 Capricorn
Dec 25 Aquarius
1940
Jan 1 Aquarius
Jan 19 Pisces
Feb 12 Aries
Mar 9 Taurus
Apr 5 Gemini
May 7 Cancer
Jul 6 Gemini
Aug 1 Cancer

Sep 9 Leo
Oct 7 Virgo
Nov 2 Libra
Nov 27 Scorpio
Dec 21 Sagittarius
1941
Jan 1 Sagittarius
Jan 14 Capricorn
Feb 7 Aquarius
Mar 3 Pisces
Mar 27 Aries
Apr 20 Taurus
May 15 Gemini
Jun 8 Cancer
Jul 3 Leo
Jul 27 Virgo
Aug 21 Libra
Sep 15 Scorpio
Oct 11 Sagittarius
Nov 6 Capricorn
Dec 6 Aquarius
1942
Jan 1 Aquarius
Apr 7 Pisces
May 6 Aries
Jun 2 Taurus
Jun 28 Gemini
Jul 23 Cancer
Aug 17 Leo
Sep 11 Virgo
Oct 5 Libra
Oct 29 Scorpio
Nov 22 Sagittarius
Dec 16 Capricorn
1943
Jan 1 Capricorn
Jan 8 Aquarius
Feb 1 Pisces
Feb 26 Aries
Mar 22 Taurus
Apr 16 Gemini
May 11 Cancer

Jun 8 Leo
Jul 8 Virgo
Nov 10 Libra
Dec 8 Scorpio
1944
Jan 1 Scorpio
Jan 3 Sagittarius
Jan 28 Capricorn
Feb 22 Aquarius
Mar 17 Pisces
Apr 11 Aries
May 5 Taurus
May 29 Gemini
Jun 23 Cancer
Jul 17 Leo
Aug 11 Virgo
Sep 4 Libra
Sep 28 Scorpio
Oct 23 Sagittarius
Nov 16 Capricorn
Dec 10 Aquarius
1945
Jan 1 Aquarius
Jan 6 Pisces
Feb 2 Aries
Mar 11 Taurus
Apr 8 Aries
Jun 5 Taurus
Jul 8 Gemini
Aug 4 Cancer
Aug 31 Leo
Sep 25 Virgo
Oct 19 Libra
Nov 12 Scorpio
Dec 6 Sagittarius
Dec 30 Capricorn
1946
Jan 1 Capricorn
Jan 23 Aquarius
Feb 16 Pisces
Mar 12 Aries
Apr 5 Taurus

Apr 29 Gemini
May 24 Cancer
Jun 18 Leo
Jul 14 Virgo
Aug 9 Libra
Sep 7 Scorpio
Oct 16 Sagittarius
Nov 8 Scorpio
1947
Jan 1 Scorpio
Jan 6 Sagittarius
Feb 6 Capricorn
Mar 5 Aquarius
Mar 31 Pisces
Apr 25 Aries
May 20 Taurus
Jun 14 Gemini
Jul 9 Cancer
Aug 2 Leo
Aug 26 Virgo
Sep 19 Lib
Oct 14 Scorpio
Nov 7 Sagittarius
Dec 1 Capricorn
Dec 25 Aquarius
1948
Jan 1 Aquarius
Jan 18 Pisces
Feb 12 Aries
Mar 8 Taurus
Apr 4 Gemini
May 7 Cancer
Jun 29 Gemini
Aug 3 Cancer
Sep 9 Leo
Oct 7 Virgo
Nov 1 Libra
Nov 26 Scorpio
Dec 20 Sagittarius
1949
Jan 1 Sagittarius
Jan 13 Capricorn

Feb 6 Aquarius
Mar 2 Pisces
Mar 26 Aries
Apr 20 Taurus
May 14 Gemini
Jun 7 Cancer
Jul 2 Leo
Jul 27 Virgo
Aug 21 Libra
Sep 15 Scorpio
Oct 10 Sagittarius
Nov 6 Capricorn
Dec 6 Aquarius
1950
Jan 1 Aquarius
Apr 7 Pisces
May 6 Aries
Jun 2 Taurus
Jun 27 Gemini
Jul 23 Cancer
Aug 17 Leo
Sep 10 Virgo
Oct 4 Libra
Oct 28 Scorpio
Nov 21 Sagittarius
Dec 15 Capricorn
1951
Jan 1 Capricorn
Jan 7 Aquarius
Jan 31 Pisces
Feb 25 Aries
Mar 21 Taurus
Apr 15 Gemini
May 11 Cancer
Jun 7 Leo
Jul 8 Virgo
Nov 8 Libra
Dec 9 Scorpio
1952
Jan 1 Scorpio
Jan 2 Sagittarius
Jan 27 Capricorn

Feb 21 Aquarius
Mar 17 Pisces
Apr 9 Aries
May 4 Taurus
May 29 Gemini
Jun 22 Cancer
Jul 16 Leo
Aug 9 Virgo
Sep 3 Libra
Sep 27 Scorpio
Oct 22 Sagittarius
Nov 16 Capricorn
Dec 10 Aquarius
1953
Jan 1 Aquarius
Jan 5 Pisces
Feb 2 Aries
Mar 15 Taurus
Mar 31 Aries
Jun 5 Taurus
Jul 7 Gemini
Aug 4 Cancer
Aug 30 Leo
Sep 24 Virgo
Oct 19 Libra
Nov 12 Scorpio
Dec 6 Sagittarius
Dec 30 Capricorn
1954
Jan 1 Capricorn
Jan 22 Aquarius
Feb 15 Pisces
Mar 11 Aries
Apr 4 Taurus
Apr 29 Gemini
May 24 Cancer
Jun 18 Leo
Jul 13 Virgo
Aug 9 Libra
Sep 7 Scorpio
Oct 23 Sagittarius
Oct 27 Scorpio

1955
Jan 1 Scorpio
Jan 6 Sagittarius
Feb 6 Capricorn
Mar 5 Aquarius
Mar 30 Pisces
Apr 25 Aries
May 20 Taurus
Jun 13 Gemini
Jul 8 Cancer
Aug 1 Leo
Aug 26 Virgo
Sep 19 Libra
Oct 13 Scorpio
Nov 6 Sagittarius
Nov 30 Capricorn
Dec 24 Aquarius
1956
Jan 1 Aquarius
Jan 18 Pisces
Feb 11 Aries
Mar 8 Taurus
Apr 4 Gemini
May 8 Cancer
Jun 23 Gemini
Aug 4 Cancer
Sep 8 Leo
Oct 6 Virgo
Nov 1 Libra
Nov 26 Scorpio
Dec 20 Sagittarius
1957
Jan 1 Sagittarius
Jan 13 Capricorn
Feb 6 Aquarius
Mar 2 Pisces
Mar 26 Aries
Apr 19 Taurus
May 13 Gemini
Jun 7 Cancer
Jul 2 Leo
Jul 26 Virgo

Aug 20 Libra
Sep 14 Scorpio
Oct 10 Sagittarius
Nov 6 Capricorn
Dec 7 Aquarius
1958
Jan 1 Aquarius
Apr 7 Pisces
May 5 Aries
Jun 1 Taurus
Jun 27 Gemini
Jul 22 Cancer
Aug 16 Leo
Sep 10 Virgo
Oct 4 Libra
Oct 28 Scorpio
Nov 21 Sagittarius
Dec 14 Capricorn
1959
Jan 1 Capricorn
Jan 7 Aquarius
Jan 31 Pisces
Feb 25 Aries
Mar 21 Taurus
Apr 15 Gemini
May 11 Cancer
Jun 7 Leo
Jul 9 Virgo
Sep 20 Leo
Sep 25 Virgo
Nov 10 Libra
Dec 8 Scorpio
1960
Jan 1 Scorpio
Jan 2 Aquarius
Jan 27 Capricorn
Feb 21 Aquarius
Mar 16 Pisces
Apr 9 Aries
May 4 Taurus
May 28 Gemini
Jun 22 Cancer

Jul 16 Leo
Aug 9 Virgo
Sep 3 Libra
Sep 27 Scorpio
Oct 22 Sagittarius
Nov 16 Capricorn
Dec 10 Aquarius
1961
Jan 1 Aquarius
Jan 5 Pisces
Feb 2 Aries
Jun 6 Taurus
Jul 7 Gemini
Aug 4 Cancer
Aug 30 Leo
Sep 24 Virgo
Oct 18 Libra
Nov 11 Scorpio
Dec 5 Sagittarius
Dec 29 Capricorn
1962
Jan 1 Capricorn
Jan 22 Aquarius
Feb 15 Pisces
Mar 11 Aries
Apr 4 Taurus
Apr 28 Gemini
May 23 Cancer
Jun 17 Leo
Jul 13 Virgo
Aug 9 Libra
Sep 7 Scorpio
1963
Jan 1 Scorpio
Jan 7 Sagittarius
Feb 6 Capricorn
Mar 4 Aquarius
Mar 30 Pisces
Apr 24 Aries
May 19 Taurus
Jun 12 Gemini
Jul 7 Cancer

Aug 1 Leo
Aug 25 Virgo
Sep 18 Libra
Oct 12 Scorpio
Nov 5 Sagittarius
Nov 29 Capricorn
Dec 24 Aquarius
1964
Jan 1 Aquarius
Jan 17 Pisces
Feb 10 Aries
Mar 7 Taurus
Apr 4 Gemini
May 9 Cancer
Jun 17 Gemini
Aug 5 Cancer
Sep 8 Leo
Oct 5 Virgo
Oct 31 Libra
Nov 25 Scorpio
Dec 19 Sagittarius
1965
Jan 1 Sagittarius
Jan 12 Capricorn
Feb 5 Aquarius
Mar 1 Pisces
Mar 25 Aries
Apr 18 Taurus
May 12 Gemini
Jun 6 Cancer
Jul 1 Leo
Jul 25 Virgo
Aug 19 Libra
Sep 14 Scorpio
Oct 9 Sagittarius
Nov 6 Capricorn
Dec 7 Aquarius
1966
Jan 1 Aquarius
Feb 7 Capricorn
Feb 26 Aquarius
Apr 7 Pisces

May 6 Aries
Jun 1 Taurus
Jun 27 Gemini
Jul 22 Cancer
Aug 16 Leo
Sep 9 Virgo
Oct 4 Libra
Oct 28 Scorpio
Nov 21 Sagittarius
Dec 14 Capricorn
1967
Jan 1 Capricorn
Jan 7 Aquarius
Jan 31 Pisces
Feb 24 Aries
Mar 21 Taurus
Apr 15 Gemini
May 11 Cancer
Jun 7 Leo
Jul 9 Virgo
Sep 10 Leo
Oct 2 Virgo
Nov 10 Libra
Dec 8 Scorpio
1968
Jan 1 Sagittarius
Jan 27 Capricorn
Feb 21 Aquarius
Mar 16 Pisces
Apr 9 Aries
May 4 Taurus
May 28 Gemini
Jun 22 Cancer
Jul 16 Leo
Aug 9 Virgo
Sep 3 Libra
Sep 27 Scorpio
Oct 22 Sagittarius
Nov 15 Capricorn
Dec 10 Aquarius
1969
Jan 1 Aquarius

Jan 5 Pisces
Feb 3 Aries
Jun 7 Taurus
Jul 7 Gemini
Aug 4 Cancer
Aug 30 Libra
Sep 24 Virgo
Oct 18 Libra
Nov 11 Scorpio
Dec 5 Sagittarius
Dec 29 Capricorn
1970
Jan 1 Capricorn
Jan 22 Aquarius
Feb 15 Pisces
Mar 11 Aries
Apr 4 Taurus
Apr 28 Gemini
May 23 Cancer
Jun 17 Leo
Jul 13 Virgo
Aug 9 Libra
Sep 8 Scorpio
1971
Jan 1 Scorpio
Jan 8 Sagittarius
Feb 6 Capricorn
Mar 5 Aquarius
Mar 30 Pisces
Apr 24 Aries
May 19 Taurus
Jun 13 Gemini
Jul 7 Cancer
Aug 1 Leo
Aug 25 Virgo
Sep 18 Libra
Oct 12 Scorpio
Nov 6 Sagittarius
Nov 30 Capricorn
Dec 24 Aquarius
1972
Jan 1 Aquarius

Jan 17 Pisces
Feb 11 Aries
Mar 8 Taurus
Apr 4 Aries
May 11 Cancer
Jun 12 Gemini
Aug 7 Cancer
Sep 8 Leo
Oct 6 Virgo
Oct 31 Libra
Nov 25 Scorpio
Dec 19 Sagittarius
1973
Jan 1 Sagittarius
Jan 12 Capricorn
Feb 5 Aquarius
Mar 1 Pisces
Mar 25 Aries
Apr 19 Taurus
May 13 Gemini
Jun 6 Cancer
Jul 1 Leo
Jul 26 Virgo
Aug 20 Libra
Sep 14 Scorpio
Oct 10 Sagittarius
Nov 6 Capricorn
Dec 8 Aquarius
1974
Jan 1 Aquarius
Jan 30 Capricorn
Mar 1 Aquarius
Apr 7 Pisces
May 5 Aries
Jun 1 Taurus
Jun 26 Gemini
Jul 22 Cancer
Aug 15 Leo
Sep 9 Virgo
Oct 3 Libra
Oct 27 Scorpio
Nov 20 Sagittarius

Dec 14 Capricorn
1975
Jan 1 Capricorn
Jan 7 Aquarius
Jan 31 Pisces
Feb 24 Aries
Mar 20 Taurus
Apr 14 Gemini
May 10 Cancer
Jun 7 Leo
Jul 10 Virgo
Sep 3 Leo
Oct 5 Virgo
Nov 10 Libra
Dec 8 Scorpio
1976
Jan 1 Scorpio
Jan 2 Sagittarius
Jan 27 Capricorn
Feb 20 Aquarius
Mar 16 Pisces
Apr 9 Aries
May 3 Taurus
May 28 Gemini
Jun 21 Cancer
Jul 15 Leo
Aug 9 Virgo
Sep 2 Libra
Sep 27 Scorpio
Oct 21 Sagittarius
Nov 15 Capricorn
Dec 10 Aquarius
1977
Jan 1 Aquarius
Jan 5 Pisces
Feb 3 Aries
Jun 7 Taurus
Jul 7 Gemini
Aug 3 Cancer
Aug 29 Leo
Sep 23 Virgo
Oct 18 Libra

Nov 11 Scorpio
Dec 5 Sagittarius
Dec 28 Capricorn
1978
Jan 1 Capricorn
Jan 21 Aquarius
Feb 14 Pisces
Mar 10 Aries
Apr 3 Taurus
Apr 28 Gemini
May 23 Cancer
Jun 17 Leo
Jul 13 Virgo
Aug 9 Libra
Sep 8 Scorpio
1979
Jan 1 Scorpio
Jan 8 Sagittarius
Feb 6 Capricorn
Mar 4 Aquarius
Mar 30 Pisces
Apr 24 Aries
May 19 Taurus
Jun 12 Gemini
Jul 7 Cancer
Jul 31 Leo
Aug 25 Virgo
Sep 18 Libra
Oct 12 Scorpio
Nov 5 Sagittarius
Nov 29 Capricorn
Dec 23 Aquarius
1980
Jan 1 Aquarius
Jan 17 Pisces
Feb 10 Aries
Mar 7 Taurus
Apr 4 Gemini
May 13 Cancer
Jun 6 Gemini
Aug 7 Cancer
Sep 8 Leo

Oct 5 Virgo
Oct 31 Libra
Nov 25 Scorpio
Dec 19 Sagittarius
1981
Jan 1 Sagittarius
Jan 12 Capricorn
Feb 5 Aquarius
Mar 1 Pisces
Mar 25 Aries
Apr 18 Taurus
May 12 Gemini
Jun 6 Cancer
Jun 30 Leo
Jul 25 Virgo
Aug 19 Libra
Sep 13 Scorpio
Oct 10 Sagittarius
Nov 6 Capricorn
Dec 9 Aquarius
1982
Jan 1 Aquarius
Jan 24 Capricorn
Mar 3 Aquarius
Apr 7 Pisces
May 5 Aries
May 31 Taurus
Jun 26 Gemini
Jul 21 Cancer
Aug 15 Leo
Sep 8 Virgo
Oct 3 Libra
Oct 27 Scorpio
Nov 19 Sagittarius
Dec 13 Capricorn
1983
Jan 1 Capricorn
Jan 6 Aquarius
Jan 30 Pisces
Feb 23 Aries
Mar 19 Taurus
Apr 13 Gemini

May 9 Cancer
Jun 6 Leo
Jul 10 Virgo
Aug 28 Leo
Oct 6 Virgo
Nov 10 Libra
Dec 7 Scorpio
1984
Jan 1 Sagittarius
Jan 26 Capricorn
Feb 19 Aquarius
Mar 15 Pisces
Apr 8 Aries
May 2 Taurus
May 27 Gemini
Jun 20 Cancer
Jul 14 Leo
Aug 8 Virgo
Sep 1 Libra
Sep 27 Scorpio
Oct 20 Sagittarius
Nov 14 Capricorn
Dec 9 Aquarius
1985
Jan 4 Pisces
Feb 2 Aries
Jun 6 Taurus
Jul 6 Gemini
Aug 2 Cancer
Aug 28 Leo
Sep 22 Virgo
Oct 17 Libra
Nov 10 Scorpio
Dec 4 Sagittarius
Dec 27 Capricorn

PART THREE
EROS

'[He] who is love, handsomest among all immortals
Who breaks the limb's strength:
Who, in all gods, in all human beings,
Overpowers the intelligence . . .'
Hesiod, *Theogony*

CHAPTER NINETEEN:

EROS – FANTASY AND THE WILD SIDE OF SEX

Eros – the Archetype

Eros is a much maligned and misrepresented god. He was an ancient symbol of potent life force, but he is now identified as the Greek equivalent of Cupid: a babyish winged youth with an arrow of desire, and with a usually flaccid penis. This compromised image defuses the power of Eros, an ancient primal and phallic deity. He was one of the earliest gods of chaos, predating Zeus and arising from the time before creation began. As a masculine generative force, he helped bring the world into creation. He was later manifested in the Olympic pantheon as the offspring of Aphrodite and Zeus. Eros symbolises the urge for life, the creation of matter out of chaos. In pre-Hellenic Greece, sexual potency was a primal life force, and Eros was honoured and revered as such.

In your birth chart, the placement by sign of the tiny asteroid called Eros represents your erotic urge and the powerful principle of erotic connection. Eros signifies how you connect things, people, places, sensations and ideas to sexuality. Eros represents the way you instinctively attach yourself to passion as a creative life force. While Venus represents the sexual act and pleasure, Eros is the unconscious choice we make about partners and environment. He is the fantasy or thoughts that trigger those sexual responses, that awakens your serpent woman.

Eros is also about wild abandon, rather than just the

sexual act itself. He is the urge for full-blown passionate arousal through sex. Eros takes you into the realms of the fantasy, the escapism, and the hunger for excessive stimulation and more ecstasy. He represents the powerful force of transformation you may experience through deeper spiritual-sexual experience. The essence of Eros is to unite the opposites, to bring together two lovers to fuse and to create a potent energy through their sexuality.

He has a dark side, like every other archetype or god/goddess. When his shadow comes into play, you can become excessive, imprisoned in your own fantasies. This is when fantasies manifest themselves as dangerous games in reality or you become obsessively attached to a person and may lose a part of yourself in sexual overkill. Eros is the god 'who overpowers the intelligence'. When he awakens, when he senses the trigger for your arousal and for your desire, you have no choice but to follow. You are awakened to sexuality as the most potent life force, the only way to unite the light with the dark, male with female, form with chaos.

In each of the following four chapters, Eros in the fire signs, Eros in the air signs, Eros in the earth signs and Eros in the water signs, you can discover your erotic triggers, fantasies, the wilder aspects of your sexual nature, and what happens if you become excessively attached to the dark side of passion.

Look up where Eros was on the day you were born in the tables at the end of this part, then turn to the relevant section to discover the wild side of your sexual/erotic profile. There is an interactive section at the end of each section to help you fill in your erotic chart. Draw the symbol for Eros in the correct sign on the chart, and fill in the key words as before with the sun and Venus sections.

The study of the placement of Eros in our birth charts is still in its infancy and research is ongoing in astrological circles. Although I have completed much research on the implications and significance of Eros, it is still a highly 'sensitive' area. You are invited to write in, in complete confidence if you wish, about the nature of Eros in your chart.

Obsession

Remember that fantasy does not necessarily have to become reality. Sexual desire needs a trigger, but when we become dependent on that trigger alone we run the risk of using our sexuality only for escapism. Eros alone is not interested in the lover or the soul mate: Eros is not interested in the reality of our sexual expression, only in the idealisation and unreal. The wild side of your sexuality is a connection to this ancient life force, yet aligning to a fantasy world alone may leave you lost in yourself, with no connection to another. Combine the expression of Eros with your sun sign's sexual purpose and your Venusian pleasure, and become more aware of your deeper sexual needs.

CHAPTER TWENTY:

EROS IN THE FIRE SIGNS

(Aries, Leo and Sagittarius)

*'She offered herself, opening her vulva with her lovely
fingers, as if she could not wait.'*
Anaïs Nin

With an Eros placement here, there will be exaggerated fantasies and a strong bias towards domination. Erotic triggers will be found in unpredictable situations or places many would not dare to even consider.

Eros in Aries – Woman

The Eros in Aries woman will prefer the ideas of aggression and impulse: perhaps the thrill of being aroused by another woman while driving a fast car, or a moment of complete self-gratification as she caresses her clitoris before an assembly of priests and nuns. The Eros in Aries woman defies many conventional fantasies, preferring to imagine herself as the leader and the seducer of both men and women. The naivety of virgin men or youths may trigger sexual arousal. It is likely that she will be turned on by the idea of sex with a whole platoon of virile soldiers. She is not averse to the idea of seducing strangers. She may imagine being the high priestess upon the altar of sexual love, about to initiate young and nubile men into the art of withholding orgasm to achieve immortality.

The kind of partner or lover who can arouse her in her fantasies may be in contrast with her Venusian values. He may be romantic, seemingly willing to pleasure her.

He will have an aura of passive seduction, as if he waits for her to dominate him. He will have beauty and grace, and may adore conversation more than body contact. He will be an idealist. She will want to seduce him, to ravish and devour, to fill his body with her fire. He will seek sexual approval and reward, but he will avoid conflict and the uglier aspects of the reality of gutsy sex.

The Eros in Aries woman may relate to her wild sexual nature easily. She may naturally respond to the eroticism of life, because it is so much a part of her imagined world. She takes both pleasure and pain in the erotic and, if she has Venus or the sun in Aries, she will discover infinite possibilities and infinite channels for expressing her truly potent wild woman. If she aligns solely to the dark side of Eros, she can become bound by her own insatiable hunger for excessive stimulation from dangerous situations or people.

Eros in Aries – Man

In his fantasies the Eros in Aries male may imagine public or exhibitionistic sex. He will respond quickly to the idea of sex with strangers. He may have fantasies about sex in dangerous situations, or a moment's opportunity for self-gratification taken without consideration. Mostly women, yet sometimes the beauty of a man, may trigger S&M fantasies. He has visions of liaisons with powerful women or perhaps with the virgin bride whom he meets at a wedding party.

The kind of partner or lover who may be an erotic trigger for this man's desire may be in contradiction of his Venusian values and sun-sign placement. She may be refined, romantic, and idealistic about life and love. She will convey an aura of intellectual superiority. She may be well-dressed and manicured. She may seem submissive, eager to do anything he desires. She will keep conversation as her erotic spur, kicking his sides with her chosen words until he can no longer wait for the moment she yields to his power.

The Eros in Aries male is an easily triggered sexual beast. He must at all costs move from fantasy to fantasy fast, before he is caught in reality's trap. He may find, however, that if he aligns solely to the intensity of Eros he may become a glutton for fantastic sex, denying himself the simplicity of sensual pleasure.

Eros in Leo – Woman

The Eros in Leo woman needs to feel the centre of attention in her sexual fantasies. She will prefer to dominate in any scenario and want it to be outrageously performed, or involve historical costumes, theatrical accoutrements or glamorous sex aids. She may imagine herself in a porn movie or on the cinema screen with famous stars. She may also enjoy sadistic fantasies: her lover tied up as he watches her seduction of another woman. She may arouse herself at the thought of pleasuring herself in a hall of mirrors, at any moment to be discovered in her moment of orgasm. She will imagine being watched by a voyeur who eventually joins in and becomes her willing slave. The Eros in Leo woman needs exciting fantasies that revolve totally around her power, whether she is the Queen of Sheba or a vampire.

Her Eros lover will trigger her erotic desire: he may not be her ideal Venus partner or the person with whom she could have a long-term relationship. The Eros in Leo woman's Eros lover would be unconventional, fixed in his radical opinions. He will be ready to try any kind of sexual experiment, but only in the pursuit of an ideal. He will prefer the good of the whole to the pleasure of the self. He is a lover who will want to change the conventions of sexuality while remaining detached and coldly glamorous.

The Eros in Leo woman can identify with her wild erotic nature, yet she prefers to keep it hidden from view. She may affirm her own eroticism in private, with a partner or lover who she feels offers complete devotion to her fantasies. If she has the sun or Venus in Leo she may find it easier to accept her highly self-pleasuring needs. If she identifies solely with the dark side of Eros, she may reject partners and seek only to gratify herself alone. Her desire for orgasm will become exaggerated and she will disconnect eroticism from relationship.

Eros in Leo – Man

His fantasy world is charged with power, control and, above all, glamour. He may enjoy the images of the courtesan or the geisha girl slaving to his every whim. He may have exhibitionistic fantasies, perhaps about having sex on the stage or in front of TV cameras. His daydreams may include scenarios where he is the dominant or master.

The kind of person who may be an erotic trigger for his passion may be contrary to his sun sign and Venus values. She may be independent, intellectually sparkling and wise. She may project an aura of glamour, sophistication and worldly success, or she may be working for the good of society rather than the needs of the individual. She may be unconventional, idealistic, and want to convince everyone of her opinions. She will expect sex to be an intellectual adventure, and desire to introduce every man she meets to the unusual and bizarre. She may want to take sex beyond human limits.

Like the other Eros in fire signs he relies on his imaginary world as a potent trigger for his sexuality to both inspire him and give him vision for the future. Yet he can become rigidly stuck in his fantasy world if he identifies too closely with the dominant roles he gives himself: the real world can never offer him such exaggerated pleasure.

Eros in Sagittarius – Woman

The woman with Eros in Sagittarius may be fascinated by images of primitive sexual orgies: men and women in total abandon, unashamedly arousing one another without jealousy or possessiveness. She will also want equality of minds and sexual needs in her fantasies, and dreams rarely about domination or submission. She may imagine a sex romp with all the professors of an elite educational establishment, or perhaps a secret liaison with every member of the government. She may even fantasise she is a spy, listening to high-powered secrets in her bedchamber. The more risqué the environment the better. She might imagine inviting the musicians in an orchestra backstage to test her sexual stamina, or the strangers on a station platform, or the crew of a flight to Australia. She may be turned on by sex on horseback, or by the thought of ravishing the head groom among the straw bales while the stallion covers his mare. Her fantasies will merge at times into reality, for she needs to express her richness of erotic connections.

The kind of person who may trigger this woman's erotic desire may be contrary to her intimate intentions or Venusian values. Her Eros man will have charm, wit and intellectual virtuosity. He will be amusing, ephemeral, able to take on any role or any disguise. He will be the illusionist who can make her disappear into fantasy and will offer myriad tricks. He will engage in all kinds of games, preferring ideas about sex to the actual performance. He will be restless, hesitant one minute, focused the next. He has the ability to traverse the darker depths of sexual passion, then return to the lighter, electrifying side.

The Eros in Sagittarius woman relates to her wildness, like the other fire signs, with truly natural passion. She is like a centaur, both animal and human, ready for anything in her erotic world. She will enjoy experiencing every new trigger of arousal, every moment of desire that flames from within and burns through her body. She will celebrate erotic joy and express her expansive wild woman. However, if she becomes excessively attached to one kind of arousal, denying herself the freedom of varied sexual experience, she may impose impossible expectations on every sexual encounter, totally suppressing her ability to be the bringer of joy.

Eros in Sagittarius – Man

His fantasies may be weighted with danger, with fast and sudden sex. He may fantasise about passionate sex in public places or having sex with a stranger he meets on a train, in a taxi, on an aeroplane. He may be fascinated by the idea of seducing the poised and the glamorous: female tycoons, city slickers or the extremely rich. He will fantasise about dangerous people and dangerous locations. An erotic trigger may be exposure to the elements: raging seas, wild woods, mountain ranges. The more boundless, the more free the fantasy, the more likely it will bring him pleasure.

The kind of person who may trigger his erotic desire may be incompatible with his Venus and sun values and needs. This is a woman of wit, conversation and charm. Someone who knows how to flirt and shock, to tease and taunt. She will seem to change roles, never really being herself: an escape artiste from any identity. She may scatter her thoughts, be restless then engaging, flighty then possessive. She will prefer not to make commitments. She will intellectualise her varied sexual desires before they have even found pleasure. She will have the capacity for the deepest emotion, and yet appear fickle and shallow.

The Eros in Sagittarius male often seeks to escape into the realm of his imagination, fired by enthusiasm for any new vision that will stimulate his easily triggered arousal. Yet if he attaches himself wholly to the world of sexual fantasy, denying the earthiness of human pleasure, he may have too many expectations and resort to living out his fantasies by indulging in sex with strangers whenever possible.

The Female Fire Fantasy

In the hall of mirrors she will wait until she is alone. Now the only observers of her pleasure are her reflections. She will be wearing stockings and suspenders beneath her voile dress, but her sex is bare. The golden belt round her waist is all she needs for pleasure. The crimson dress reflects a thousand fiery flames in the mirrors. Now she is ready to honour her lonely one-woman show. Yet someone will crouch down at the doorway just as she begins to unfurl one stocking down her leg. The rustle of the silk cannot smother the gasp of someone's breath. She will smile, for knowing she is being watched by another is as exciting as watching herself. Now she will enjoy the art, the danger. She will abandon herself to this unknown watcher.

She dances towards two mirrors, angled to reflect a view of her buttocks as she raises her skirt above her waist. There she begins to remove the other stocking, careful not to reveal her sex, careful not to show she is already wet with pleasure. The voyeur at the door will want to move closer, to see every curve of her body as she bends forward, the mirrors moving in time, a hundred emanations of herself. She focuses on herself in the longest mirror, unclasps the golden belt, then licks her fingertips. Knowing that the voyeur still gazes at her buttocks, she unzips her dress. The crimson voile glides to the floor and she stands only in her suspenders and the golden-clasped belt round her waist.

In the mirror she sees the voyeur, sees his excitement at the sight of her pubis. His arousal will not be silent, she is sure. Down the curves of her buttocks, to the most dark and secret of places, she begins to explore with her wet fingers. Then, bending forward, she licks and stabs with her tongue at her own reflected face on the mirror. She unclasps the gold belt and lets it fall down over her hips and across her belly. The gold is cold, hard against her flesh. She hears the voyeur shuffle, move his coat to feel for his own pleasure. She thrusts her hips forward towards the mirror and gazes at her pubic valley, the mound of hair soft like velvet, the ruby-red lips waiting to be caressed, parted and teased. The reflection of her own sex sends shudders of warm pleasure down to her clitoris and she moistens her fingertip with saliva and plays with the swelling folds around her bud.

Yet he cannot resist, this stranger. He comes up behind now, his arrogance startling as he pushes himself against her buttocks. In the mirrors she sees his mastery, sees the hugeness of his cock. She wants to possess his power, to take it for herself. She swirls round, kneels before him and drives his penis into her mouth. Sucking and teasing, she watches herself in the mirror. The great phallus is swollen, engorged with desire for explosive orgasm. Now she has him. There in the hall of mirrors she has a hundred visions of her power as she brings him to his climax. He sways back, unable to stop the sweetness from flowing into her mouth.

Now she has feasted upon him she must pleasure herself alone. Again she turns to the mirror, takes the golden belt and begins to pull it rhythmically back and forth across her sex, one hand behind her buttocks, the other in front of her belly. The gold clasp catches on her swelling bud with every move. She moistens the gold with her fingers, then watches her image in the mirrors as she moves the belt faster and faster. Now she wants to merge with her mirror image. She presses herself against the mirror and glides her sex up and down the glass, turning it misty, steamy with her desire. The haze of the voyeur in the background vanishes as she reaches her moment of surrender. The full pleasure of her clitoris explodes as she rams her body again and again at the enflamed and pulsating woman reflected before her.

Interactive Section
Eros in Fire

As in the other chapters, choose the words with which you most identify and fill in your erotic-profile chart accordingly.

Eros represents my fantasies and the wild side of my sexuality.

I am turned on by _____

Choose from: being dominant, excitement, danger, unpredictability, being the centre of attention, romance and glamour, social celebrations, myself.

My fantasies include _____

Choose from: exhibitionism, dangerous locations for sex, historical or dramatic sex, dominance, sex with strangers, group sex, being sexually served, initiation and ritual sex.

My erotic triggers include _____

Choose from: beauty, the great outdoors, rebels, intellectuals, mind games, power games, freedom, strangers.

Questions

- Do you find your erotic nature easily assimilated into your sexual relationships?
- Do you tend to impose your favourite fantasy on your partner, or do you listen to and share in theirs?
- Are your fantasies usually filled with excitement, dazzle and glamour?
- Do you rebel against the power of Eros? If so, has your need for self-control ever made you feel guilty about or threatened by erotic desire when it overwhelms you?

CHAPTER TWENTY-ONE:

EROS IN THE AIR SIGNS

(Gemini, Libra and Aquarius)

'Both bodies in a single body mix,
A single body with a double sex.'
Ovid

*T*hose with Eros in the air signs easily connect to Eros's power over the mind, and often indulge in lengthy fantasy as part of their sexual foreplay. They may prefer sexual fantasy to the reality.

Eros in Gemini – Woman

The woman with Eros in Gemini may find an erotic connection in every experience or idea. The more she indulges in her mental pictures, the more she will find the bizarre and the curious are as arousing as the normal. She has a powerful imagination which crosses boundaries that she might not dare to in reality. She may have fantasies about sudden and spontaneous sexual encounters while on her travels. She is most likely to be in the dominant role. The bisexuality of the air signs is most predominant in Gemini, and she may prefer fantasies that involve her own sex but strongly resist or not enjoy the actual reality. Erotic literature, films and photographs may be important stimulants. She may fantasise about erotic phone conversations with a stranger. She may imagine board and party games that involve sexual forfeits of group sex for the losers.

The kind of person who may trigger this woman's erotic desire may be in contrast to her intentions or long-term sexual values. This person would be wild and adventurous, willing to take her anywhere she desires. He will be outspoken, brash and arrogant, seemingly irresponsible and apparently lacking in emotion. He will be fiery, a visionary with big ideals and high expectations. He would rather ride bareback through the desert than sit in a restaurant, yet he will delight in revelry and the celebration of sexual euphoria. He will insist on equality of mind and body, but may prefer brief encounters and dangerous liaisons to long-term commitments.

The Eros in Gemini woman relates easily to the power of her mind and the wildness of her fantasies. Her intellectual fascination with sex means she can live every joy in her head, and often finds the loneliness of her wild nature only revived by verbal stimulation. If she becomes excessively attached to her fantasy world, denying herself a partner to share her pleasure, she may rush from encounter to encounter. She will believe she is experiencing true pleasure while it is only her mind that is being stimulated, rather than her emotions or body.

Eros in Gemini – Man

Intellectual and abstract fantasy is a great pleasure for this man. He indulges in the images and thoughts of a wide variety of erotic acts: anything from sex with strangers and bisexuality to bondage and sadism. He may prefer imagining himself as the wielder of sadistic yet genuine pleasure: a row of women each waiting for the touch of his spurs upon their thighs, or the roughness of his leather belt across their breasts. He will enjoy fantasies that ensure he is centre stage, whether as the slave-driver, or the youth ravaged by an older woman or man behind the library shelves.

The kind of person who may trigger this man's erotic desire may be a contradiction of his long-term intimacy intentions or sexual values. This woman would be extrovert, wild and untamable. She will roam through life like a huntress, eager to catch her prey and eager to have fun. She may be impulsive, inspiring and daring. She will want everything now and live only for the next moment, never looking back to the past. She will want complete equality in her relationships, but she may also prefer the danger of the unknown, of never committing herself truly to another.

The Eros in Gemini male may need to share his erotic thoughts or fantasies frequently with his partner, for he may bore quickly if his mind is not fed with new delights. Whatever his partner's favourite fantasy, he will quickly find it becomes his, too. If he aligns solely to Eros he may forget his deeper sexual needs and expect all his fantasies to be lived out, however bizarre they may be.

Eros in Libra – Woman

This woman needs to feel in control and usually to dominate in her fantasies. In reality she is often fearful of being overwhelmed by passion and so asserts her need for controlling her partner in her mind. Her imagination is as vivid as the other air signs, and she is strongly aroused by bisexual images. She may prefer the idea of initiating women into ritual sex, of magically controlling their orgasm. She may even imagine herself with a vast penis and indulge in a fantasy of exhibitionist masturbation before a group of subjugated women. Yet she will also want her fantasies to be beautiful, to arouse her highly aesthetic sense of pleasure. She may imagine herself held captive in a high tower, with a beautiful youth visiting her each night. There will need to be a sense of etiquette and morality, a need for order however forbidden the imagery.

The man who can trigger her Eros arousal may be in conflict with her sun-sign intention and her Venus values. This Eros person would be self-centred and romantic, yet potent and masculine. He would be fiery and impulsive in his approach to sex. He would want to dominate and to assert his masculinity. He would prefer sex to be simple, hard penetration. He would be impatient with lengthy stimulation. He will be bold and prefer the hunt to the kill. He will want total sexual commitment from her, but may not offer it himself.

The Eros in Libra woman usually enjoys her wild Eros side. The imagery of sexual ecstasy comes easily to her but she may have trouble relating to Eros in her day-to-day sexual lifestyle unless she has the sun or Venus in a powerful sign like Leo or Scorpio. If she identifies solely with the dark side of Eros, she may, like her airy sisters, rush from one erotic encounter to another to suppress her mental anxiety. Orgasmic release will become dependent only on herself, and she may be unable to connect erotic desire with relationship, seeking only to release her wild passions in obsessive patterns of sexual behaviour.

Eros in Libra – Man

Like the other air signs, the Eros in Libra man may intellectualise rather than physically experience erotic arousal. He may enjoy the idea of the spontaneous arousal of passing strangers. He may prefer images of submission, his own and others'. He may enjoy the images of bondage, of being held down by two women, or two men, while another androgynous and masked person pleasures his sex. However bizarre or perverse the imagery, it must be ordered, designed, and in line with his own high ideals. All his fantasies will involve beauty and aesthetic refinement. He will imagine the decoration and the perfect taste and sophistication of the place where his fantasies are played out, whether it is a grandiose palace or a Far Eastern temple. His women will be powerful, able to dominate and force him into orgasm over and over again. He may also fantasise about men for, like the other air signs, bisexuality may be integrated into his fantasy world, however much he does not align to it in reality.

The kind of person who may trigger his erotic desire may be in contradiction of his sun-sign intention or

Venusian values. This woman would be fiery, impulsive and dangerous. She would want to dominate and lead. She would expect no compromises, no indecision. She would be forceful and dedicated to herself, often egocentric and crusading, yet fearful of her femininity and her vulnerable feelings.

If he aligns solely to Eros, he may become addicted to the romance and abstraction of his fantasies, fearing the humanness of sensual and physical bonding.

Eros in Aquarius – Woman

The Eros in Aquarius woman has a deeply powerful mind that may bring the most bizarre and obscure fantasies to her world. She will prefer to be in control in her imagination, to be the instigator of outrageous acts performed by other people under her control. She may see herself as a powerful businesswoman analysing each employee's sexual performance, experiencing their vulnerability with complete and utter detachment. She may fantasise about running a whorehouse, subjugating all the clients to her own sexual perversions. She may fantasise about organising the most outrageous orgy, where men and women indulge in S&M fantasies while she watches with pleasure. In her imagined world she will want to shock rather than to enjoy. Her fantasy pleasure is in the unimaginable, rather than in the tried and trusted.

The person who may trigger her erotic desire may be in conflict with her sun-sign intentions and Venus values. He would be glamorous, aloof and often obsessed with his own body. He may appear self-centred and vain, preferring to look in the mirror at himself rather than at others. He will be unconcerned with the world or the environment. Sexually, he will want all and demand the best. He will lead rather than follow and be an exhibitionist in all ways, perhaps theatrical, exuding prestige and worldly power. His forwardness will be intrusive yet magnetic, his fiery sexuality inescapable and yet daring.

If she has either the sun or Venus in Aquarius she may be able to align her rather dissident fantasy world with her detachment in one-to-one relationships. But this is a remarkably powerful placement for Eros, and one that requires deep understanding of what Eros really symbolises. The woman with Eros in Aquarius seeks a fantasy world where she is approved for being different, for standing out from the crowd which she wants to control. If she aligns solely to the dark side of Eros she can become obsessive in her need for power trips over others, for proving her validity as someone who sexually deviates from the norm, rather than accepting she is just another vulnerable human being.

Eros in Aquarius – Man

The mind of the Eros in Aquarius male is a potent cauldron of erotic thought. He may invent many images that others would find bizarre or perverse. His fantasies would involve orgies of sexual experimentation involving toys and devices but little emotional contact or sensual pleasure. He will always be the orchestrator, and the wielder of power. He may prefer voyeurism to his own participation. He will enjoy the idea of watching two women, two men, or a combination of all. The more outrageously he can control others, the more pleasure he will derive from this fantasy world of detached, yet potent power.

The kind of person who may trigger his erotic desire may be a contradiction of his sun-sign intention or Venusian values. She would be passionate and dramatic. Her appearance would be dazzling and ostentatious, yet highly individual. She would be vain and proud, someone who wants the limelight only for herself. She will want the best and demand exclusivity in all relationships. Yet her charismatic and flamboyant style often hides a vulnerable and lonely child.

If the Eros in Aquarius male aligns solely to his fantasy world, he may withdraw completely from sexual experience, preferring total abstinence. He may need to learn to share his fantasy world with a partner who is prepared to accept his often weird and unusual imagination.

The Female Air Fantasy

There will be a temple dedicated to Dionysus and the art of sexual pleasure. She will be the high priestess, her white robe covering her nakedness except for the opening down the front of the muslin dress. As the breeze lifts the flames of the temple fire it will also swirl her robe across her body, revealing her shaven pubis and her rouged nipples, the honours of being the chosen one. She will stand beside the altar to hold out the chalice of wine to those who come to be initiated. She is the one who will show them the beauty of arousal, of their own deeply hidden desire. They will be mostly women who come to this altar. She has no fear, this priestess, for each experience will be utterly controlled, her pleasure gained through the power of showing others her way.

There are five who must watch as they wait for their turn, for by their very observation they will want to succumb to the devouring torment themselves. She turns to the first beautiful woman, a houri. She will take the houri's hand as the girl lies down upon the altar, she too only clothed in a white robe, the ribbon ties falling open around her belly and the soft mound of pubic hair. She binds the houri's wrists and ankles to the stone cross.

Slowly at first, she touches the girl's skin with her lips, her fingers pushing back the white robe carefully to reveal her nakedness. She sees the others entranced: the women look away at first, then back, tempted, tantalised, aroused by the sight of the naked woman. The priestess glides her fingers across the houri's skin, teases her breasts with just the edge of her nails. From beneath her robe she reveals a huge phallus. It is crudely carved from an olive tree. The wood is oiled, gleaming and hard. She lays it beneath the houri's sex, nestled between her white thighs.

The priestess feels the surging waves of her own pleasure, yet her mind is in control and she will not surrender. There is music now, candles lit, flames of desire burning. The houri is entranced, captivated by the torment of this woman's power as she swirls above her, never resting, not yet touching her secret place. Now the priestess removes her robe, the glow of the candles illuminating fully her naked vulva, hairless, the folds of her sex-lips. Her mouth salivates with desire as she stands beside the woman, her sex only centimetres from the houri's warm silken belly. She releases the ties on the houri's robe and, as it drops to the floor, she gazes with desire upon her exquisite nipples.

The houri is breathless, dazed with waves of frenzied desire as the priestess begins to tongue her nipples. Then the priestess pushes her fingers between the younger woman's labia, begins to circle her clitoris, teasing it out of its petals. The houri arches her back with pleasure. With one hand the priestess takes the huge phallus and begins to push it between the houri's swollen labia until she moans with delight. With the other hand the priestess begins to flick her fingers against the houri's hard bud. Her mouth is within inches of the houri's sweetest taste. The priestess lowers her mouth to the houri's sex, her tongue exploring the darkness, licking the wetness from the young woman's inner sanctuary.

The houri is ready for ecstasy and surrender as the priestess now tongues her clitoris, licking, teasing, rhythmically caressing the protruding bud. With the last flickering of the priestess's tongue the houri begins to moan, her orgasm an ecstasy of knowing she cannot stop her pleasure now. The priestess's power is complete. She will remain moist, the first hardness of desire in her own clitoris held in suspense, powerful and pleasurable. Once she has initiated all the houris, she will lie naked and prostrate upon the stone altar herself, pushing her sex into the rough stone of initiation to welcome the pleasure of both body and mind.

Interactive Section
Eros in Air

As in the other chapters, choose the words with which you most identify and fill in your erotic-profile chart accordingly.

Eros represents my fantasies and the wild side of my sexuality.

I am turned on by _____

Choose from: my mind, bizarre thoughts, conversation, beautiful bodies of both sexes, pleasing others, my own self-control, experimentation, dissent.

My fantasies include _____

Choose from: orchestrating group sex, bisexuality, cross-dressing, exhibitionism, sex with strangers, sadism, voyeurism, initiation, sexual forfeits.

My erotic triggers include _____

Choose from: the curious and the different, intellectual rapport, erotic literature and movies, fiery people, opportunists, dangerous encounters, potently beautiful men and women, powerful people, watching others' perversions

Questions

- Do erotic triggers play a big part in your sexual relationships?
- Do you find you prefer the imagined world to the real one?
- Do you become frustrated if your partner doesn't understand your erotic needs?
- Do you find it easy to identify with Eros?
- Does mutual masturbation have to involve your fantasy world?

CHAPTER TWENTY-TWO:

EROS IN THE EARTH SIGNS

(Taurus, Virgo and Capricorn)

*'To lie naked on the furs, to be taken there lying on this
animal smell, caressed by the furs.'*
Anaïs Nin

*T*hose with Eros in the earth signs have tactile fantasies, nurtured by the thoughts of sensual torment
and earthly delights. All the pleasures of wicked and
forbidden sex are triggers for erotic arousal. Wild abandon and the cults of ritual ecstasy may entice them, as
do bondage and subjugation, either as dominatrix or
slave.

Eros in Taurus – Woman

She will prefer images of wickedness behind the curtains
and the sins of the flesh. She may imagine being ravished
by a lover with bestial desires, and be aroused by the
idea of anal sex. She may turn her imagination to mud-
wrestling with another woman, the masseur or the
masseuse, the aromatherapist who seduces her on the
bed. She may even fantasise about the psychotherapist
as she lies on the leather couch revealing her darkest
sexual fantasies to him. Her surroundings are important:
there must be oils and perfumes, gold and silver jewels
for her labia, or the clinking of chain mail or armour
against her pubis. Food is also an erotic connection for
her: feasts of oysters, aphrodisiacs and champagne, or
grapes deseeded by a nubile lover while she bathes in
musky oils. She may also imagine a vampire lover or
insatiable sex god, draining her of her sexual energy

while she lies submissive on her bed studded with golden coins.

The kind of person who may trigger her unconscious erotic desire may well be contrary to her needs and expectations and to her Venus and sun-sign placements. He may be darkly secretive, have hypnotic eyes and the steely hardness of a glinting sword. He may be dignified and dangerous. She will sense his deep intensity, his need to probe every fathom of her body. He may be one who treasures his woman's body like a shrine, yet will be demanding and irresistible. He will be a sexually powerful demon or a magus, and she will be compelled to feast with him.

The Eros in Taurus woman has a natural awareness of her wild erotic nature, for it is an essential part of her sexuality. Without Eros she would be lost. She does not aspire to erotic arousal simply for the sake of it, however: she merges the pleasure of the mind with her sensual needs. If she becomes excessively attached to Eros's dark side as a means of avoiding close intimacy she may become addicted only to her fantasy world. She may reject the ordinary needs of human sexual energy, denying anyone or anything that cannot turn her on.

Eros in Taurus – Man

This is a man whose fantasies will be deeply sensual. He may like the images of licking and sucking peanut butter, oils, oysters and pomegranates from his lover's sex. He may imagine the feeling of leather, lace, satin, rubber, furs, jewels and the delights of candlelight and wine. He may enjoy the idea of being chained to a four-poster bed, the incense and the perfumes heady and intoxicating as he lies, submissive, before a masked woman dressed in black. He will imagine being touched with whips, then flogged with feathers. He will need to imagine feasts and banquets, orgiastic lovers drunk with desire upon the table. Yet he will prefer the image of himself apart from the others, wandering through their revelry in search of the one who will smell of wild sex.

The kind of person who may trigger his erotic desire may be contrary to his long-term intentions or Venusian values. She will be mysterious, cool and remote, yet intensely powerful. She may have a hypnotic voice and send shudders of dangerous pleasure down to his sex as she fixes her penetrating gaze upon him. She may penetrate his soul and his sexuality with ease, and he will be unable to resist her charisma as he is drawn to the darkness of her sexual secret. She may desire only a dance of sheer demonic pleasure with him.

If he aligns solely to erotic thoughts and rejects his own need for pleasure, he can become addicted to egocentric behaviour, ignoring the sexual needs of others.

Eros in Virgo – Woman

The woman with Eros in Virgo has a need for images and fantasies of perfection, of purity versus ugliness, or the sacred versus the profane. Her fantasies may revolve around submission and sadomasochism. She may prefer the idea of being tightly bound by chains to beds and railings. She may enjoy the images of whips and leather thongs, of being subjugated to a sexual deviant who desires only to masturbate over her face or breasts while she is held down by two women. If she prefers the dominant role she may imagine herself wearing stilettos and using huge dildos. She may imagine being pierced for her lover, in her nipples, her labia, her clitoris, while she submits to the pleasure-pain. There may be much torment invoked in her fantasies to compensate for the guilt she feels for enjoying the associated pleasure.

The kind of person who may be a trigger for her erotic desire will often be contrary to her Venusian values and her long-term sexual intentions. This man may be romantic, an escapist poet. He may be easily led into her perfect world, for he is imperfect, flawed by genius or by emotion. He will both submit to her and oblige her. He may be powerless and yet be on a quest for a divine experience, to find a partner who can release his hidden sexual energy. This man will bring ritual and release to her erotic rigidity.

The Eros in Virgo woman may feel acutely uneasy with erotic desire. Her relationship to Eros will be tinged with her need to find the perfect image or the perfect connection. She will use her fantasy world mostly when engaged in intimacy, rather than as a device for self-pleasure. Her mind is so powerful that she may begin to fear the invasion of Eros into her sieved thoughts. She may try to suppress these erotic instincts. This may result in guilt or sexual abstinence. If she can learn to identify with her erotic nature, she may discover a rich and powerful source of creative energy.

Eros in Virgo – Man

He may prefer purist fantasies, where he experiences the perfect woman or the ideal sexual encounter. He may enjoy the idea of being served and yet also yielding to a greater power. He has a need for images of excellent sexual techniques, or perhaps of S&M roles, where he alternates between dominant and submissive. He may enjoy the idea of surgical sex changes, of the precision of body piercing, of being tattooed between his buttocks or on the end of his penis. He may prefer to indulge in fantasies set in a sterile environment: the operating table, the dentist's chair, or among the white linen of an untouched bedchamber. He may imagine crisp and fresh sheets, the woman who lies beneath naked and bathed in the purest of essences. He may have fantasies of tortured sexual penetration, or of total abstinence.

The kind of person who may be a trigger for his erotic desire may be contrary to this man's Venusian or sun-sign needs. This woman would be elusive, scattered and ephemeral. She would seem disorganised, poetic and artistic. Gullible and dreamy, she may seem the most feminine and divine of women. She may be emotional, compassionate and willing to please, and she may reflect his own desires quickly, knowing how to bring him pleasure without demands. She will flow with the ambience, the romance, yet she will always seem far from the world of reality. She is flawed and yet enchanting: a woman he will want to sexually re-create.

The Eros in Virgo male finds his erotic fantasies disturbing, for they force him to contemplate the stirrings of his intellectual arousal. He will attempt to analyse them over and over again. If he identifies only with Eros, he may become obsessed with pornography, sex toys and aids as his only means of arousal.

Eros in Capricorn – Woman

This woman will have ambitious fantasies about being in a position of power. She will imagine being so successful and wealthy that she can indulge in any chosen pleasure. She will imagine herself as a film star, porn queen or the richest business woman. Her imagination may insist on having sex on the boardroom table after the meeting, or in the lift on the way to her penthouse office suite. She will imagine having limousines and country houses filled with lovers. She will fantasise about tying up her lover and disciplining him. Her partner may be clothed in leather or rubber, his penis revealed to her through a special opening as he is chained to an iron bed. She may insist in her fantasies on anal sex, and imagine the men she couples with as powerful, brutish, and blessed with thrusting powerful cocks. She may imagine a chess game, both players naked. She will win this game and her partner will have to perform a sexual forfeit. The power of winning is her greatest erotic trigger.

The kind of person who may be a trigger for this woman's erotic desire may be contrary to her long-term intentions for intimacy as shown by her sun sign and

Venus placement. He will be quietly mysterious, sensitive and cautious. He may seem as if he is hiding behind an image of glamour or success, fearful of his vulnerability being unmasked. He will be easily dominated, easily subjugated to any whim.

The Eros in Capricorn woman may find difficulty in connecting to Eros rather than directly to her simple sexual drive. She may avoid erotic conversation and may appear detached from any suggestions of wickedness. Yet this underlying erotic energy needs to be balanced with her earthy sexuality. If it is not, she can become underhand and wilfully destructive. She can attach herself to sex as a means of climbing ladders and gaining money and success, purely to bypass the deeper instincts of her powerful eroticism.

Eros in Capricorn – Man

This man fantasises about control and power. In his dreams he must have the stamina for long periods of penetration, unstoppable and unbreakable. He may enjoy setting his daydreams at the film set, or a yacht harbour in the South of France. He may imagine the chic and glamorous, the powerful and the corrupt. He will imagine sex on the stock-market floor, enjoying magnificent arousal as his shares are on the brink of collapse or growth. The women in his fantasies may be ready to submit to his control, follow every device, every desire of his plan. He may even enjoy the idea of having masochistic partners. He may imagine bondage and anal sex, simple animal lust, and little romance. Bodies will be earthy, gutsy. Flesh will be inviting, lusciously covered in stimulating creams or powerful aphrodisiacs.

The kind of person who may be a trigger for this man's erotic desire may be contrary to his long-term intentions for intimacy. She may be darkly sensual, richly emotional and yet deeply secretive. She will seem ultra-feminine. She will willingly submit and seem ready to placate and to give. She is highly receptive and acutely sensitive, as if she knows exactly what is needed of her to ensure his pleasure, and ensure they unite. She will be bonding and tenacious, yet fearful of her hidden power being unmasked.

One of his erotic triggers may be masochistic partners. If he becomes addicted to Eros solely, he may use his power unwisely, manipulating others to achieve satisfaction.

The Female Earth Fantasy

There will be a deserted bar in the wild country, a dusty road and a dead-end sign. She will have travelled all night and be ravenous for food, hungry for pleasure. Her hair will be in wild tangles down her sweating back. She pushes open the bar-room door and two strangers turn to look. Both are leather-clad bikers, fragrant with grease and sweat. She smiles: an opportunity for fun and for excitement. The three of them drink Tequila at the bar together. The leathered men, one dark, one blond, drop their ice cubes down the back of her T-shirt. She will touch them both, running her fingers down their leather jackets. She begins to unzip the black leather of the dark-haired one.

He is beautiful, his chest hairless, muscled and tanned. The line of hair from his navel drops down into his tight leather trousers. She knows what is pulsing there, can almost feel it inside her, can almost imagine the vastness of his cock. She pushes herself up against him, his smell intoxicating as he grasps her face and licks her lips. The other biker cannot resist as she sways her hips into his friend. He stands behind her, gently kneading her buttocks with his erect shaft, his leather jeans bulging with his desire. They watch her, hypnotised by her artistry and impetuosity. She begins to caress the dark one, pushing her hand down his trousers to feel the heat and power of his penis as it begins to extend above the top of his belt.

Her desire is sensational: she must have them simultaneously. There is no other way. The dark one lifts her on to the table and she opens her thighs ready for his touch. He unzips his trousers, unleashes his huge penis and rubs it against her thigh. She rips off her wet knickers and her skirt, takes the other biker's hand and guides his fingers deeper and deeper between her moist lips, until he gasps with an urgent need for orgasm. They both want to enter her, to thrust hard and to release themselves into her wildness.

She wraps her legs round the dark one's hips, and he gently lowers her on to his cock. Now she rises and falls upon him, skilfully riding him. Now she is like water, flowing, caught on a crescendo of ecstasy as the ride gathers strength and frenzy. The blond one cannot resist any longer: he grasps her from behind and pushes his penis up the cleft between her buttocks. He enters her, the force of his penetration stretching her to oblivion, sending waves of spasmodic delight through her body as he rides with his dark friend.

This is sweet for her; this is torment for her. Yet it is glorious torment. She watches the dark rider's penis as it enters her powerfully again, unstoppable. She clutches both their cocks in her hands, one from the front of her belly, one from behind her aching buttocks. As they ride into frenzied orgasm, she cannot stop her own release, the leather zip rubbing, chafing at her clitoris, until she lets the waves of pleasure sweep violently through her body.

Interactive Section
Eros in Earth

As in the other chapters, choose the words with which you most identify and fill in your erotic-profile chart accordingly.

Eros represents my fantasies and the wild side of my sexuality.

I am turned on by _____

Choose from: sensuality, purity, rituals, feasting, success, power, romance, being in control.

My fantasies include ————————————————

Choose from: food and drink, nudity, S&M, body piercing, pornography, sexual surrogacy, whips and leather, bondage, disciplined sex, anal sex.

My erotic triggers include ————————————————

Choose from: mystery, wickedness, my own submission, bisexuality, people who are dominating, people who are powerless, power.

Questions

- Do you fear your fantasies or are you able to treat them as part of your sexuality?
- Do you suffer guilt and shame when you are aroused by erotic thoughts?
- Do you prefer to keep your imagined world to yourself, or to expose it to your partner?
- Are you uncomfortable with your own arousal when turned on by other people?

CHAPTER TWENTY-THREE:

EROS IN THE WATER SIGNS

(Cancer, Scorpio and Pisces)

'Unclasps her warmed jewels one by one,
Loosens her fragrant bodice; by degrees
Her rich attire creeps rustling to her knees;
Half hidden, like a mermaid in seaweed'
John Keats, *The Eve of St Agnes*

*T*hose with Eros in the water signs have an emotional reaction as well as an intellectual one to sexual desire. These signs have a mysterious, intangible eroticism about their fantasies. Erotic triggers will be found in anything from the macabre to the fantastic, and from submission to domination.

Eros in Cancer – Woman

The Eros in Cancer woman may have fantasies about secret sexual acts where she is a submissive participant. She may be aroused by imagery of rituals, Dionysian cults and orgies, and the early pagan sexual rites of passage. She has a highly evolved imagination and will often live totally in a world of fictitious characters and historical scenes of dangerous, passionate romance. She will enjoy the thought of love potions and philtres, and the poignancy of unrequited love. Food may play a great part in her erotic triggers: she may enjoy the idea of eating aphrodisiacs or hallucinogenic herbs. She will like dressing in silks, satins, lace and rubber. Yet she can also veer towards powerful domination fantasies involving anal sex and aggressive or sadistic role-playing, if she feels comfortable with her wild Eros nature.

The kind of person who may trigger sexual desire in this woman may be contrary to her long-term sexual needs and values as shown by her sun sign and Venus placement. This man will be ambitious and successful. He will be ferociously demanding about his sexual needs. He may be strong and masterful, exuding an aura of accomplished sexual performance and complete discretion. He will have little time for sexual pedantry and will prefer the rough and powerful passion of bestial sex to emotional and mysterious intimacy.

The Eros in Cancer woman may identify with her wild erotic nature if she can surrender to the power of her mysterious heritage. Her energies are powerful, and she may keep her fantasies shrouded in secrecy rather than opening up to her own needs and sharing her imagined world with others. Once she feels secure and cherished, she may begin to honour her wildness and acknowledge the gift of Eros in her sexual relationships. If she also has the sun or Venus in Cancer, she may feel locked into patterns of conventional behaviour, but understanding that her fantasies can be as ambitious as she wants them, rather than feeling she has to control the flow of her thoughts and vivid imaginings, may liberate her to the wildness she truly seeks. However, if she lives only in her fantasy world, preferring her dreams and images to reality, she may begin to withdraw from close intimacy or become highly tenacious, manipulative and demanding.

Eros in Cancer – Man

The Eros in Cancer male may imagine being dominated, controlled by powerful and often macabre women. He may imagine he is with a heroine from history or literature: he finds the fictitious or ancient world a place where he can relax and explore his gentle erotic fantasies. He may imagine himself a pharaoh or a Roman emperor but, whatever the guise, he will be the submissive participant, led by the splendour of a wild and powerful Amazonian woman, or a goddess. He may enjoy the idea of theatrical costume, rich and sumptuous bedding, silks and lace, rubber and leather.

The kind of person who may trigger his sexual desire may be a contradiction of his sun-sign intention for long-term intimacy or his Venusian values. This woman may be demanding and ambitious. She may have a successful career, or plummet into every mode of life with integrity and purpose. She has glamour, a cool and often powerful energy that can overwhelm others. She needs to feel accomplished and controlled in all she does. She will be sexually demanding, passionate and forceful. She may be highly discreet and conventional, yet hiding an inner wildness. She will be dominating and enjoy the role of initiating and controlling her partner's pleasure.

The Eros in Cancer male may find it difficult to accept his fantasy world. He will have a powerful urge to escape into his dreams but may fear his images. He may also find it difficult to allow anyone access to his very private and hidden imagination, such is his fear of his own power.

Eros in Scorpio – Woman

This woman has intensely polarised fantasies, ranging from the macabre and demonic to the beautiful. She has a highly volatile and compulsive erotic connection to people and the world, and often finds herself aroused by the perverse and the taboo. Dominatrix roles and the domain of S&M are included in her favourites. She may enjoy outrageous clothes or fantasies about vampires. Gender is indistinct and irrelevant. One of her beautiful fantasies may be of being an Inca priestess ravished in the exotic ruins of a Peruvian temple. The most potent erotic fantasy or trigger for the Eros in Scorpio woman is undoubtedly her need to assert her power over others, particularly women. She can also submit to fantasies of masochistic delight to counter her guilt for the pleasure she associates with power. She may imagine herself possessed by sadists, demons, Mephistopheles, or the wild orgiastic rituals of Dionysus.

The kind of person who may trigger this woman's erotic desire may not necessarily align with her intentions for sexual intimacy nor her Venusian values. Often the person who becomes a potent hook for our erotic fantasies or desire is the kind of person we believe we detest. This man would be richly sensual. He would be manly, potent, demanding and have a high sex drive. He will be patient, testing, cautious and able to be at peace with the moment. He will appear to have no thoughts on the future or memories of the past. He will seem grounded, centred and in touch with the earth. He will prefer the solitude to the crowd, and the darkness to the light.

The Eros in Scorpio woman has little problem integrating her erotic nature into her sexual lifestyle, unless she has Venus or the sun in Virgo or Libra. If this is the case she might find that accepting the darkness of her erotic fantasies seems incompatible with her sexual idealism. But if she begins to work with Eros she may begin to access her wild woman, and acknowledge the deeper issues surrounding her sexual guilt. If she aligns to the dark side of Eros, however, she can become hungry for power through obsessively playing out her weirdest fantasies. When this becomes addictive, she may assume that everyone is part of her fantasy world. She may imagine that her real partners are as disposable as those in her daydreams.

Eros in Scorpio – Man

This is a man with powerful fantasies that range from the macabre to the pure and the divine. The further removed from the norm, the more erotic the fantasy. The more fetishistic and intense the images, the more aroused he may become. He may imagine himself in power, as a magus, a demon or a shaman, his pleasure taken with the young and innocent, or those eager to delight in the wilder darkness of S&M. He may like the fantasy of anal sex, or his own imagined involvement in pornographic films. He may like the idea of transforming others, as a sexual surrogate or teacher.

The kind of person who may trigger this man's erotic desire may be a contradiction of his long-term intimacy intentions or Venusian values. This woman may be voluptuous and enticing, yet deeply possessive. She will be nourishing, grounded and richly feminine. On the surface she may seem serene and dignified but still she conveys an aura of dark and mysterious sensuality. Her earthiness may excite him and her sexual containment may drive him crazy with desire.

If he becomes obsessively hooked on Eros, he may insist that his fantasies become reality, often resulting in destructive relationships and, ultimately, complete abstinence.

Eros in Pisces – Woman

The woman with Eros in Pisces has probably the richest source of fantasies upon which to draw. She is the ultimate escapist, preferring to live in the world of imaginings than in depressing reality. Her fantasies flow around water, mermaids, drowning and orgasm as sacrifice. She may indulge in bisexual scenes. She enjoys the beauty of women, and men who are in touch with their feminine side, such as poets and artists. Powerful triggers for her erotic arousal are scenes of extreme romantic passion from *Tristan and Isolde* or *Romeo and Juliet*. The more painful and the more esoteric the image, the more stimulated she will become. She may have many dreams of forced submission and masochistic delights. Although she often denies it, she may be turned on by watching S&M sex, she as the 'madame' or voyeur. She may dream of being a temple harlot or a high-class whore.

The kind of person who may trigger her sexual desire

may not necessarily be aligned to her Venusian values or her long-term relationship needs. The man who may irresistibly attract her would be refined, gentle, and yet emotionally detached. He may be a demanding perfectionist, allowing few close to him. He may be dedicated to his work or his body, often obsessed with detail and the rituals of daily life. He will prefer sex to be a perfect experience, untouched and pure, meticulous and timed to the moment. He wants his partner to be flawless, excelling in the art of technique rather than feeling.

The Eros in Pisces woman relates to her erotic nature well. She lives in a world of fantasy where reality barely exists. She often feels guilt for being so aroused by her own fantasies, and may prefer to ignore them as a means for masturbation, relying on them only for mutual arousal. If she aligns solely to Eros, she may begin to act out her fantasies in real life, in the belief that she can achieve sensual pleasure only through the painful excesses of her mind. If she can learn that her wildness *is* compatible with pleasure, that she can both dream and enjoy guilt-free sex, she may begin to discover the deeply healing power of her feminine eroticism.

Eros in Pisces – Man

The Eros in Pisces male may find pleasure in romantic and ideal images. Sacrifice, masochism and surrender to a higher force or divine power may be strong ideas in his ephemeral world. He may refuse to admit his fantasies include sadistic pleasure and bisexuality, often along with a bias towards exhibitionism. One day he may prefer the simple imagery of a woman's lips across his penis, and then the next he will imagine being bound to a cross and ravished by a powerful warrior woman. He may prefer in his thoughts and dreams to be the watcher of others' forbidden joy. He may play with the idea of sexual encounters in a monastery. The more forbidden the pleasure, the more arousing the fantasy.

The kind of person who may trigger this man's erotic

desire may be a contradiction of his long-term intimacy needs or Venusian values. She would be elegant, discriminating and discreet. She may be fascinated by perfection and ready to criticise and find fault with anything less than ideal. She may want a perfect lover and a perfectly divine experience. Her mind will be incisive and calculating, and her emotions may seem locked for ever in a hidden chamber. Her passion may be cool and remote, but her desire will be chiselled to a point of complete precision, beautiful and immaculate.

His fantasy world will play a huge part in his sexual encounters. If he aligns solely to Eros he may become lost in a dream world, ever more remote from his partner and fearing the difficulties of intimate relationship.

The Female Water Fantasy

There will be a knock on the great oak door of her bedroom. The curtains are billowing across the stone floor as the wind whistles wildly outside. The chateau of the Marquis de Cadres is lit only by candlelight. She will have met him at the masked ball in Limieux. She knew him to be insatiable, filled with desire and greedy for feasting on women. She was compelled by his voice, his intense passion and his ice-cold eyes. Lured by his hypnotic quality and his strange potions, she had fallen into a trance. Now the night storm wakes her to the sound of his steps pacing the corridor outside her chamber. He knocks again, louder this time, demanding. He is intent on her soul.

She lights the candle, closes the shutters of the great window and pulls her white muslin gown round her, her nipples hardened by the cold night air. She unlocks the door. He comes to her now, his purple cloak sweeping behind him, a vampire mask still upon his face, his tousled black hair soaked from the storm outside. His linen shirt is open at his chest. Sweat and rain drips to the floor as he takes her arm roughly with his hand. Had he been pleasuring another, or is this desire for her alone that she smells on his breath? Pulling her to him, he takes off his mask. His eyes are wild, lit with desire, as she feels his mouth hard and fierce upon hers. There is no love, no honey sweetness, only the power of possession.

Yet she will willingly submit to his power. She will let him take pleasure from her. He pushes her down to the chaise longue and binds her legs and arms to the carved sofa with golden ropes. She feels exposed, vulnerable, possessed. In the candlelight she catches only glimpses of his eyes, his smile, his lust. He rips open her muslin chemise, the cloth tearing across her breasts. The gold rope sears her skin. The first waves of passion fill her body with a burning desire. He kneads her breasts with his strong hands, her nipples firm buds in the coldness of the night. He fingers her throat and kisses her neck like a vampire lover. She catches a glimpse of his magnificent penis, well-formed, already hard and swollen with desire as he opens the buttons of his velvet breeches. His leather boots push against her thighs. His spurs tear her skin.

She moans, filled with a glow of pleasurable fear at the growing arousal of her sex. He fingers her nipples, twirls, pulls and bites, until the spasm of pleasure begins to flow down to her clitoris. She arches her back to him, desperate for him to touch her there, to take her to oblivion. But he torments her with the lightest of touches now, furling his fingers around her pubis, always avoiding her bud and the moistness of her secret pillow. He holds her arms tightly, forcing her back against the roughness of the sofa cushions.

Suddenly he sits astride her, ready to force his swollen manhood into her. He unleashes his phallus and begins to masturbate, his foreskin glinting in the candlelight as he draws it back, again and again. Suddenly she sees glinting in the dull flickering light the two rings on the end of his pierced glans. Two silver coils tinkle as he moves his hand up and down, making his own pleasure a torment. She wants him in her now, the fear of his pierced body now becoming a powerful arousal.

With one thrust he forces his penis in between her labia, the rings stabbing her flesh, the great width of his phallus ramming her whole body into the end of the sofa, until she can only cry out for more, her muscles holding him, kneading him, sucking him of his sweetness. The silver rings slide against the inside of her sex then, as he withdraws slowly, carefully, they dart like two tongues against her clitoris. With each movement, and each thrust, his rhythm quickens, the rings creating a delicious friction against her swollen bud as he withdraws ready to enter her again. Now she has no choice but to surrender herself to him at last, as his breathing becomes faster and his body is frenzied by his own pleasure. She shudders as the first waves of orgasm sweep down through her clitoris, the pulsating of her sex round his pierced glans engulfing him with bittersweet pain as he reaches his fiercely powerful peak.

Interactive Section
Eros in Water

As in the other chapters, choose the words with which you most identify and fill in your erotic-profile chart accordingly.

Eros represents my fantasies and the wild side of my sexuality.

I am turned on by _____

Choose from: hidden passion, the intangible, submission and domination, sensual stimulants, sex toys, taboo subjects, romanticised sex.

My fantasies include _____

Choose from: voyeurism, exhibitionism, sex around water, domination, S&M, bisexuality, torture, vampirism, piercing, leather and rubber, ritualistic sex, the macabre.

My erotic triggers include _____

Choose from: powerful people, spontaneity, sensuality, possessiveness, solitary people, beauty, emotional pain, dangerous liaisons.

Questions

- Do you find your body, soul and mind are overwhelmed when you desire?
- Do you relate uneasily to this powerful force, or do you accept that it is an energy to be honoured, like Eros the god?
- When in a sexual relationship, do you find it easy to reveal your darkest fantasies? Do you fear rejection if they are exposed?

EROS TABLES 1935–1985

*L*ook up your date of birth to find out which sign Eros was in on that day.

For example, say you were born on 20 March 1973. The dates before and after this date are when Eros moved from one sign to another. You can see Eros was in Taurus from 22 February to 28 March. So on 20 March 1973 Eros was in Taurus.

If you were born on the day before the changeover day or the actual changeover day itself, it is possible that Eros was in the following or previous sign to the one given. If this is the case, simply read the relevant sections for both the given sign and the adjacent one to determine which you think is most like you.

1935
Jan 1 Sagittarius
Jan 26 Capricorn
Mar 19 Aquarius
May 25 Pisces
Aug 15 Aquarius
Nov 29 Pisces
1936
Jan 1 Pisces
Jan 19 Aries
Feb 28 Taurus
Apr 3 Gemini
May 6 Cancer
Jun 7 Leo
Jul 11 Virgo
Aug 15 Libra
Sep 23 Scorpio
Nov 4 Sagittarius
Dec 21 Capricorn
1937
Jan 1 Capricorn
Feb 8 Aquarius
Apr 2 Pisces
May 26 Aries
Jul 21 Taurus
Sep 19 Gemini
1938
Jan 1 Gemini
Feb 21 Cancer
Mar 30 Leo
May 7 Virgo
Jun 19 Libra
Aug 5 Scorpio
Sep 25 Sagittarius
Nov 15 Capricorn
1939
Jan 1 Capricorn
Jan 6 Aquarius
Feb 25 Pisces
Apr 14 Aries
May 28 Taurus
Jul 8 Gemini

Aug 13 Cancer
Sep 16 Leo
Oct 18 Virgo
Nov 19 Libra
Dec 23 Scorpio
1940
Jan 1 Scorpio
Feb 1 Sagittarius
Mar 25 Capricorn
Jun 5 Sagittarius
Sep 28 Capricorn
Nov 29 Aquarius
1941
Jan 1 Aquarius
Jan 20 Pisces
Mar 7 Aries
Apr 17 Taurus
May 24 Gemini
Jun 28 Cancer
Jul 31 Leo
Sep 1 Virgo
Oct 5 Libra
Nov 10 Scorpio
Dec 19 Sagittarius
1942
Jan 1 Sagittarius
Feb 2 Capricorn
Mar 26 Aquarius
Dec 10 Pisces
1943
Jan 1 Pisces
Jan 27 Aries
Mar 7 Taurus
Apr 12 Gemini
May 15 Cancer
Jun 16 Leo
Jul 20 Virgo
Aug 24 Libra
Oct 1 Scorpio
Nov 12 Sagittarius
Dec 28 Capricorn

1944
Jan 1 Capricorn
Feb 15 Aquarius
Apr 9 Pisces
Jun 5 Aries
Aug 9 Taurus
Nov 7 Aries
1945
Jan 1 Taurus
Feb 14 Gemini
Mar 20 Cancer
Apr 21 Leo
May 25 Virgo
Jul 3 Libra
Aug 16 Scorpio
Oct 3 Sagittarius
Nov 22 Capricorn
1946
Jan 1 Capricorn
Jan 12 Aquarius
Mar 3 Pisces
Apr 20 Aries
Jun 5 Taurus
Jul 16 Gemini
Aug 22 Cancer
Sep 25 Leo
Oct 27 Virgo
Nov 28 Libra
1947
Jan 1 Scorpio
Feb 11 Sagittarius
Oct 10 Capricorn
Dec 7 Aquarius
1948
Jan 1 Aquarius
Jan 27 Pisces
Mar 13 Aries
Apr 24 Taurus
Jun 1 Gemini
Jul 6 Cancer
Aug 8 Leo
Sep 9 Virgo

Oct 13 Libra
Nov 17 Scorpio
Dec 26 Sagittarius
1949
Jan 1 Sagittarius
Feb 9 Capricorn
Apr 4 Aquarius
Aug 25 Capricorn
Oct 10 Aquarius
Dec 18 Pisces
1950
Jan 1 Pisces
Feb 3 Aries
Mar 15 Taurus
Apr 19 Gemini
May 23 Cancer
Jun 24 Leo
Jul 28 Virgo
Aug 31 Libra
Oct 8 Scorpio
Nov 18 Sagittarius
1951
Jan 1 Sagittarius
Jan 3 Capricorn
Feb 22 Aquarius
Apr 17 Pisces
Jun 17 Aries
Nov 12 Pisces
Nov 21 Aries
1952
Jan 1 Aries
Jan 24 Taurus
Mar 1 Gemini
Apr 2 Cancer
May 4 Leo
Jun 7 Virgo
Jul 14 Libra
Aug 25 Scorpio
Oct 10 Sagittarius
Nov 28 Capricorn
1953
Jan 1 Capricorn

Jan 17 Aquarius
Mar 9 Pisces
Apr 27 Aries
Jun 13 Taurus
Jul 25 Gemini
Sep 1 Cancer
Oct 5 Leo
Nov 6 Virgo
Dec 8 Libra
1954
Jan 1 Libra
Jan 11 Scorpio
Feb 25 Sagittarius
May 17 Scorpio
Aug 13 Sagittarius
Oct 19 Capricorn
Dec 14 Aquarius
1955
Jan 1 Aquarius
Feb 2 Pisces
Mar 21 Aries
May 2 Taurus
Jun 9 Gemini
Jul 14 Cancer
Aug 17 Leo
Sep 18 Virgo
Oct 21 Libra
Nov 25 Scorpio
1956
Jan 1 Scorpio
Jan 3 Sagittarius
Feb 17 Capricorn
Apr 15 Aquarius
Jul 22 Capricorn
Oct 28 Aquarius
Dec 26 Pisces
1957
Jan 1 Pisces
Feb 10 Aries
Mar 22 Taurus
Apr 27 Gemini
May 31 Cancer

Jul 2 Leo
Aug 4 Virgo
Sep 8 Libra
Oct 15 Scorpio
Nov 25 Sagittarius
1958
Jan 1 Sagittarius
Jan 9 Capricorn
Feb 28 Aquarius
Apr 25 Pisces
Jul 5 Aries
Sep 12 Pisces
Dec 23 Aries
1959
Jan 1 Aries
Feb 5 Taurus
Mar 12 Gemini
Apr 14 Cancer
May 16 Leo
Jun 18 Virgo
Jul 25 Libra
Sep 3 Scorpio
Oct 18 Sagittarius
Dec 5 Capricorn
1960
Jan 1 Capricorn
Jan 24 Aquarius
Mar 15 Pisces
May 5 Aries
Jun 22 Taurus
Aug 5 Gemini
Sep 13 Cancer
Oct 17 Leo
Nov 18 Virgo
Dec 20 Libra
1961
Jan 1 Libra
Jan 26 Scorpio
Aug 29 Sagittarius
Oct 27 Capricorn
Dec 20 Aquarius

1962
Jan 1 Aquarius
Feb 8 Pisces
Mar 27 Aries
May 9 Taurus
Jun 17 Gemini
Jul 22 Cancer
Aug 25 Leo
Sep 26 Virgo
Oct 29 Libra
Dec 3 Scorpio
1963
Jan 1 Scorpio
Jan 10 Sagittarius
Feb 25 Capricorn
May 5 Aquarius
Jun 18 Capricorn
Nov 9 Aquarius
1964
Jan 1 Aquarius
Jan 3 Pisces
Feb 18 Aries
Mar 29 Taurus
May 5 Gemini
Jun 8 Cancer
Jul 10 Leo
Aug 12 Virgo
Sep 15 Libra
Oct 22 Scorpio
Dec 2 Sagittarius
1965
Jan 1 Sagittarius
Jan 15 Capricorn
Mar 7 Aquarius
May 4 Pisces
1966
Jan 1 Pisces
Jan 4 Aries
Feb 14 Taurus
Mar 21 Gemini
Apr 23 Cancer
May 25 Leo

Jun 28 Virgo
Aug 3 Libra
Sep 11 Scorpio
Oct 25 Sagittarius
Dec 11 Capricorn
1967
Jan 1 Capricorn
Jan 30 Aquarius
Mar 22 Pisces
May 13 Aries
Jul 2 Taurus
Aug 18 Gemini
Sep 29 Cancer
Nov 4 Leo
Dec 8 Virgo
1968
Jan 1 Virgo
Jan 15 Libra
Jul 12 Scorpio
Sep 9 Sagittarius
Nov 4 Capricorn
Dec 26 Aquarius
1969
Jan 1 Aquarius
Feb 14 Pisces
Apr 2 Aries
May 16 Taurus
Jun 24 Gemini
Jul 30 Cancer
Sep 2 Leo
Oct 4 Virgo
Nov 6 Libra
Dec 10 Scorpio
1970
Jan 1 Scorpio
Jan 18 Sagittarius
Mar 6 Capricorn
Nov 17 Aquarius
1971
Jan 1 Aquarius
Jan 10 Pisces
Feb 24 Aries

Apr 6 Taurus
May 13 Gemini
Jun 16 Cancer
Jul 19 Leo
Aug 21 Virgo
Sep 24 Libra
Oct 30 Scorpio
Dec 9 Sagittarius
1972
Jan 1 Sagittarius
Jan 22 Capricorn
Mar 13 Aquarius
May 15 Pisces
Sep 3 Aquarius
Nov 20 Pisces
1973
Jan 1 Pisces
Jan 13 Aries
Feb 22 Taurus
Mar 29 Gemini
May 1 Cancer
Jun 3 Leo
Jul 6 Virgo
Aug 11 Libra
Sep 19 Scorpio
Nov 1 Sagittarius
Dec 17 Capricorn
1974
Jan 1 Capricorn
Feb 5 Aquarius
Mar 29 Pisces
May 21 Aries
Jul 13 Taurus
Sep 4 Gemini
Oct 27 Cancer
1975
Jan 1 Cancer
Feb 24 Leo
Apr 20 Virgo
Jun 8 Libra
Jul 29 Scorpio
Sep 19 Sagittarius

Nov 11 Capricorn
1976
Jan 1 Capricorn
Jan 2 Aquarius
Feb 21 Pisces
Apr 9 Aries
May 23 Taurus
Jul 2 Gemini
Aug 7 Cancer
Sep 10 Leo
Oct 12 Virgo
Nov 13 Libra
Dec 18 Scorpio
1977
Jan 1 Scorpio
Jan 26 Sagittarius
Mar 16 Capricorn
Jun 26 Sagittarius
Sep 19 Capricorn
Nov 25 Aquarius
1978
Jan 1 Aquarius
Jan 16 Pisces
Mar 3 Aries
Apr 13 Taurus
May 20 Gemini
Jun 24 Cancer
Jul 27 Leo
Aug 28 Virgo
Oct 1 Libra
Nov 6 Scorpio
Dec 15 Sagittarius
1979
Jan 1 Sagittarius
Jan 29 Capricorn
Mar 21 Aquarius
Jun 1 Pisces
Aug 1 Aquarius
Dec 4 Pisces
1980
Jan 1 Pisces
Jan 22 Aries

Mar 2 Taurus
Apr 6 Gemini
May 9 Cancer
Jun 11 Leo
Jul 14 Virgo
Aug 18 Libra
Sep 26 Scorpio
Nov 7 Sagittarius
Dec 23 Capricorn
1981
Jan 1 Capricorn
Feb 11 Aquarius
Apr 4 Pisces
May 29 Aries
Jul 27 Taurus
1982
Jan 1 Taurus
Jan 31 Gemini
Mar 9 Cancer
Apr 11 Leo
May 16 Virgo
Jun 25 Libra
Aug 10 Scorpio
Sep 28 Sagittarius
Nov 18 Capricorn
1983
Jan 1 Capricorn
Jan 8 Aquarius
Feb 27 Pisces
Apr 16 Aries
May 31 Taurus
Jul 11 Gemini
Aug 17 Cancer
Sep 19 Leo
Oct 22 Virgo
Nov 23 Libra
Dec 27 Scorpio
1984
Jan 1 Scorpio
Feb 4 Sagittarius
Apr 3 Capricorn
May 18 Sagittarius

Oct 2 Capricorn
Dec 2 Aquarius
1985
Jan 1 Aquarius
Feb 22 Pisces
Mar 9 Aries
Apr 20 Taurus
May 27 Gemini
Jul 1 Cancer
Aug 3 Leo
Sep 5 Virgo
Oct 8 Libra
Nov 13 Scorpio
Dec 22 Sagittarius

EPILOGUE:

WORKING WITH YOUR EROTIC-PROFILE CHART

Now that you have read through the sections of the book that refer to you and your partner and have filled in your erotic profile, you can begin to work with the different aspects of your sexuality.

This book has been an introduction to the deeply complex alchemy of sexual relationships. By combining the richness of your sexual reality (i.e. Venus pleasure and the sun's sexual identity) with your erotic impulse (i.e. Eros), you can begin to honour your own wild female soul and heritage of ancient sexual forces.

You may not immediately connect to the portrait painted on your erotic profile. If you feel at all hesitant, consider whether you are perhaps denying your deeper instincts, suppressing your desire, or channelling your sexual energy into another area of your life – perhaps work, creative pursuits or physical exercise.

The likelihood of the sun, Eros and Venus all being in the same sign is very small, but if they do coincide then you may find the harmony of your inner needs, sexual purpose and erotic triggers makes them balanced and easy to work with. It is when the sun and Venus are at odds that you may find difficulty integrating all three.

Eros is usually neutral because he is just a catalyst for the individual's first steps on the journey towards pleasure. However, Eros can be in stressful aspect to Venus, the sun, or any of the other planets used in astrology. This is why your own unique birth chart holds many more intricate sexual clues and secrets than can be given here.

Conflicting Values

Identifying with only one heavenly body or archetype at the expense of the others can cause conflicts in your sexual relationships. You may be hooked on Eros yet denying your true sexual values (i.e. Venus placement); you may be searching for your purpose in life (the sun) at the expense of honouring your erotic impulse (Eros); you may be suppressing sensual pleasure (Venus) in the misguided belief that it is somehow wrong, fearful, or out of line with your social or cultural expectations of sexual behaviour.

There can be problems integrating your sun-sign purpose and identity with your sensual and pleasure values. These are a few examples of tension between the sun and Venus:

The sun is in a FIRE sign and Venus is in WATER
The sun is in an AIR sign and Venus is in EARTH
The sun is in a WATER sign and Venus is in FIRE
The sun is in an EARTH sign and Venus is in AIR

If the asteroid Eros is three signs away from Venus, there may be difficulties in integrating erotic arousal with sensual pleasure. Look at your chart and count the signs from where Venus is placed in an anti-clockwise direction to see how far away Eros is. If, for example, your Venus is in Aries, then count the next sign, Taurus, as one, Gemini as two and Cancer as three. Venus is here in fire and 'uncomfortable' with the nature of Eros in water. However, remember Eros is impartial, and is always a catalyst.

Harmonious Combinations

If you have each heavenly body in three consecutive signs (i.e. Sun in fire, Venus in earth, and Eros in air), there may be a balanced flow of energy. Other harmonious combinations are:

Venus in FIRE and the sun or Eros in AIR
Venus in AIR and the sun or Eros in FIRE
Venus in WATER and the sun or Eros in EARTH
Venus in EARTH and the sun or Eros in WATER

You and Your Partner

Again, looking at the synastry of two birth charts is highly complex. However, here are some pointers to understanding the flow of erotic and sensual pleasuring between two people:

1. If your partner's Eros is in the same sign as your Venus, or your Eros is in the same sign as his Venus, then this is an excellent trigger for sexual arousal.
2. When *your* sun and *his* Venus are in the same sign, or both of your Venuses or suns are in the same sign, you can easily relate to the same sexual issues, needs and values.
3. Take all same-sign contacts between two charts as harmonious, nurturing and sexually aligned.
4. If your Venus is in the sign opposite his Eros, this can be a highly potent and powerfully erotic relationship. For example, say you have Venus in Aries and he has Eros in Libra. Aries is naturally opposite Libra in the zodiac, as you can see by looking at the chart. If other combinations of heavenly body are in opposition, like your sun and his Venus, his sun and your Venus, or his sun and your Eros, your sun and his Eros, or your Venus and his Venus, etc., then work on the assumption that these are all powerful positions for potent sexual relationships.
5. However, the opposition between heavenly bodies may be magnetic and transformative, but also requires deep understanding of your very different sexual needs.

Afterword

Astrology relies on many other heavenly bodies and many other aspects in a birth chart to complete a total picture of our psyches. That is why you should take what I say here as only the beginning of the journey of finding out about yourself.

Enjoy the knowledge you gain from this book. The secrets of female desire are yours to work with. Even if you are not ready to analyse your own erotic profile, I hope that you have found reading this book an enriching experience and that it has given you more knowledge of the wild woman of your sensual and erotic psyche.

We hope you enjoyed reading *Women, Sex and Astrology*. It is the first non-fiction Black Lace book. Black Lace is the first series of erotic books written exclusively by women, for women. We have published 120 titles in the series and have storylines and settings to suit all tastes and fantasies. For a complete guide to storylines of all available titles, please send a large SAE to the following address:

Black Lace
332 Ladbroke Grove
London W10 5AH

If you are not resident in the UK, please send two International Reply Coupons.

BLACK
lace

BLACK LACE BOOKLIST

All books are priced £4.99 unless another price is given.

Black Lace books with a contemporary setting

ODALISQUE	Fleur Reynolds ISBN 0 352 32887 8	☐
VIRTUOSO	Katrina Vincenzi ISBN 0 352 32907 6	☐
THE SILKEN CAGE	Sophie Danson ISBN 0 352 32928 9	☐
RIVER OF SECRETS	Saskia Hope & Georgia Angelis ISBN 0 352 32925 4	☐
SUMMER OF ENLIGHTENMENT	Cheryl Mildenhall ISBN 0 352 32937 8	☐
MOON OF DESIRE	Sophie Danson ISBN 0 352 32911 4	☐
A BOUQUET OF BLACK ORCHIDS	Roxanne Carr ISBN 0 352 32939 4	☐
THE TUTOR	Portia Da Costa ISBN 0 352 32946 7	☐
THE HOUSE IN NEW ORLEANS	Fleur Reynolds ISBN 0 352 32951 3	☐
WICKED WORK	Pamela Kyle ISBN 0 352 32958 0	☐
DREAM LOVER	Katrina Vincenzi ISBN 0 352 32956 4	☐
UNFINISHED BUSINESS	Sarah Hope-Walker ISBN 0 352 32983 1	☐
THE DEVIL INSIDE	Portia Da Costa ISBN 0 352 32993 9	☐
HEALING PASSION	Sylvie Ouellette ISBN 0 352 32998 X	☐
THE STALLION	Georgina Brown ISBN 0 352 33005 8	☐

Black Lace books with an historical setting

---------- ✂ ----------------------------

Please send me the books I have ticked above.

Name ....

Address ....

....

....

.... Post Code ....

Send to: **Cash Sales, Black Lace Books, 332 Ladbroke Grove, London W10 5AH, UK.**

US customers: for prices and details of how to order books for delivery by mail, call 1-800-805-1083.

Please enclose a cheque or postal order, made payable to **Virgin Publishing Ltd**, to the value of the books you have ordered plus postage and packing costs as follows:

UK and BFPO – £1.00 for the first book, 50p for each subsequent book.

Overseas (including Republic of Ireland) – £2.00 for the first book, £1.00 each subsequent book.

If you would prefer to pay by VISA or ACCESS/MASTERCARD, please write your card number and expiry date here:

....

Please allow up to 28 days for delivery.

Signature ....

---------- ✂ ----------------------------

BLACK
lace

WE NEED YOUR HELP . . .
to plan the future of women's erotic fiction –

– and no stamp required!

Yours are the only opinions that matter.

Black Lace is the first series of books devoted to erotic fiction by women for women.

We intend to keep providing the best-written, sexiest books you can buy. And we'd appreciate your help and valued opinion of the books so far. Tell us what you want to read.

THE BLACK LACE QUESTIONNAIRE

SECTION ONE: ABOUT YOU

1.1 Sex (*we presume you are female, but so as not to discriminate*)
Are you?
Male ☐
Female ☐

1.2 Age
under 21 ☐ 21–30 ☐
31–40 ☐ 41–50 ☐
51–60 ☐ over 60 ☐

1.3 At what age did you leave full-time education?
still in education ☐ 16 or younger ☐
17–19 ☐ 20 or older ☐

1.4 Occupation _____

1.5   Annual household income _____

1.6   We are perfectly happy for you to remain anonymous;
      but if you would like to receive information on other
      publications available, please insert your name and
      address

      _____

      _____

      _____

      _____

SECTION TWO: ABOUT BUYING BLACK LACE BOOKS

2.1   Where did you get this copy of *Women, Sex and Astrology*?
      Bought at chain book shop   ☐
      Bought at independent book shop   ☐
      Bought at supermarket   ☐
      Bought at book exchange or used book shop   ☐
      I borrowed it/found it   ☐
      My partner bought it   ☐

2.2   How did you find out about Black Lace books?
      I saw them in a shop   ☐
      I saw them advertised in a magazine   ☐
      I read about them in _____
      Other _____

2.3   Please tick the following statements you agree with:
      I would be less embarrassed about buying Black
      Lace books if the cover pictures were less explicit ☐
      I think that in general the pictures on Black
      Lace books are about right   ☐
      I think Black Lace cover pictures should be as
      explicit as possible   ☐

2.4   Would you read a Black Lace book in a public place – on
      a train for instance?
      Yes   ☐   No   ☐

SECTION THREE: ABOUT THIS BLACK LACE BOOK

3.1 Do you think the sex content in this book is:
        Too much   ☐   About right   ☐
        Not enough   ☐

3.2 Do you think the writing style in this book is:
        Too unreal/escapist   ☐   About right   ☐
        Too down to earth   ☐

3.3 Do you think this book is:
        Too complicated   ☐   About right   ☐
        Too boring/simple   ☐

3.4 Do you think the cover of this book is:
        Too explicit   ☐   About right   ☐
        Not explicit enough   ☐

Here's a space for any other comments:

SECTION FOUR: ABOUT OTHER BLACK LACE BOOKS

4.1 How many Black Lace books have you read?   ☐

4.2 If more than one, which one did you prefer?

4.3 Why?

SECTION FIVE: ABOUT YOUR IDEAL EROTIC NOVEL

We want to publish the books you want to read – so this is your chance to tell us exactly what your ideal erotic novel would be like.

5.1 Using a scale of 1 to 5 (1 = no interest at all, 5 = your ideal), please rate the following possible settings for an erotic novel:

Medieval/barbarian/sword 'n' sorcery ☐
Renaissance/Elizabethan/Restoration ☐
Victorian/Edwardian ☐
1920s & 1930s – the Jazz Age ☐
Present day ☐
Future/Science Fiction ☐

5.2 Using the same scale of 1 to 5, please rate the following themes you may find in an erotic novel:

Submissive male/dominant female ☐
Submissive female/dominant male ☐
Lesbianism ☐
Bondage/fetishism ☐
Romantic love ☐
Experimental sex e.g. anal/watersports/sex toys ☐
Gay male sex ☐
Group sex ☐

5.3 Using the same scale of 1 to 5, please rate the following styles in which an erotic novel could be written:

Realistic, down to earth, set in real life ☐
Escapist fantasy, but just about believable ☐
Completely unreal, impressionistic, dreamlike ☐

5.4 Would you prefer your ideal erotic novel to be written from the viewpoint of the main male characters or the main female characters?

Male ☐   Female ☐
Both ☐

5.5 What would your ideal Black Lace heroine be like? Tick as many as you like:

Dominant	☐	Glamorous	☐
Extroverted	☐	Contemporary	☐
Independent	☐	Bisexual	☐
Adventurous	☐	Naïve	☐
Intellectual	☐	Introverted	☐
Professional	☐	Kinky	☐
Submissive	☐	Anything else?	☐
Ordinary	☐	_____	

5.6 What would your ideal male lead character be like? Again, tick as many as you like:

Rugged	☐		
Athletic	☐	Caring	☐
Sophisticated	☐	Cruel	☐
Retiring	☐	Debonair	☐
Outdoor-type	☐	Naïve	☐
Executive-type	☐	Intellectual	☐
Ordinary	☐	Professional	☐
Kinky	☐	Romantic	☐
Hunky	☐		
Sexually dominant	☐	Anything else?	☐
Sexually submissive	☐	_____	

5.7 Is there one particular setting or subject matter that your ideal erotic novel would contain?

_____

SECTION SIX: LAST WORDS

6.1 What do you like best about Black Lace books?

_____

6.2 What do you most dislike about Black Lace books?

_____

6.3 In what way, if any, would you like to change Black Lace covers?

_____

6.4   Here's a space for any other comments:

_____

_____

_____

_____

_____

Thank you for completing this questionnaire. Now tear it out of the book – carefully! – put it in an envelope and send it to:

Black Lace
FREEPOST
London
W10 5BR

No stamp is required if you are resident in the U.K.